DEEP ROMANTIC CHASM

James Lees–Milne in his Bath library

Deep Romantic Chasm

DIARIES, 1979–1981

James Lees-Milne

Edited by Michael Bloch

JOHN MURRAY
Albemarle Street, London

First published in 2000
by John Murray (Publishers) Ltd
50 Albemarle Street, London W1S 4BD

Reprinted 2000
Paperback edition 2003

A catalogue record for this book is available from the British Library

ISBN 0-7195-6211 2

Typeset in 11.5/13pt Bembo by Servis Filmsetting Ltd, Manchester
Printed and bound in Great Britain by Butler and Tanner Ltd, Frome and London

Contents

Preface

This is the eighth volume of James Lees-Milne's diaries to be published. It opens in 1979 when he was seventy years of age. For three years, he and his wife Alvilde had been living at Essex House on the Duke of Beaufort's Badminton estate, where she had created a celebrated garden. They had also kept the flat in which they had formerly lived at 19 Lansdown Crescent, Bath, where Jim retreated most days to work in his beloved library. Since the summer of 1976 he had been absorbed in research for a biography of his old friend Harold Nicolson; and these diaries cover the writing of that monumental work and its publication in two volumes. His industry was astonishing: each of the Nicolson volumes, amounting in their unedited state to more than half a million words, was completed in a matter of months. At the same time he produced a number of smaller works, wrote a stream of articles and reviews, visited London regularly, travelled in England and abroad, served on several committees (notably the National Trust Properties Committee of which he had once been Secretary), read prodigiously, maintained a voluminous correspondence, led a busy social life, and kept up with a wide circle of friends. And he kept these diaries.

Jim had already achieved some celebrity as a diarist with the appearance of the two volumes of his wartime journals, *Ancestral Voices* and *Prophesying Peace*, in 1975 and 1977. He had published these with misgivings, and was surprised at their success and the stir they created. Before the present volume ends, he had decided to publish sequels covering the immediate post-war years: these appeared in 1983 and 1985 as *Caves of Ice* and *Midway on the Waves*. After that, it was not initially his intention to release more diaries in his lifetime. Those he had kept in the 1950s and 1960s were sporadic; and they told the story of an unusual marriage which, though generally close, had often been turbulent and at one moment looked as if it might come to grief. One day in the late 1980s he destroyed much from this period in a fit of remorse; and although he had resumed his regular journal in the summer of 1971, this was not at first intended for twentieth-century consumption. But a few years later, encouraged by his old school friend and new publisher John Murray, he relented. *A Mingled Measure*, containing surviving fragments from the 1950s and 1960s together with his diaries for 1971 and 1972, appeared in 1994, soon after Alvilde's death; *Ancient as the Hills*, covering 1973 and 1974, followed in 1997. Shortly before his own death in December 1997, in his ninetieth year, Jim edited another volume with the assistance of his great-nephew Nick Robinson: this was published posthumously in 1998 as *Through Wood and Dale*, and brought the sequence up to 1978.

Rather to my surprise, for we had not seen much of each other for several years, Jim bequeathed his literary estate to me, along with the unpublished diaries for the last nineteen years of his life. It has therefore fallen to me to continue the process of preparing volumes for publication. It has been a curious task; for I met Jim in February 1979, and these diaries include a personal record of the friendship which sprang up between us. He was the finest person I ever knew; and he conceived feelings for me the nature of which I hardly grasped at the time (but now understand all too well). Going through his pages has been an intense experience, a Proustian journey in time, reviving a host of precious memories while provoking not a few soul-searchings and regrets.

During the three years covered by the present volume, Jim kept his diary in the form of a typescript which he updated on average once or twice a week. I have reduced this to about four-fifths of its original length, removing material which struck me as repetitious, hurtful, excessively personal or otherwise unsuitable, and tidying up (as Jim would have done) a text which was often dashed out in haste. When he went abroad, however, he usually kept another sort of diary, filling pocket notebooks with detailed handwritten travelogues. For these years, such notebooks exist for two visits to Mount Athos, one to Normandy and one to Calabria. (Another notebook to which he refers in the typescript, covering a trip to Australia in November 1980, appears to be lost.) So different in character are these from the regular diaries that the choice appeared to lie between cutting them drastically and publishing them separately. As they may be of interest to other travellers in these regions, I have reproduced them, substantially as they were written, as a series of appendices.

Any errors or lapses of taste resulting from my editing and foot-noting (or lack of them) are my own responsibility, but I am indebted to Stephen Carroll, the Duchess of Devonshire, Fred Grubb, Bruce Hunter, John Kenworthy-Browne, R.B. McDowell, Grant McIntyre, Liz Robinson, Nick Robinson, John Saumarez Smith, Tony Scotland and Alexander Titov for their invaluable guidance. I hope I have done a suitable work for Jim's memory which will not cause offence to the living – though these diaries would not be true to form were they incapable of giving rise to some fluttering in the dovecotes.

Michael Bloch
London
February 2000

But oh! that deep romantic chasm which slanted
Down the green hill athwart a cedarn cover!
A savage place, as holy and enchanted
As e'er beneath a waning moon was haunted
By woman wailing for her demon-lover!

Samuel Taylor Coleridge, *Kubla Khan*

1979

A[lvilde] went to Holy Communion at Big Badminton this morning at eight. The congregation consisted of herself and Mary Beaufort only.* I walked across the park to Little Badminton at ten. Besides myself, there were three old women. If I were to live another twenty years there would, I dare say, be no church services functioning in England at all. Now I keep asking myself, are we churchgoers better than those who don't go? I don't think we are, if one takes a cross-section of both parties. Women like Peggy[†] who don't go are gener-ous, cheerful, hard-working, honest, honourable. I am rather mean, gloomy, hard-working yes, at my own work, and lazy if it comes to doing things for others, honest in my way but generally dishonour-able. In balance I come out lower on the scale than Peggy. Yet I worry inordinately about spiritual problems, traditional manners and the Faith. I may not be as good as Peggy, but I think, and she doesn't. I measure the depreciation of standards since my youth. She does not. Does this make her inferior to me? I think not.

Today the thaw has come after ten days of bitter cold and frosty roads and snow. All is grey and slush. On Thursday, as I was returning from Bath, just past the Lansdown Tower in the darkness, a blizzard started. I was almost blinded. I saw ahead a stationary car, abandoned, half on the verge, half on the road. I skidded into it, going possibly 25 mph, and badly buckled my front mudguard and the passenger door. The total estimate for repair is £100.

At this particular moment the political situation in this country is about as menacing as it has ever been.[‡] The lorry drivers are on unoffi-cial strike for higher wages. Already petrol is scarce, and by the end of

---

* The Duchess of Beaufort (1897–1987); Lady Mary Cambridge, dau. of 1st Marquess of Cambridge (brother of Queen Mary, consort of King George V); m. 1923 Henry Somerset, subsequently 10th Duke of Beaufort (1900–84), known as 'Master' on account of his long years as MFH and Master of the Horse, owner of the Badminton estate.
† The L.-Ms' daily help, Peggy Bird.
‡ It was the so-called 'winter of discontent', the chaotic period of severe weather and unofficial strikes marking the last months in office of the Labour Government.

the week there will be none on sale at all. The food shops' stock is exhausted. I suppose the Government will give way. If they stand firm there will be a general strike. All communication, all industry will cease. People will not be able to get to work. We shall be stuck here.

John [Kenworthy-Browne]* has presumably not returned from America yet: at least he has not telephoned. I have felt uneasy and unhappy. It is absurd that after twenty years and more I should mind as much as I do. I miss being out of touch with him. Yet when I am with him I am frequently irritated. I just long for him to telephone and say he is glad to be back, and did not enjoy his visit much; and above all that John Pope-Hennessy† was hell to him.

Monday, 8th January

Having written these uncharitable words I go to Bath this morning, and there I find a letter from John written in New York. It must have been waiting for me over the weekend. All my anxieties are allayed. I feel relieved and happy. I have made a plan to see him next week. Already I am in no haste to see him. The assurance of his affection is enough. It is all very stupid, but strange.

Sunday, 21st January

Last weekend George Dix‡ stayed. At 2.30 a.m. on Sunday I was woken by a tap at my bedroom door. George in his pyjamas to say there was a burst pipe in his room. Feverishly we try to stop the gush by sticky-tape. No avail. I am obliged to wake up Alvilde who reminds me that the water tap controlling the whole supply to the house is in the downstairs lavatory. This succeeds. In the morning Gerald§ comes round at once and miraculously mends it. He points out that this pipe, made of copper, put in three years ago by us, in a warm room too, should not have burst. He, a plumber, says that manufacturers pur-

---

* Born 1931; formerly on staff of N.T. and Christie's; expert on neo-classical sculpture; close friend of J.L.-M. since 1958.
† Sir John Pope-Hennessy (1913–95); Chairman of Department of European Paintings, Metropolitan Museum, New York, 1977–86.
‡ Friend of J.L.-M. since 1945, at which time he was a US naval officer.
§ Gerald Bird, husband of Peggy.

posely make pipes with flaws so that they will not last long and will have to be replaced by the customer.

I drive George to Holy Communion at Acton Turville. On the way he tells me that, as an Anglo-Catholic who has not been to confession, he won't communicate. I said, what have you been doing? He said, something I ought not to have done, last Wednesday night. We get to the church first, meeting a farmer in brown breeches and a pipe in his mouth on the way out. The Vicar comes up to me and says he has forgotten to bring the wafers, but the farmer, a bell-ringer, will get some bread from the pub. The result is I am nearly choked by a huge piece of Mother's Pride.

A wretched week for interruptions, caused by snow, ice and fog. Went to London for Wednesday night and stayed with John [Kenworthy-Browne]. We dined cosily at Brooks's. Went to the shop in the King's Road recommended by David Somerset* for trousers, called the Jean Machine. Blaring hot music. Nice polite young man told me that my waist, being 36 inches, was too large to allow much choice of trouser. Ended buying a fawn pair of corduroys which I did not really want. Wanted some exotic trousers, but they were too small round the waist.

Sunday, 28th January

The bitter cold persists. This morning at breakfast the thermometer outside my window registered 13 degrees Fahrenheit. With a few days' break over Christmas we have endured this extreme cold for six weeks. I now keep my working library in the boot of my car, for I never know, when I leave Bath, whether I shall be able to return next morning.

On Thursday Tom Gibson, the Vicar, was sitting in his study at 7.30 p.m. His wife is in South Africa recuperating and his children all away. He heard a noise in the kitchen and thought his son Angus had turned up as he said he might. Vicar went to the hall, and was confronted with an awful looking blaggard carrying a strip of exhaust pipe. There were two confederates behind him. With astonishing presence of mind Vicar said 'Wait a minute, old chap', retired behind

---

* Born 1928; cousin and heir of 10th Duke of Beaufort; m. 1950 Lady Caroline Thynne (1928–1995), dau. of 6th Marquess of Bath; lived at The Cottage, Badminton.

the door and seized some awful implement of his own, an iron bar. Came back and without a moment's hesitation dealt the first man a devastating blow on the shoulder. He yelled but put up no resistance, and the three fled. Jumped into a small grey van which they had backed to the outer kitchen door, and drove off. Vicar hurled implement at the car, and struck it. Then telephoned police. Police asked his age, the colour of his skin, the maiden names of his two grandmothers, and then told him he had committed a serious offence, and could be sued by the assailant for unprovoked aggression with intent to hurt. 'I only wish I had hurt him more,' Vicar said. He is sure he broke the man's collarbone. Yet no hospital has admitted a man with this injury.

That very evening at 7.20 A. and I were sitting in the drawing room. Suddenly Folly* stood up and barked ferociously, her alarm bark, and when we let the dogs out of the front door they rushed to the gate. We think the burglars wanted to raid us, and were deterred by our dogs. Seems to me unlikely three men would specially invade the rectory.

Yesterday we lunched with Ann Fleming† at Sevenhampton. John Sparrow,‡ John Gere, nice clever man from the British Museum, and the Roy Jenkinses.§ I sat next to Ann and Mrs Jenkins, whom I liked immensely. Very intelligent, a little 'blue', dressed in subfusc, no nonsense, and no trailing of coat, sympathetic. A sort of Girton girl. We talked about the Historic Buildings Committee and the National Trust. She said that the HBC Secretary, clever young man of thirty and no Socialist, is shocked by the aristocratic, paternalistic constitution of the Trust. I said I used to be worried by this before the war when every chairman of committee had to be an earl.

After luncheon, A., Mrs J. and Ann went for a walk with the dogs. We four men stayed indoors and had a long talk. Rather fascinating. Talked of politicians and great statesmen. Macmillan modelled himself on A.J. Balfour to the extent of folding his bow tie under the points

---

* Folly and Honey were the L.-Ms' whippets.
† Ann Charteris, dau. of Hon. Guy Charteris, m. (3rd) Ian Fleming (1908–64), novelist.
‡ Warden of All Souls College, Oxford, 1952–77 (1906–92).
§ Roy Harris Jenkins; b. 1920; Labour politician and cabinet minister; President of European Commission, 1977–81; Leader of Social Democrat Party, 1981–3; cr. Lord Jenkins of Hillhead (Life Peer), 1987; m. 1945 Jennifer Morris (b. 1921; DBE 1985), Chairman of N.T., 1986–90.

of his collar when a younger man. Jenkins has a great admiration of Baldwin; has written a 60,000-word monograph on him. He said Baldwin was a very tragic figure in the end. Retired aged seventy in a blaze of glory, KG and earldom. Then his last ten years a purgatory: reviled and harassed very unfairly. Told story of Baldwin in first-class carriage from Worcester to London when Prime Minister. A man got in and sat opposite. Kept on looking at Baldwin. At last tapped him on the knee and said: 'Baldwin?' B. said yes. Man said: 'Harrow 1885?' Baldwin said yes. 'And what, pray,' asked the man, 'are you doing now?'

Jenkins spoke about interpreters at important meetings with heads of state. Whenever he is talking to Giscard* he insists on speaking in English through an interpreter the moment questions of intricacy arise. G. speaks fluent English but won't, because he believes every foreigner ought to speak French. Does not like Giscard; finds him proud and icy cold. I asked if a good interpreter imitated the intonation of the speaker, put on a voice of anger, impatience, cynicism, etc. He said the good ones do not do this. Jenkins knows that when a colleague says 'I understand French though I don't speak it well', he cannot understand at all. Just as when a foreigner speaking English does not occasionally ask what exactly some expression means, he really does not know our language well.

Annie says Roy Jenkins is shy. This may account for his behaviour when they were announced. He shook hands with a perfunctory smile and flew to the drinks table and mixed himself a stiff martini. Sat down and read the newspaper, while we were left talking to Mrs.

For some odd reason he thinks highly of my two books of diary. 'They give the best impression of life in London at that period I have ever read.' Thinks *Prophesying Peace* a bad title, and asked what it meant. I said 'Peace' should be read as meant caustically. He said Ann lent him her copy of *Ancestral Voices*. He left it behind in the train, then had to buy two more copies, one for her and the other for himself to keep. Flattering.

I asked if he was sensitive to criticism in the press. He said it depended. If it was a leader in *The Times* he minded. If it impugned his integrity he minded. If it merely disagreed with his policy, he didn't mind at all. It also depended who the critic was.

---

* Valéry Giscard d'Estaing, President of France 1974–81.

Friday, 2nd February

In a sense I have today finished the first volume of my Harold [Nicolson] book. By which I mean that I have typed down the last chapter and corrected it. Now I have to go through the whole thing, trying to reduce it drastically, correct again, and re-type from beginning to end, before I can send it to Chatto's. I know it to be far too long, and I have the utmost misgivings. A. has read each chapter and says she enjoyed them all. She was only bored by the political sections, some of which I may be able to reduce. I see that I began the actual writing on 20 June last year, so it has taken me a little over six months. This means that had I not had interruptions, like going abroad, going to London, etc., I could have written it in four months.

Saturday, 17th February

On Friday the 9th, A., Caroline Somerset and I went to Berlin for a long weekend on package terms, that is to say a cheap ticket, amounting to £154 inclusive of flight and hotel, the Savigny in Brandenbergerstrasse, modest and clean. We came back on the Monday afternoon.

It was bitterly cold, and when the wind blew straight from the Steppes the very marrow of the back was pierced as with knives. But the hotel, the museums, cafés, shops, buses were very hot, so I never once wore the fur lining I had dragged all the way to Berlin. It is the most hideous city I have ever seen, worse than Constantinople, even Athens, though more agreeable than either. I refer to the West Sector, which is a hotchpotch of the worst-taste modernistic buildings, evidently put up in a hurry after the war by speculative builders. Our last morning we went to the East Sector, and I regret to say that the Communists have done far better. Their new buildings are commonplace enough, but they conform in height and scale to the fine wide boulevards. Many of the houses of faience, which instead of giving a public lavatory look are almost pleasing. They also had better old buildings in their sector, and gradually they are reproducing them exactly as they were. Berlin, which I had always supposed to be ugly – i.e., before 1939 – must have been a fine city. Many of the early nineteenth-century palaces, the Schinkel School ones, very impressive indeed.

In the West, Tiergarten scruffy, barbed wire and no statues that I

could see. Stunted trees all new since the war, old ones cut down for
firewood. Walked to look at Brücken-allee where Harold's apartment
was. Gone completely, even the street, and site occupied by tower
blocks. Reichstag impressive, though of William II date, and melancholy next to the Wall. Wall not quite so terrifying as I had expected,
because white cement, with rounded capping. A sad, moving little
group of crosses marking the site where fugitives from the East were
shot down by the stinking Communists. The area by the Wall very
desolate, a sort of no-man's-land, blighted. In fact the scruffiness is
beyond all belief.

Spend one day in Staatsmuseum. I suppose one of the best picture
galleries in Europe. Rembrandt's man in a gold helmet. Helmet looks
gold from a few feet away, and green when peered into. Rembrandt
self-portrait. What an insignificant face for the greatest painter genius.
Pig eyes, commonplace features, like a major in the Pioneer Corps,
mousy little moustache. Not unlike Harold entirely. I loved early
nineteenth-century paintings in the National Gallery, conversation
pieces of *gemütlich*, cosy Biedermeier rooms.

The Charlottenburg Castle, which the West Germans have rebuilt
from the gutted ruin it was reduced to, has been restored, redecorated
and refurnished in a most commendable way. The exterior has been
done perfectly. The replacement of the long first-floor galleries, the
gold and white stucco rooms of Frederick the Great, remarkable. Also
wonderful are the smaller more intimate rooms downstairs, into
which they have put back red damask wall hangings with rich gold
braid, and above all the Chinese rooms. Here they have replaced all
the blue-and-white china, which had been reduced to rubble, by
buying presumably old blue-and-white from other sources. Almost a
miracle, down to the little porcelain tassles hanging from the window
pelmets. The quality of some of the stucco on walls and ceilings is
coarse. Nevertheless, the work is a triumph.

Stayed Monday night with Eardley [Knollys],* and on Tuesday to the
Properties Committee. Michael Bloch,† the young man who had
written to me about Harold and Philip Guedalla,‡ whose biography he
is writing, lunched at Brooks's. Suave and dark, with large luminous

---

* Painter; formerly on staff of N.T. (1902–91).
† Born 1953; student (undergraduate and postgraduate) at St John's College, Cambridge,
1971–9; called to the Bar by Inner Temple, 1978.
‡ Historian and essayist (1889–1944).

eyes like Brian Howard's,* but not chi-chi like Brian. Quiet, soft-spoken so that I strained to hear, and very intelligent. Unfortunately Alvilde called punctually at 2.30 to motor me home and I had to dismiss him, not without arranging to take him to see Rosamond [Lehmann]† whom he pines to know.

The Persian catastrophe is one of the worst since the War.‡ What I knew would happen is happening. The Marxists are taking over. A People's Republic has shot four generals and announces that more executions will follow. Of course it is not a revolution of the right but of the left. The mullahs will not succeed in establishing order. Whole thing organised by Russia, via Afghanistan. And our Government and the Americans have already recognised the Ayatollah's regime. Never have I despised and loathed a Government more than this one. Rhodesia, capitulation everywhere, to Marxism, the Unions. And yet they muster a majority at the end of every debate in Parliament, and can't be removed, though they represent a minority in the country.

Thursday, 22nd February

On 3 January I took John Cornforth§ to lunch with Dorothy de Navarro in Broadway after a year or more of nagging him to visit the house, with a view to an article in *Country Life* on the Court Farm. Both de Navarros were longing for this. John thought there was not enough data; but had he not procrastinated, we could have got the data from Toty.¶ That day he was in bed with heart trouble. Dorothy let us peer at him through his bedroom door. He was lying supine and wan. With his wonted courtesy he just raised himself to shake my hand and laugh. He has now died, and today I go to his funeral in Broadway.

---

* Aesthete and dilettante (1905–58); the model for Anthony Blanche in *Brideshead Revisited*.
† Novelist (1901–90).
‡ Following the flight of the Shah, an Islamic Republic hostile to the West was established that month under Ayatollah Khomeini.
§ Architectural historian and contributor to *Country Life* (b. 1937).
¶ José Maria de Navarro (1896–1979), only surviving son of the actress Mary Anderson (1859–1940) who retired from the stage in the 1880s to marry Antonio de Navarro (1860–1932), a wealthy Spanish-American, and settle at Court Farm, Broadway, Worcestershire. 'Toty', archaeologist and Fellow of Trinity College, Cambridge, m. 1940 Dolores MacKenzie Hoare (1901–87), Fellow of Newnham College, Cambridge.

I was never intimate with Toty, but always liked him. He was a dear man, and a really virtuous man, staunch Papist, and I would say without an evil thought in his head all his eighty-three years. His death brings back memories of Mamie, his mother, who befriended me when I became a Papist in 1934 and was for a period not allowed to go home to Wickhamford. I used to stay with her in Broadway, which annoyed my father as I had intended, and distressed my mother. I am sorry now for having done these things. Mamie de Navarro was a very affected woman, not an intellectual but with a genuine liking for intellectuals. She entertained all the intellectual and social nobs since the 1890s in this house. I met Elgar there at a concert once in the Twenties, and George Arliss the actor, and [J. M.] Barrie. The old father was a distinguished little Spanish grandee with a neatly trimmed pointed beard. There was always something a little too good to be true about this household, and one felt that with one misplaced word one might outlaw oneself from it for ever. Any disparagement of the Holy Father or any anti-Catholic remark would have broken the sweet spell and brought instant exclusion. Nevertheless I owe a deep debt of gratitude to Mamie de Navarro, who helped me at a difficult time, gave me little holy books with wishes for the salvation of my soul inscribed, books which had been given her years before by the Duchess of Newcastle and Baroness von Hügel, etc. I think I affronted her at the beginning of the War with my pacifist tendencies, and I am sure I shocked Toty and Dorothy with my novel and autobiography* (which is not in fact an autobiography, for I do not regard it as such any more than Harold's *Some People*† was meant to be).

Sunday, 25th February

Went to Toty de Navarro's funeral on Thursday, Requiem Mass at Broadway. Not a soul I knew except Alice Fairfax-Lucy‡ and she not a local. It was strange being in the church which I used to frequent

---

* J.L.-M's memoir *Another Self* (1970), and *Heretics in Love* (1973), a novel on the theme of incest.
† Harold Nicolson's celebrated work of semi-fictionalised autobiography, first published in 1927.
‡ Hon. Alice Buchan, dau. of 1st Baron Tweedsmuir (the author John Buchan); m. 1933 Brian Cameron-Ramsay-Fairfax-Lucy, later 5th Bt (1898–1974), of Charlecote Park, Warwickshire.

when I lived at Wickhamford, during weekends, with my parents, after they forgave me. What a dreary, thin, tasteless, unspiritual building. Its flat roof ceiled with cheap wood, its Stations of the Cross made of plasticine and painted mustard. Hideous Romanesque altar. Toty's coffin standing below the altar steps on the Gospel side. A poor organ, a limited choir in the loft. Dreariness, dismalness, death and shoddiness. A ghastly service which lasted an hour and a half. And when we left, poor Dorothy and her son stood at the gate after the committal and she said to me: 'What a beautiful service it was. We were so lucky: we got special permission from the Bishop to have it in Latin.' Now why the hell should they have to get the Bishop's consent for the Mass to be sung in the language it always was sung in since the first century AD?

Took the train from Gloucester to Derby. Stayed night at Midland Hotel. Was joined for dinner by Christopher Wall* who drove me to Sudbury [Hall, Derbyshire] next morning. Meeting there. Debo [Devonshire]† came and said: 'But why did you not come and stay with me?' I replied that I didn't like to presume. 'What! Presume? You who have known me since I was three weeks old?'

In that Broadway church I did not experience one second of spiritual devotion, not one flicker. Just irritation and revulsion. I wonder, did I ever like the cheap mumbo-jumbo in the days when I got used to it? I am really quite anti-Catholic now. How my great-aunt Katie would smirk.

Saturday, 10th March

On 1 March 1938 I met Rick Stewart-Jones.‡ On 1 March 1979 I went to Chippenham Hospital to have a number of little warts removed, not cauterised as I expected, but frozen off by a sister. The effect would be that of frostbite. One or two of the warts tingled badly

---

* Born 1929; on staff of N.T., 1956–94 (Representative for Thames and Chiltern Region, 1971–94, formerly for N.W. where his responsibilities had included Sudbury).
† The Hon. Deborah Mitford, youngest of the Mitford sisters; b. 1920; m. 1941 Lord Andrew Cavendish, who succeeded his father as 11th Duke of Devonshire, 1950; member, with J.L.-M. and Wall, of the N.T's Sudbury Hall Advisory Committee.
‡ Richard Stewart-Jones (1914–57), architectural conservationist. In *Fourteen Friends*, J.L.-M. writes of him: 'It was on St David's Day that I met him . . . so that on each anniversary I recall the occasion as if it were yesterday.'

for several days. Then I went to a chiropodist in Bath to have two corns removed. O the squalors of the septuagenarian body. But one must persevere to keep it decent.

Now, on the 7th I motored up to London to meet by appointment at Brooks's Michael Bloch. I got there at six and he had already arrived. I had forgotten what he looked like. He is slim and willowy. His Brian Howard eyes are large and luminous and fine. He has an oval face, alabaster skin. Don't know how handsome. Full, dark hair, cut like nephew Nick's.* We talked in the upstairs Subscription Room, he drinking Bloody Marys, until we drove at eight to pick up Rosamond for dinner. I lost the way: he who cannot drive was no help, not knowing where any street was. We took Rosamond to dinner round the corner. Over £16 it cost. They sat together and I opposite. I could barely hear for the noise. The meeting was a success. She liked his intelligence and positive views.

Last week we had one lovely day, sun and calm, without a breath of wind. Honey and I went for a walk this evening just before sunset, in Vicarage Fields. Coming back, facing the sky, which was a gash of crimson and orange, the darkness was creeping up from the grass, and I had the sensation of walking in space. I moved very fast, without the least effort, racing across the fields, Honey beside me, like wind through wheat, feet barely touching the ground, without effort, without breathlessness. It was almost a mystical experience. March has always been a queer month for me, full of emotional events and portents. What is this one to bring?

A. and I dined with the Julian Fanes† in their nice large flat in Eccleston Square. Julian told me that Leslie Hartley‡ never corrected what he wrote, which accounted for the dreadful trouble Hamish Hamilton had with his MSS when he went gaga. Julian said he would write his novels in highly concentrated spurts, while others were in the room laughing and talking. It was as though they did not exist for him, unless they left the room. At the end of each spurt he would stop, get up, join in the conversation, and then return to the desk for another spurt. His power of concentration and fertility of imagination were prodigious.

---

* J.L.-M's great-nephew Nicholas Robinson, son of his sister Audrey's daughter Prudence; b. 1955; then working for Chatto & Windus, J.L.-M's publishers.

† Hon. Julian Fane (b. 1927); yr son of Diana, Countess of Westmorland; writer.

‡ L.P. Hartley (1895–1972); novelist; author of *The Go-Between*.

Sunday, 11th March

This morning at eight o'clock Communion I awoke to hear myself reciting the last lines of the General Confession without knowing what I was saying or how I got to this passage of the service.

The Arthur Duckworths* lunched. She sympathetic and gentle; he a sad, disillusioned man with a huge ungainly house (Orchard Leigh) and no staff, and three gardeners whose wages rise without warning three times a year, whereas rents are fixed at absurdly low figures by statute. Iniquitous. Elspeth Huxley† and John Gwynne also lunching with us. Elspeth looking the spit of Iris Murdoch whom we saw and listened to interviewed on telly last night. These lady novelists with fringes cut awry, wearing stained, untidy blouses, trousers and no attempt at dress or make-up.

Monday, 12th March

I have that ache in the abdomen, but I will not allow myself to go over the brink. Unfortunately I sense that damned spring approaching, and that awful wanderlust feeling, that misery which I never seem to grow out of. How I hate the unsettling, beastly reminder of lost opportunities, the reminder that there can be no further opportunities, that bloody spring.

Tuesday, 13th March

A letter this morning. I could not bring myself to open it until after luncheon. Took a strong drink. Was ever a man of seventy more blessed? It is going to be a platonic relationship, and possibly the deepest of my whole life.

Saturday, 17th March

Telephoned J[ohn Kenworthy-Browne] and talked to him about a bust of John Francis's‡ which I have found in a junk shop in Bath and

---

* George Arthur Victor Duckworth (1901–87), of Orchardleigh Park, Frome, Somerset; MP for Shrewsbury, 1924–45; m. (2nd., 1968) Mary Buxton.
† Elspeth Grant (1907–94); m. 1931 Gervas Huxley (d. 1971); writer.
‡ Sculptor (1780–1861); executed, *inter alia*, busts of Prince Albert and Queen Victoria.

asked his advice. He gave it at length. Then I said I supposed he was busy packing for his jaunt to Sicily tomorrow. He said: 'No, I fear it is off. My father died half an hour ago. The person I was going with is dreadfully put out.' He thought his father's funeral would not be for ten days (which is unusual) and supposed he could go to Sicily just for the week. I said I really did not think he could. He agreed, but it is sad for him.

We dined at Berkeley Castle on Friday. Lennox and Freda* staying, Freda in one of her bored moods. I would say John Berkeley† is as good as gold, and A. who talked at dinner with him says he is intelligent, with a great sense of responsibility and of what is expected of him.

Sunday, 18th March

When we last parted M. said, 'Do let's write.' Well, my trouble is that I find it easier to write every day than to write once in a while. Moreover, trite observations and sentiments seem less trite in a daily missive than in an occasional missive, from which more is expected.

Saturday, 24 March

Lunched with the Mayalls.‡ Lees is a gentle, sympathetic, unsocial sort of being. I had a long talk with Priscilla Bibesco that was. She told me that her father after the last war, when very hard up, sold all the letters he received from Proust to an American library. Tony Powell§ said to me that his 'book', as he calls the twelve volumes, was to be filmed for television in 1982.¶ He said he would like to live to see it, but were

---

* Sir Lennox Berkeley (1903–90), composer; nephew of 9th and last Earl Berkeley (d. 1942) but unable to inherit title and estates owing to his father's illegitimacy; m. 1946 Freda Bernstein (b. 1923).

† Born 1931; distant cousin of 9th Earl Berkeley (see preceding note) from whom he inherited Berkeley Castle, Gloucestershire.

‡ Sir Alexander Lees Mayall (1915–93); diplomat; m. (2nd) Hon. Mary Ormsby-Gore, dau. of 4th Baron Harlech.

§ Anthony Powell (1905–2000); novelist; m. 1934 Lady Violet Pakenham.

¶ Having bought an option on the television rights to Anthony Powell's twelve-volume novel sequence *A Dance to the Music of Time*, the BBC decided their proposed serial would be too expensive to produce. A much acclaimed serialisation by Alvin Rakoff finally appeared on Channel Four in 1997.

it not for that, he would be content to die now. He does not the least wish to see more of this disagreeable world. Told me this in greatest good humour, with a cocktail in the hand; and I knew he was speaking the truth and not for effect. I said, 'I expect you get letters from strangers saying what a snob you are.' 'I do,' he said, 'but this morning I received a letter from a black man in New York saying how much he appreciated the sort of people I wrote about, and ending "Your brother". '

Thursday, 29th March

Joan Drogheda* lunched with me at a strange underground restaurant called Joe Allen behind Covent Garden. Joan always accommodates herself to anything and was amused by the ambience. No menu but a list of things chalked up on a board. We ordered the salad of the day, neither of us being great midday eaters. We were served the salad in enormous shaving-bowls like troughs, and could barely get through the surface. Good talk, easy, affectionate. She is a darling.

Friday, 30th March

Learned that Michael Rosse has been ill again. I telephoned and spoke to Anne† in London. Indeed, he nearly died of kidney trouble. His children were summoned. Anne desperate; but he got through an operation miraculously. She told me to telephone him, which I did. The frailest, most laboured, tiredest voice answered. I merely said a few words of greeting, hope and comfort, and rang off, feeling very sad. He is shortly being taken back to Birr.‡ Poor Michael.

Tuesday, 3rd April

The Vicar stopped me in the village street, full of complaints about the Duke having invited the Bishop of Gloucester to preach on the Sunday when the Queen comes, and a choir from Cheltenham,

---

* Joan Carr, pianist (d. 1989); m. 1935 Garrett Moore, later 11th Earl of Drogheda (1910–89).

† Anne Armstrong-Jones (*née* Messel), m. 1935 Michael Parsons, 6th Earl of Rosse (1906–79).

‡ Birr Castle, Co. Offaly; Irish seat of the Rosses.

without so much as a by-your-leave. The Vicar rebuked him on the telephone, and Master white with rage said, 'You seem to forget that I am the Duke of Beaufort.' Vicar claimed to have replied, 'So what? The Church is my concern, not yours.'

Monday, 9th April

The weekend is over. I drove in pouring rain, without once stopping, to Cambridge. Arrived at 7.15, put car in a multi-storeyed carpark, and walked to 9 King's Parade. An opening opposite the gate of King's led down a passage. No. 9 painted over a door. I rang. Presently M. appeared, smiling. Led me to his charming room with two Georgian windows facing the Parade. Typical undergraduate's room, cheap but not unattractive, flowered wallpaper *à la* Zuleika Dobson, dresser of art nouveau, hideous modern chandelier from supermarket, comfortable stuffed chairs, one very large table covered with typewriter and papers. Books everywhere, on shelves and on floor. We drank whisky. We talked. He is easy to talk to. At 9.30 we went to dine at a disgusting place down the street where we ate lamb goulash and drank red plonk. Afterwards we visited a Russian lady he knows, Vera Traill, living in penury and surrounded by empty bottles of *vin rosé*.[*] She intelligent and sharp. Much badinage. She is a friend of John Lehmann,[†] that sinister figure which looms, and of Moura Budberg,[‡] who was a kleptomaniac following her menopause. When after her death friends went to her flat, they found their choicest possessions lying around.

Then M. and I went back to No. 9. One dim lamp, the gas fire and Bach played softly on the gramophone. The whole occasion like that of any undergraduate, though he a graduate. He told me about his life. We talked till 2 a.m. by the fire. He read me from the beginning of a play he is writing, and from books, including my own. Then he accompanied me to St John's College, to the guest room where I spent the night. The moon was scurrying through the clouds as we strolled through the deserted quadrangles, lit by the single passageway lamp. He fetched me in the morning and took me back to his rooms to have

---

[*] Film critic (1906–87); daughter of the Tsarist politician Alexander Guchkov.
[†] Author, publisher and critic (1907–87); brother of Rosamond. Michael Bloch had briefly been his secretary.
[‡] Baroness Budberg (1892–1974) *née* Maria (Moura) Zakrevskaya, Russian *émigrée* active in London literary circles and sometime mistress of H.G. Wells.

breakfast, the landlady, who clearly adores him, talking beside the table. He says she does not mind how many male friends he has in his room, but hates girls, and whenever they telephone him says he is out.

Sunday spent wandering around the Backs, visiting the Fitz-William, too crowded; had a luncheon–tea there in basement café, and at five I left.

13th April (Good Friday)

Eardley and I spent two days this week motoring in Somerset. Like old times. How often have we two not done this in the old days, thirty-five years ago. We spent Tuesday night with the Stones.* Were shocked to discover that Reynolds is inexplicably senile. At breakfast on Wednesday he insisted on reading a passage from K. Clark's† book on Beardsley, and could not get the words out. It was like a child suffering from the inability to co-ordinate. The words just meant nothing to him. Janet seized the book in her bossy way, but he would not let her take it, and persisted. Eardley and I did not dare look at each other. However, Reynolds was able to tell me a charming story while showing me a nice panel of early Renaissance tapestry they have hanging over their staircase. It belonged to Dr Luxmoore, who culti-vated the garden at Eton in which I used to sit for dreamy evening hours with dear friends like Tom and Desmond.‡ He was very fond of it, but during the First World War decided he ought to sell it in aid of the Red Cross. His friends, led by Reynolds' mother, knew what its loss would mean to him. They clubbed together and bought it. One afternoon while Luxmoore was out they re-hung it in its old place on the staircase. Nothing was said. No thanks, no reference to what they had done came from Luxmoore. One day three months later Mrs Stone happened to accompany Luxmoore upstairs. She noticed that as he climbed the stairs he shielded the left side of his face with his hand. The top of the stairs reached, Mrs Stone wheeled him

---

* Reynolds Stone (1909–1979); designer, graphic engraver and printer; m. 1938 Janet Woods.

† Baron Clark of Saltwood (Life Peer, cr. 1969); best remembered as Sir Kenneth Clark, art historian (1903–83).

‡ Hon. Thomas Mitford (1909–45), only brother of Mitford sisters; Hon. Desmond Parsons (1910–37), brother of Michael Parsons, 6th Earl of Rosse: J.L.-M's closest friends at Eton.

round and took his hand away from his face. Luxmoore was amazed. In gratitude he left the tapestry to the Stone family in his will.

Much talk about K. Clark. Great complaints of his new wife* who, both Stones claim, is making him unhappy, keeping him away from Saltwood, making him travel ceaselessly and preventing him from writing.

I received a letter from Ros [Lehmann] which slightly upset me – that Misha† had been to see her again, as indeed he told me. She can't make him out: he is like a character in a novel who is not fully formed. Her brother John says he is mad. Now mad is the last adjective I would apply. Emotionally unstable, possibly. He reminds me more and more of Jamesey [Pope Hennessy],‡ without any of the bitchiness.

Tuesday, 17th April

Bank Holiday. Motored up to London alone. Stayed the night with John [Kenworthy-Browne], at his nicest and best. Following afternoon the N.T. Properties Committee. Virginia Woolf's house at Rodmell under discussion. I have never been inside, but from knowledge of outside am dubious. However, she must be the greatest literary genius of the century in English. Just re-reading *Mrs Dalloway*. No writer has thrown such vibrant, impressionistic light on everyday things as she. I marvel over every sentence. Not that I am not at times bewildered and bored by the narrative.

Met M. for tea at his club and had dinner cooked by him at his flat, excellent dish with caraway. Not entirely satisfactory evening. A handsome young friend of his, Charles Orwin,§ who works at Faber's and is a fan, joined us. Somehow I felt out of my element. At 10.45 said I must go home. We talked of promiscuity, whether it blunts the sensibilities. I said I was not sure, but I am. It must. It does.

Saturday, 21st April

Today Papa would be ninety-nine. Pray God forgive me for the unfilial way I treated him when he was alive, and since his death.

---

* Nolwen, Comtesse de Janzé (1925–90); m. Lord Clark 1977 as his 2nd wife.
† Michael Bloch.
‡ James Pope-Hennessy (1916–74); writer; younger brother of Sir John P.-H.; close friend of J.L.-M. in 1940s; done to death in January 1974.
§ Publisher (b. 1951).

Ros is in my confidence. She is a rock of fortitude, of sympathy and good advice. She is very unhappy about her sister Beatrix who has had a bad stroke, and may never act again, which is her life. A hard woman, I gather, and her whole face contracts when Ros dares to mention that her friends pray for her.*

We have Jimmie Smith† staying for the Badminton Three-Day Event. Although the weather is warm, Jimmie seldom goes out of doors. He has become fearfully old, or rather death-wishy. He walks with a stick even indoors, though can do perfectly well without it. Otherwise full of chat, and his friendship with the Queen Mother. We were thereby invited to take him to the Beauforts' after-dinner party which they gave for the Queen's birthday. Mary Beaufort had hired a 'funny man', as she called him, from Bristol. It was rather painful. All one-person performances have to be extremely good or they are embarrassing. This little man was no Ruth Draper, and signally unfunny. Only the Royals in the front row were holding their sides; whether out of pity, good manners or enjoyment, who can tell? Twice the performer called for assistance from the audience. Each time Prince Andrew and Prince Charles volunteered to go forward. Both very good, un-shy, and the Prince of Wales was frankly funnier than the 'funny man' in his clowning. A ghastly party, and we had drinks afterwards in the dining room. What was nice was that the Beauforts had asked people from the estate, Leslie the butler's wife and two sons, farmers, estate servants, their wives dressed to kill and talking away with the Royals at their ease. I did not speak to one Royal: had my eye on one or two, female, but was not presented.

Thursday, 26th April

To London today. Went straight to Chatto's where I delivered into the hands of Norah‡ my typescript. In fact I had not quite finished correcting it. That done, to London Library and took out Siegfried Sassoon and Paul Valéry's poems. Then to annual meeting of the [Society of] Antiquaries, which I had not attended for ten years. Even

---

* Beatrix Lehmann (1903–79), actress known for macabre roles. She was a militant atheist.
† Hon. James Smith (b. 1906); Governor of Sadler's Wells Theatre and member of the Royal Opera House Trust.
‡ Norah Smallwood (1909–84), the dragon-like Chairman of Chatto & Windus.

so was bored to tears and left after half an hour. Drove to Eardley for a cup of tea with him. Cold worse. Dosed myself with Beecham's Powders. Then to Johnnie Churchill's* in Tite Street to a ghastly party given for Kay Halle.† Old, old crocks like John Foster,‡ that exhausted stallion, half-dead with decay, and Duncan Sandys,§ stone deaf. Then on to Brooks's. M. very smart in his tweed suit and full of confidences. I have trouble hearing him: the voice like pattering raindrops.

Monday, 30th April

Now that I have divested myself, temporarily I suppose, of Harold, I am at a loss. Feel bereft, with no purpose in life, in spite of my reviews for *Apollo* and articles for *Country Life*. I understand how Virginia Woolf had a breakdown when she finished a book. Only she didn't have hers returned, underscored, or larded with requests to rewrite parts. Non-writers don't understand how writers feel like emigrants in an alien world, having left forever the shores of yesteryear.

Wednesday, 2nd May

Still bitterly cold. Wearing thickest winter clothes. Everything nature-wise most backward. Snowdrops only just dead; the wind-flower out, and primroses; bluebells sprouting. Motored to Bath this morning in a snow blizzard. Today exchanged my old white Renault for a new one, blue with a special paint to prevent rust. Did not feel as sad parting with the old friend as I would have been twenty-five years ago, when I was dreadfully attached to my cars. Now they are merely vehicles of convenience.

Hardy Amies¶ lunched here last Sunday, bringing a delightful woman, Countess Bernstorff, English married to a German. She

---

* J.G. Spencer-Churchill (1909–94), nephew of Sir Winston; artist; friend of J.L.-M. since they had crammed together for Oxford in 1927.

† American writer on Churchill family (d. 1992).

‡ (1904–82); QC and Conservative politician.

§ (1908–87); Eton contemporary of J.L.-M.; Conservative cabinet minister, 1951–64; m. 1935 Diana, dau. of Winston Churchill; cr. Lord Duncan-Sandys, 1974.

¶ Hardy Amies (b. 1909); Dressmaker by Appointment to HM The Queen; KCVO 1989.

remained in Hamburg throughout the last war. The Germans were nice to her. Her only compatriot, whom she met constantly without causing suspicion, was the Princess of Hesse.* Hardy has been in Monte Carlo. There saw Alan Searle,† who with Willie's royalties is rich as Croesus. All he does is eat in different restaurants and become enormous. But he remains incredibly generous. One day he met a young pianist and asked him the time. Pianist said he did not know as he didn't possess a watch. 'What!' said Alan. 'Come with me at once to Cartier.' They went. Alan chose the watch, but it had no gold bracelet. Cartier said they would have one made specially. Alan paid down £3,000. Some time later, Alan called at Cartier in the company of another young man, and was told the watch would be ready next day. Next day Alan called again. 'Oh,' said Cartier, 'we handed over the watch this morning to the young friend who accompanied you yesterday.' Neither young man nor watch was seen again. Alan however assured the pianist that he had ordered another watch for him.

Sunday, 6th May

We played a small part in the General Election, acting in turn as tellers at the village hall, used as the polling station. Bywater, the Duke's secretary, knows which way every single inhabitant of the village voted. He said that several of them subscribe to Tory funds yet vote Labour – out of fear of the Duke, I suppose. Wonderfully cheered by the victory.‡

Tuesday, 8 May

Today I motored in my new Renault to lunch with Elspeth Baldwin.§ I endeavoured to sort through her books, for she is too blind to read the names on the spines. She wants to reduce the number and yet to

---

* Hon. Margaret Geddes, m. 1937 the Prince of Hesse and the Rhine.

† Secretary-companion and heir of W. Somerset Maugham ('Willie'), whom the L.-Ms had known in the south of France in the 1950s.

‡ At the general election on 3 May, the Conservatives under Mrs Thatcher were returned to power with a parliamentary majority of 43.

§ American-born widow of 3rd Earl Baldwin ('Bloggs'), who had died in 1976: at the time of their marriage in 1936 her father-in-law, Stanley Baldwin, was Prime Minister.

keep any books with family associations. There are many given to her
father-in-law, others autographed by Kipling, Burne-Jones, etc. I
could have got through the whole library during this visit had E. not
interrupted with a flow of chat. But I wouldn't have stopped her for
the world, she is so amusing.

Over a cup of tea she confided that her and Bloggs's relations with
their only child Edward had not been good. Bloggs made very
unhappy by the boy's apparent indifference. He has never read a single
book of Bloggs's and always resented being a Baldwin, his grandfather's prime ministership, and the title. Now poor Bloggs is dead he
has been very kind and good to his mother. About time, too. He is
over forty.

E. is getting rid of the Baldwin papers and treasures – silver caskets,
etc., given to Stanley Baldwin in dozens. Bloggs left them all to her
to dispose of. Among the papers she quite unexpectedly came across
a day-to-day account of the Abdication which Baldwin had commissioned Sir Horace Wilson* to compile. For some reason this was not
put among the Cabinet Papers, but kept by Baldwin. Elspeth notified
Tommy Lascelles.† He said 'You must give it to the Queen', which E.
has now done. Directions on the outside that it was not to be read
before 1983. E. however read every word, then tied it up and sealed
it. Has never told a soul what it contains. She says, having read it, that
no one could make out a good case for the Duke of Windsor or Mrs
Simpson. Before he abdicated, the King was 'mad' and a physical
wreck. He ought to have been shut up. No one knows the awful time
Mr Baldwin went through.

Elspeth very sweetly told me to take away any books I wanted. So
I took Siegfried Sassoon's three autobiographical books, *Jean Santeuil*
of Proust, and John Heygate's *Decent Fellows* in original paper cover,
price 2/6d. Anyway I was able to save for her a bound proof copy of
Brideshead Revisited with a letter from Evelyn to Bloggs inside it. I told
her this was worth more than £100.

---

* (1882–1972); influential civil servant of 1930s and confidant of Macdonald, Baldwin
and Chamberlain, with deceptive title of Chief Industrial Adviser to HM Government.
† The Rt Hon. Sir Alan Lascelles (1887–1981); courtier; Private Secretary to King
George VI and Queen Elizabeth II (1943–53) (having earlier been Assistant Private
Secretary to Edward VIII as both Prince of Wales and King).

Tuesday, 15th May

Nigel Nicolson* stayed last night. Very appreciative guest. Is amazed that I have taken H.N. only down to 1929 in Vol. I and wonders if three vols will be necessary, as the most important part of H.N's life was in the 1930s and '40s. This may be so, but I maintain that thereafter until his death there is not much for a biographer to say, except about his books, for his life was one of lecturing and attending committees, not of great interest to readers. I am apprehensive about Ian's† verdict. Surely if he thought it any good he would have sent a p.c. to say so by now.

Trained to London. At 6.30 M. came to Brooks's. He gave me a chapter of his Guedalla book. Very well done. He has great descriptive powers, imagination and perception. If only he perseveres, he may be as good a writer as Jamesey. But he must work like a daemon, I have told him.

Monday, 21st May

A disagreeable incident. I took the dogs round the village. Crossing the recreation ground, they bolted towards Vicarage Wood. I heard furious yells. Stalked cautiously round the entrance gates and saw the Duke with a pair of binoculars. I retreated, coward that I am. Alvilde very boldly decided she must look for the dogs; ran into the Duke, who was beside himself with passion. He had been watching his cherished vixen and cubs. He was almost apoplectic. Said he would not have our bloody dogs on his land. Bloody this and bloody that. He would get his gun and shoot them. A. kept her head and temper, apologised and said what a good idea. Then he called at the house. I went to the door. Again he ranted. He sent the keeper after the dogs; keeper called and also said he would shoot them if ever again they were seen loose. Duke then telephoned, abused A., and slammed down the receiver. All for a trivial cause, in concern about some cubs which his hounds will tear to pieces before the autumn is through. Ghastly values, ghastly people. How I hate them. I shall never set foot

---

* Born 1917; yr son of Harold Nicolson and Vita Sackville-West; politician and author, then editing the letters of Virginia Woolf in six volumes; resident at Sissinghurst Castle, Kent.
† Ian Parsons, editorial director of Chatto & Windus.

in the big house again, in the unlikely event of being asked, and shall never speak to the hell-hound again beyond a curt good-morning if I pass him on the road.

Thursday, 24th May

We motor to London for dinner at the Droghedas'. Some ten in all. Derry there with his Alexandra,* whom I sat next to, and intelligent she undoubtedly is. She talked of her schooldays when her father was Ambassador to Poland. Said Poles not deeply religious, as people here supposed, but they identified the Catholic Church with Polish nationalism. Their hatred of Russians universal and strong. On my other side Marilyn Quennell, who was sober and sensible. Peter Q.[†] told me he had virtually been sacked from *History Today*, and felt aggrieved. His co-editor Alan Hodge, who because his home life was unhappy had come to identify himself with the magazine, was so upset that he developed a tumour on the brain and has been given one month to live. Clarissa Avon[‡] there, friendly but very sharp. Chief guest was Tito Gobbi, operatic singer. We had a long talk when dinner over and the women left the room. He has now retired. I asked if he constantly listened to records of himself in his famous roles. He said never. Why? I asked. Because he would be so critical of certain passages that it would upset him. Said the only critic to whom he paid the slightest attention was his wife, a dear old soul who was also present, she a pianist from a well-known musical family. He said that Callas's life was a tragedy, all because of love going wrong. She was left with no friends, except possibly himself. One evening at the Savoy a few friends gave him a supper party. Suddenly Callas appeared in the foyer and asked if she might join the party, as she was staying there and had just arrived from Milan. He was delighted. Next morning he asked for some flowers to be sent to her room. The hall porter told him Madame Callas had left for Milan at 7.30.

---

* Viscount Moore (b. 1937); photographer; son and heir of 11th Earl of Drogheda; m. (2nd) Alexandra, daughter of Sir Nicholas Henderson, diplomatist.
† Sir Peter Quennell (1905–94); author and journalist; editor (1951–79) of *History Today*; and his 4th wife Marilyn.
‡ Clarissa Churchill (b. 1920); sister of J.L.-M's friend Johnnie Churchill; m. 1952 Sir Anthony Eden, later 1st Earl of Avon (1897–1977).

Friday, 25th May

A. and I fly to Bulgaria for package tour of three days and nights, staying at Hotel Sofia, Sofia. Terence Mullaly* our guide. Intelligent, agreeable man. Sofia an attractive town in centre with many decent early nineteenth-century, neo-classical buildings. Periphery horrid, tower blocks rising in ever-increasing numbers and heights. Extremely clean cobbled streets which are hosed at night and even during the day by stalwart women wielding heavy hose-pipes. First thing one sees in early morning is these women sweeping up ends. Heavy fines for throwing litter. The buildings are colour-washed tawny yellows and orange. We watched the *jeunesse dorée* strolling arm-in-arm in front of the hotel, facing the statue of Alexander II which has been allowed to survive. Bulgarians just as well-dressed as the English plebeian young. City full of parks and gardens, densely tree'd and freshly green. Archaic Roman fragments in the underpasses, Roman bas-reliefs. Imagine how they would be vandalised in London. Mosque Jami-demi [?Tcherna Djamía] by architect of Blue Mosque. But disappointing. We could not enter. Portico of three bays, with ablution niches honeycombed. The Church of Santa Sophia dates, we are told, from Constantine the Great; but the interior walls are plastered over and painted a dreary brown.

On Saturday we dined at a Folk Music restaurant just outside Sofia. Frightfully hot and airless. Bulgarian band and professional dancers in national dress laid on. The native guests, full of vodka, joined in and danced and sang with abandon. The English party sat looking on with selfconsciousness and embarrassment.

This trip has put me in a bit of a quandary. Made me ask myself whether these apparently happy people are not right to be Communists. They have no one to whom they feel inferior. Of course they are regimented. But it does possibly mean the greatest happiness of the greatest number. Mullaly told me that his opposite number in the Communist equivalent of the *Daily Telegraph* is paid what amounts to £20,000 p.a., far more than he earned. The privileged here lead luxurious lives, and are allowed to leave their earnings to their children. Thus a meritocracy, not to say a new aristocracy, is being established.

At Plovdiv, the old town is preserved. We walked through it,

---

* Born 1927; art correspondent of *Daily Telegraph*, 1956–86.

between ancient houses with overhangs. Entered one, decorated in
Turkish style about 1840. An old woman spoke to me in French. She
said she admired our Queen. I said we did too. She keeps a photograph in her bedroom where it cannot be seen by strangers. A man
selling cherries in the market to Kate Vestey* said, when told she was
English, 'Maggie Thatcher, she great, she great'.

The women work in the fields, hoeing the hard earth; no modern
agricultural implements, but donkeys abound. The provincial towns
very poor-looking, poor quality of modern buildings, crumbling.
Beautiful countryside. Masses of wild flowers. Hedges of syringa
along the roadways. Dog-roses, lavender and the Valley of the Roses,
about ten miles of fields of the little white and pink musk rose, picked
for their essence. Acacia in flower, and elder. The Monastery of Rila's
splendid situation in the basin of steep mountains with snow on their
tops. Like the Mount Athos monasteries. This one 1373, but burned
several times. Church restored about 1840, beautifully, in traditional
manner. Opulent carving of iconostasis.

We returned on Monday evening. Bulgarian food absolutely ined-
ible.

Thursday, 29th May

Feel fearfully depressed, because I unwisely telephoned Norah at
Chatto's to ask if Ian had finished with my typescript. She was short
and curt. Said it was too detailed and much too long. A young man
came from London to photograph me for some article in *Harper's
Bazaar*. Nice attractive-plain young man aged thirty-one from
Stourbridge in Worcestershire. Worcestershire was a bond. Told me
his parents poor miners or the like. All his childhood he knew he must
get away from Black Country. Was sensitive, liked poetry and painting but, being semi-educated, could not express himself or his feelings. Told me he had no emotional life, never suffered from love, only
from anxiety about his profession. Complimented me on the structure of my head. Then said sweetly, 'You are an eccentric. I mean this
as a compliment.' The reason being that I keep the Max Jacob painting in the fireplace because there is no room to hang it. Second time
called an eccentric in two days. Lady Vestey said I was, on account of
my grey hair being all over the place. When I took the photographer

---

* Kathryn Eccles, m. (1970–81) 3rd Baron Vestey, of Stowell Park, Gloucestershire.

back to the station he thanked me profusely for making the appointment so enjoyable.

Wednesday, 30th May

Went to London for the day. M. met me at Brooks's. We lunched
alone, happily, until at 2.15 Alan Pryce-Jones* joined us for a quarter
of an hour, with non-stop flow of talk which fascinated M. But he
told me nothing about H.N. Said he would look out letters from him
and bring them over in July to the Magdalen Gaudy which we are
both attending. There is something tiresome about his manner.
Brilliant conversationalist though he be, his talk conveys the impression of being turned on and off like a tap. Insincerity? Certainly.
Vanity? Yes. Joy in communication? Yes. He said the Laureate
[Betjeman] was the most selfish man he knew, though qualified this
remark by saying he was also the dearest. I felt that his quarter of an
hour's call on me at Brooks's was a gracious concession.

Tuesday, 5th June

We went with the [Lennox] Berkeleys to Sir Robert Mayer's†
Centenary Concert at the Festival Hall. Splendid from beginning to
end. Began with a fanfare of trumpets specially composed by Walton,
invigorating if nothing else. Then *Meistersinger* Overture, Janet Baker
singing Berlioz's Gauthier poems, then Yehudi [Menuhin] and Isaac
Stern playing concerto for two violins. Geraint Evans made entertaining speech from the rostrum which was replied to by Sir Robert, in a
strong voice amplified. Berkeleys witnessed him receiving KCVO
from Queen personally in the interval.

Thursday, 7th June

Joined National Trust Arts Panel party for Plymouth, spending the
day at Saltram, which is beautifully kept, then Penheale to visit
Mrs Colville who surprisingly remembered me visiting the house

---

* (1908–2000); contemporary of J.L.-M. at Eton and Magdalen College, Oxford; author
and journalist; editor, *Times Literary Supplement*, 1948–59.
† Musician, writer and musical philanthropist; b. Mannheim, Germany, 1879; he had
been knighted as long ago as 1939; m. for the 2nd time in 1980.

years ago. Looked at her Italian drawings, Leonardo, Raphael, and Donatello model of the Gatemalata equestrian statue. We stayed the night at the Bedford Arms where Eardley and I so often stayed. In the morning to Cotehele. Strange to be there after so many years, for I originally arranged this house, having done all negotiations with the dear old Mount Edgcumbes.* I suggested that the N.T. put up a memorial tablet to them in the chapel at Cotehele, which was accepted.

These all-male parties depress me somewhat. And I have been feeling deeply depressed about my book and Ian Parsons' comments. But have decided to wait till I pick up the MS with his suggestions for cutting on Friday, and devote all next week and most of the following to deciding whether or not to chuck the whole thing. I think with no work I would be too unhappy to continue living, and so must make every effort to resume. Am depressed too about M. and how little I see him.

Saturday, 9th June

The Downers† are staying the weekend. Alec has been extremely ill but now appears quite cured. Went for a long walk with me in the park in the morning. Said his illness had clarified his spiritual condition and sharpened his mind, which is now working better than he ever remembers. Has a great admiration for Mrs Thatcher. Thinks she has the qualities of Queen Elizabeth I. Has asked her for an interview in a fortnight's time. Wants to tell her that a large section of the Australian people still hold this country in high regard, and her government must not let this affection evaporate. Last time she came to see him when she was Leader of the Opposition she brought a foolscap pad and filled three pages of notes during their talk. Is greatly disappointed by Heath. I said he was pig-headed. That is the very expression Carrington‡ used of him to Alec the other day.

---

* These are recounted in J.L.-M's diaries for 1946–7, *Caves of Ice*.
† Sir Alexander Downer (1910–81); son of Sir John Downer, Premier of South Australia; Australian politician and diplomatist; Minister of Immigration, 1958–63; High Commissioner in London, 1964–72; m. (1947) Mary, dau. of Sir James Gosse.
‡ Peter Carington, 6th Baron Carrington; Conservative politician; Secretary of State for Foreign and Commonwealth Affairs, 1979–82.

Sunday, 17th June

Passed on the road what I think was a dead chaffinch, with its mate hovering over it. I have never before actually seen a bird positively grieving. A distressing spectacle.

Tuesday, 19th June

To London last evening and met the Rosses at Brooks's. Had I not been pre-warned I would never have recognised Michael. His declension is pitiable and terrible. I do not suppose he can live more than a few months. He is more like a corpse than a living being, tiny drawn face with tight slit of a mouth, unsmiling. When he stands up he is a bag of bones. Anne incredibly brave, but told me she had been knocked endways first by Oliver's* death last year, then by parting with Stafford Terrace,† and now by Michael's condition. It was difficult to know what to say. Yet Michael is lucid and compos, and talks perfectly well and sanely.

I had John K.-B. and Nick Robinson to dine with me. Introduced them to the Rosses. Nick very smart for the first time ever in a nice blue suit and looking extremely handsome. I felt proud of him. Yet I don't think John cared for him; thought him arrogant, which is of course nonsense.

Left last chapter of H.N. for J.K.-B. to read for his candid opinion. He made some sound criticisms and thinks it can do with some pruning. Thinks too much of Vita in it. And curiously does not like my mentions of Vita's love affairs nor of Eddy [Sackville-West]'s making up his face in Berlin days. Thinks such items should be omitted. I don't find myself in agreement here.

Thursday, 21st June

Listened while shaving this morning to Handel's 'Lascia ch'ia pianga' from *Rinaldo*. Was moved to tears by the beauty. Handel so often repetitive and dog-trotting; but this somehow inspired with desperate

---

* Her brother, the theatrical producer, designer and artist Oliver Messel (1904–78).
† A house with a perfectly preserved late Victorian interior which had belonged to Anne Rosse's grandfather Linley Sambourne, *Punch* cartoonist of the 1880s.

love and sadness. O the hell of love, hoping for the letter. Will there be one this morning? No. Will there be one tomorrow? There is – which may be worse than if there hadn't been one. And so the agony goes on.

Received a sweet letter from Janet Stone about Reynolds' stroke. My first, horrid thought was this. Supposing Reynolds dies, supposing Michael Rosse dies, and the funeral means putting off my visit to Cambridge next week, I shall make every excuse and endeavour to go to Cambridge. Just like the Duc de Guermantes' behaviour when his cousin Amanien d'Osmond was dying and he dismissed all remonstrances in a determination to attend a costume ball. So here is inconstancy, disloyalty: putting someone I have known for a few months before old friends of a lifetime. But the truth is that friends of a lifetime become a duty, not a pleasure. (Eardley is the exception.) My old friends are becoming gaga, when they don't die. Joan Drogheda cannot take down a telephone number and has to call Lady Poole to do it for her. Anne Rosse mumbles about my coming to Nymans and does not explain whether she wants me to stay or merely lunch, not taking it in that that luncheon would mean a drive of three hundred miles in one day from Badminton.

Robert Henshaw* telephoned me that he had seen a portrait in a shop in Gay Street purporting to be of William Beckford. Would I have a look at it? I went. Found it to be [Sir Joshua] Reynolds' portrait of Beckford as a young man. It came from Hamilton Palace, as I saw from a torn label on the back.† Shop asking only £500 or so for it. Unfortunately for me Henshaw had asked the shop to hold it for him while he made enquiries. I advised him to buy it immediately, which he did. I am sure he will not keep but sell it, as he is a sort of dealer on the sly.

Tuesday, 26th June

Poor Reynolds has died, and will be buried next Friday. Alvilde said to me rather tartly, 'Lucky for you the funeral is not to be when you

---

* Resident of Bath; musician and conservationist.
† J.L.-M's library at 19 Lansdown Crescent was originally made for the writer and collector William Beckford (1760–1844) when he retired to Bath from Fonthill Abbey; Beckford's 2nd dau. m. the 10th Duke of Hamilton.

are going to Cambridge. Would you chuck your new friend?', etc. Indeed, just what I had been debating with myself. She divines my thoughts if she does not read my diary.

Thursday, 28th June

I am now back from Cambridge, and feeling so-so. Spent two nights there, one in a room in M's lodgings, the second in his college. We breakfasted together each morning in his college cafeteria. No breakfasts in Hall these days, but a squalid makeshift place where one fetches a tray, as at a railway station, and sliding it along a bar takes Weetabix, horrid soggy toast and a too-sweet marmalade in a tiny plastic pillbox, and a brown beverage masquerading as coffee.

Our first evening we walked through the fields to Grantchester where we dined expensively at the pub for £15. We walked back across the fields in the dark, arm-in-arm, the lights of Cambridge guiding our footsteps. Yesterday I went to Wimpole for the day. He all day read the first half of my H.N. book, and absolutely contrary to Ian Parsons deplores the excisions. What am I to do? He says all the cut-out bits are the most interesting bits. He has found several mistakes of mine concerning the Balkan Wars. What a clever youth he is. But I gave him a talking-to about his life of restlessness and procrastination.

Saturday, 30th June

Went to Oxford for the Magdalen Gaudy, the first time I ever attended such a thing. It was both boring and interesting. Arriving at five, I parked the car the far side of Magdalen Bridge and introduced myself at the Porter's Lodge. Was directed to the President's Garden where tea in progress on the lawn. Sunny but a cold wind. Shook hands and chatted, then slunk off. Took my luggage to the room allotted me. Large sitting room and bedroom, panelled. Could be so nice, but is horrid. Broken-down furniture, dirty carpets, sofa legs propped up by telephone books. In the bedroom, no back to the bed, no bedside lamp, naked bulb hanging from ceiling. No wash-basin. No amenities. No scout, of course. To wash and pee, was obliged to descend three flights of stairs, walk along open colonnade, plunge downstairs to a basement and lavatories. Here two cracked wash-basins, a leaking urinal and baths too squalid even to be considered. Almost as comfortless as Mount Athos, and without the spirit.

Luckily Alan Pryce-Jones was present. At dinner he sat at High

Table. But first there was Evensong in the Chapel, candles in hurri-
cane globes, all lit. Singing by choir first-rate. By now I had changed
into a dinner jacket. Alan opposite me in tweed jacket, no porter
having been found to direct him to his room. Then sherry drunk in
the Cloister garth. Met and knew a mere handful of friends – Oliver
van Oss, George Coulson, Lawrence Radice. Dinner in Hall went on
for three hours. This was the worst part because I had boring neighbours, one a parson, the other a don, botanist, both nice but dull.
They undoubtedly thought the same of me. Loving-cup sent round
after toasts. Then two of the worst speeches, Alan agreed, we had ever
listened to, one by Greenham, RA, the other by the President. I could
have done far better.

At 11.15 this was over. With luck, among the 150 guests, all ancient,
I re-found Alan and sat in his room in St Swithin and gossiped for an
hour. He was just off next day with Mollie Buccleuch.* Showed me a
scurrilous reference to her in *Private Eye*, stating that she was the randi-
est duchess since Lady Castlemaine, or words to that effect. I asked if
she had seen it. He thought not, for no one would show it to her. Alan
amused because he noticed among the guests an ancient man bent and
walking on two sticks. When he [A.P.-J.] was taking his College Exam
in Hall, this man came to his room at night and slipped, without a word
of by-your-leave, into A.P.-J's bed. Told me that Lord X was charming and might be 'a friend of Mrs King', as he expressed it.

Sunday morning after Holy Communion in Chapel I motored
home.

Sunday, 1st July

Badminton gardens open today. A beautiful day and our garden better
than ever seen, in spite of the odious winter. Sat at the gate selling
tickets with Bob Parsons† to help. A number of people stopped to talk
about my books. Always embarrasses me, and sometimes irritates.
Same thing happened yesterday at Magdalen. And now my fear is I
may never write another, the H.N. one never to be published.

---

* Vreda Esther Mary ('Mollie') Lascelles (1900–93); m. 1921 Walter Montagu-Douglas-
Scott (1894–1973) who in 1935 s. his father as 8th Duke of Buccleuch and 10th Duke of
Queensberry. She was a cousin of Alan Pryce-Jones.
† American architect (1920–2000); tenant and repairer of Newark Park, Glos., N.T.
property.

Monday, 2nd July

A. walked into my bedroom at eight to say Anne Rosse had telephoned. I said. 'Then Michael has died?' 'Yes,' she said. 'Anne wanted
you to know.' Wept while I shaved. For no man was better than
Michael, unless it was Reynolds, or is Lennox. I rang up Tony
Snowdon* to find out where Anne was. He said Michael died
walking up the steep steps of Stafford Terrace. I then spoke to Anne,
who was very brave as I would expect, and said how happy she was
that he did not have to return to hospital. Funeral to be at
Womersley† by Michael's choice, because apparently the family
mausoleum at Birr has been vandalised, that dreadful cave full of
coffins where we buried Demond in 1937 which I remember too
well, having travelled to Birr with Robert Byron.‡ I suppose no
woman ever loved her husband more than Anne. Find myself thinking of the Rosses all day, and their consistent goodness to me
throughout the long years.

Wednesday, 4th July

To London for the day. Straight to V&A to see Garden Exhibition.
Well arranged but too many books displayed which can't be taken in.
To Brooks's came Derek Drinkwater, Australian thesis writer, who
had lent me his dissertation on H.N. as classical diplomatic theorist,
very good but heavy and full of bibliographical references I never
knew about, including articles by H.N. on diplomacy in obscure journals like *The International* and *Foreign Affairs*. This boy ordered brandy
and soda, large, which he left undrunk. It cost me £1.20, so I made
him lap it up before he went. Lunching hurriedly in library at Brooks's
I saw John Saumarez Smith§ who asked how H.N. getting on. John is
a sort of biographical barometer. I told him about the excessive length.
He offered to cut the MS for me, for a fee. I wondered whether it
would not be wise to let him, for as a bookseller he knows more than
anyone alive what the reading public needs, or thinks it does. So if

---

* Anthony Armstrong-Jones; b. 1930, son of Anne Rosse by her 1st marriage; photog-
rapher; cr. Earl of Snowdon in 1960 on his marriage to HRH Princess Margaret, who
divorced him in 1978.
† Womersley Park, near Doncaster, Yorkshire, the Rosses' English seat.
‡ Travel writer, Byzantinist and aesthete (1905–41).
§ Managing Director of G. Heywood Hill Ltd, booksellers in Curzon Street.

Nigel confirms that it is too long and himself makes no particular suggestions, I had better put myself in John S.S's hands.

At 2 p.m. meeting of Corsham Trustees which lasted till 4.45. Very
critical of large endowment asked for by N.T. They will contest it.
Then I rushed to tea with Hugh Montgomery-Massingberd* at
Travellers'. He looking tired and anxious. Is worried about Country
House *Index*, which looks as though it may collapse. There has been
terrible row between *Burke's Peerage* people and Compton Press. H.
thinks latter may go bust. I advised him to accept Burke's offer to
become editor of the *Index*, which Burke's want to issue on its own.
Then to Berkeleys' dinner to meet Maud Russell.† I could have done
without this. Maud arrived tottery, and mind awry. Did not know
who I was. Had to ask Freda. Then made little sense. Arrived home
at 1 a.m.

Friday, 6th July

I left home at 7.30 in my little Renault for Womersley. Arrived about
noon. Waited in the road outside the village so as not to get there too
early. It was boiling hot and I was in a muck sweat. House full of
black-dressed people; mostly family, Susan de Vesci‡ and children of
all sorts. All very sweet to me, except old Lady de Vesci,§ very formal
and stiff, well over ninety but I fancied not pleased to see me. Tony
Snowdon came up and kissed me on both cheeks. Then Anne entered
in black, wearing her pearls and diamonds, a little veil over her face,
but looking so pretty. Her courage stupendous. I heard her say, 'Where
is Jim?', so I presented myself. She dragged me into her little sitting
room, that little room where she and I used to dine and gossip during
the War, under Oliver's portrait of her, so white and fluffy. Told me
how poor Michael collapsed climbing the steps to Stafford Terrace,
and she had to hail a young man passing by to help her carry him
upstairs, where he died in her arms. She feels relief now the strain is
over. The service a beautiful one. When the coffin was taken out I

---

* Born 1946; writer and genealogist; Obituaries Editor of *Daily Telegraph*, 1986–94.
† Maud Nelke (1892–1982); art collector and patroness; donor (1957) of Mottisfont
Abbey, Hants., to N.T.; m. Gilbert Russell (d. 1942).
‡ Dau. of Anne Rosse by her 1st marriage; m. John Vesey, later 6th Viscount de Vesci.
§ Lois Lister-Kaye, mother of Michael Rosse, who as widow of 5th Earl of Rosse m.
1920 the 5th Viscount de Vesci.

waited behind, disliking the committal at the graveside. But evidently the coffin was taken away in the hearse for cremation, because I saw Anne standing inside the west door shaking hands with the congregation as they passed out. When the last person left I had to go too. Then the fatal thing. Anne clasped me in an embrace and wouldn't let go, and said, 'Do come and see me in London next week', and sobbed; and I broke down too. Felt ashamed, couldn't reply but just nodded my head affirmatively.

I drove on to Flintham to stay the night. Myles [Hildyard]* had staying his niece and Andrew Murray-Thriepland whom Myles has long loved in vain. He has lost his looks, which must have been considerable. We began dinner late, and sat over the dinner table till one o'clock. It is years since I have done such a thing.

Sunday, 8th July

Derry and Alexandra Moore staying the weekend. Derry very restless like his father and dashing from place to place. Not such fun as when he stayed with us as a bachelor. We all went to the Hollands' evening concert.† Pianist Howard Shelley, like a young handsome Beethoven, playing Chopin. Joan Holland telephoned begging us to come early as she had reserved us to talk to Prince and Princess Michael of Kent,‡ guests of honour. Needless to say they came just before the concert began, so our presence was of no account. But during the interval I was sent for. We were presented to the Prince, a nice-looking, vacant young man. A. talked with him while *she* collared me. She was very effusive about my books, said she had read them all (they all say this) and had always wished to meet me, etc. Said she had a mind to send me *Ancestral Voices* for my autograph. She is larger than I thought from photographs, but profile very good. Wore a sort of Druid's robe, with her long fair hair down her back. Certainly agreeable to meet, but very un-royal. Too much enthusiasm, too little dignity. But I liked her. Eardley tells me she is tough and acquisitive. She did tell me that the moment she

---

* Squire of Flintham Hall, Nottinghamshire; war hero and local historian (b. 1914).

† Sir Guy Holland, 3rd Bt (1918–2002); farmer and art dealer; m. 1945 Joan Street.

‡ HRH Prince Michael of Kent (b. 1942), and his wife Marie-Christine von Reibnitz, whom he had married in June 1978, renouncing his right of succession as she was a Roman Catholic.

married she went straight to the V&A, where she had worked in her humble days, and requested the return of those pictures and works of art given to the museum [by her husband's family] on semi-permanent loan, making herself unpopular in consequence with John Pope-Hennessy.

Monday, 9th July

A delicious day with Eardley. Met him at Swindon at 10.30. While I went to telephone I told him to sit in the car, forgetting Folly in back seat. She bit him through the upper lip, which bled profusely. Obliged to stop at chemist to buy and apply TCP. We walked along the Ridgeway for twelve miles. Ate picnic which E. carried in his knapsack. Beautiful day, not too hot, sun out and clouds in distance. Distant views of Downs. Wild flowers in profusion – eglantine, blue vetch, yellow bedstraw, wild mignonette. We gossiped ceaselessly. No one in the world with whom I am happier than with E. For his seventy-seven years he walked like a stripling. Neither of us a bit tired. Folly the tiredest.

Tuesday, 10th July

Tiresome day at re-opening of Bath Assembly Rooms. Decorated by young Mlinaric.* Not good work. Posh luncheon. Hanging about for Princess Margaret. I felt sorry for her. She looked extremely nervous. On the platform her hand was shaking. Making strange grimaces with her mouth. I suppose she is frightened of insults, and somebody told me that when she visited Bristol lately, a person in the crowd shouted 'Whore!' I am sorry for under-dogs. She is her own worst enemy of course, and if you are royal you must be immaculate, or expect the consequences. But she consorts with the raffish, and this the public do not like.

Wednesday, 11th July

Motored to Oxford. Met M. by appointment in the art section of Blackwell's. We strolled down Ship Street and ate a strange dish of

---

* David Mlinaric (b. 1939); fashionable designer and interior decorator.

salad and cream. Chatted away about our various doings since we last wrote and met. Each time I see him I feel wound up like an old grandfather clock. He accompanied me as far as OUP [Oxford University Press], where I had interview with Jeremy Lewis,* nice, extrovert young publisher, and Richard Brain,† whom I liked for his handsome face and merry, mischievous eyes. They explained the 'Country House Anthology' I am to do – 30,000 words only.

Sunday, 15th July

How long am I to suffer? The last spell endured fifteen years at least, and is not entirely over today. Does this mean that I shall be eighty-five before I have recovered from this one? In other words, are all my remaining years to be spent aching, waiting for the post, the telephone call, the fleeting meeting, the mild jealousies, the angst? Pray to God, No. I remember in 1958, when I was last smitten, Richard Rumbold‡ advised me to record every sensation in my diary. I don't think I did so then. And now that I do so, it makes a catalogue of moans – not attractive, or an inducement to sympathy.

Yesterday morning A. went to the Warrender wedding at Widcombe.§ Juliet Nicolson¶ was there. A. said to her jokingly, 'What are you doing here? You are supposed to be taking Jim's MS to Sissinghurst.' She said, 'I'm going to Sissinghurst this evening and have got the MS safely in the car.' This means Nigel will read it in the course of the week, and as he is so quick and prompt I may hear by Saturday. I feel certain he will think little of it. I have just finished Bates's Life of Dr Johnson, on the jacket of which is an appreciation by Nigel. He rightly gives it unstinted praise, for it is a very superior work, and as far above mine as Tolstoy is above Barbara Cartland.

Last night we dined with the Somersets. The Beits** staying. Clementine told me that she read Proust over and over again. He was

---

* Publisher and author (b. 1942).

† Editor (b. 1928); J.L.-M. had possibly forgotten that they had met in the 1950s, through Harold Nicolson.

‡ Journalist and writer; committed suicide, 1961.

§ Annabel, dau. of Hon. Robin Warrender, of Widcombe Manor, Bath, m. Hon. Alastair Campbell, e.s. of 3rd Baron Colgrain of Everlands.

¶ Nigel Nicolson's dau.; m. 1977 James MacMillan-Scott (m. diss. 1995).

** Sir Alfred Beit, 2nd Bt (1903–94), art collector and sometime Conservative MP; m. 1939 Clementine Mitford (cousin of the Mitford sisters).

the greatest novelist in the world, and George Painter's biog. the greatest biog. ever written of a novelist. I sat between Daphne* and Caroline. With Daphne I refrained from mentioning the death a week ago of her son Valentine Thynne, and talked about the Rosses. Then I turned to Caroline, who immediately wanted to talk about her brother's death, which she has dreadfully on her mind. She said candidly that she had not loved him. But she was filled with guilt; feels she ought to have bothered more about him; is appalled by the manner of his death (by hanging). Explained that when found his face was peaceful. No tongue hanging out, protruding eyes or look of agony. Is therefore satisfied that he did not suffer. They do not know why he did it. He was drunk at a charity ball, and rather a nuisance following his brother Christopher and Princess Margaret. So Christopher turned on him and said, 'For God's sake behave yourself and fuck off.' Valentine walked home and killed himself. Christopher is distraught, feels responsible. He wrote a touching letter of regret and love which he put in the coffin. Caroline was irritated by the widow's theatrical behaviour at the funeral. She prayed by the graveside with her hands clasped above her head, heavily veiled. When she unveiled herself her face was the studied Madonna Dolorosa. Whereas the seventeen-year-old boy's face was contorted by the sobs he vainly tried to control.

Tuesday, 17th July

Nigel telephoned me in Bath this morning in his polite, precise way to say he has received my MS but would be unable to peruse it until next week. Meanwhile it was in front of him, unopened. He would devote three days to reading it carefully and we could discuss it on the telephone on the Thursday. I am lunching with Anne Rosse at Nymans on the Friday, and could go over from there to Sissinghurst.

Thursday, 19th July

Took afternoon train to London and went straight to Anne Rosse at Stafford Terrace. She was in her drawing room on the first floor

---

* Caroline Somerset's mother, Hon. Daphne Vivian; novelist and fellow resident of the Badminton estate; m. (1st) Henry Thynne, later 6th Marquess of Bath; (2nd) Xan Fielding, war hero and author.

writing letters. She answers sixty a day, which her doctor tells her is
too much, for her blood-pressure has gone up. Was candid and at
times funny about her children. Quite clearly does not like Tony, and
says she always lamented that he was made an earl for 'stud purposes'.
Says that John Cornforth has taken her in hand and runs her life.
Having been used to Michael running it, she is grateful, but apprehensive. Apparently Michael died leaving no money in the bank, but
a large overdraft. She can't bear old Lady de Vesci, who was so cruel
to Desmond and unloving with Michael. Lady de V. asked Martin*
the very morning before the funeral whether Michael's death would
mean her jointure being reduced.

Tuesday, 24th July

John Cornforth telephoned to ask if I thought [Simon] Verity would
be a suitable designer of the memorial to Michael which Anne wants
in Womersley Church. There is not much time, said Cornforth
piously, because Anne's blood-pressure is high. Which I considered a
little patronising and pragmatical, to say the least. Yet his intentions
are of the kindest.

On Sunday we lunched with the Nicky Johnstons† the other side
of Faringdon. Enormous party of fourteen in the kitchen. Terrible
noise. Ann Fleming said before the coffee came that she could hear
nothing and was moving to the drawing room. If one can't do what
one wants at one's age, she said, when can one? Talked to Paddy Leigh
Fermor‡ about Brian Howard, whom he mimics to perfection. Paddy
said his achievement was not in his writing, or even his conversation,
but in the penetrating phrase. He uttered splendid sentences, without
hesitation or forethought, but always with a sting in the tail. Was once
overheard criticising the RAF, when himself in uniform, by an irate
air marshal, who came forward and said, 'Who are you? Give me your
name at once!' Brian answered, 'Mrs Smith.' That is quite funny, but
does it merit immortality? Kelly Clark there.§ Said she was afraid her

---

* Hon. Martin Parsons (b. 1938), yr s. of 6th Earl of Rosse.
† Architect (b. 1929); m. 1958 Susanna Chancellor.
‡ Patrick Leigh Fermor (b. 1915); writer living in Greece; m. 1968 Hon. Joan Eyres-
Monsell.
§ Hon. Colette, daughter of Lord Clark of Saltwood.

father's mind was going. Which means that, although he makes sense still, he probably will not be able to write another book, or produce new ideas.

Last night, while walking the dogs in the lower woods, I thought dispassionately that I would commit suicide if only I knew how, and if by so doing I might not cause distress to A. Talked to Diana W[estmoreland] at tea yesterday about June's terrible depressions.[*] Junie admits that she has every reason to be blissfully happy – she has a husband and a son whom she adores, a house she loves and enough money – yet she undergoes depressions in fits. I suppose I am the same and have always been so, only my depressions are presumably less dire, and cannot be strictly measured by fits or seasons.

To my immense surprise, while I was reading after dinner last night the telephone rang and I was read a telegram from Nigel Nicolson: 'Half way through. Marvellous. Nigel.' Now, what a reassuring message to get. How charming of him to bother. He knew I was in a state of anxiety. But he would not have sent it if he did not mean it. Of course, there is still the second half to be read. Still, I *am* pleased.

Wednesday, 25th July

Motored with A. to London this evening. Occasion was *the* meeting with M.B. We had John B[etjeman][†] and Elizabeth C[avendish][‡] to dine with us at Brooks's. I think A. liked M., though she finds him looking, as she says, unhealthy. After dinner, M. and John had a long talk about Uranian verse, and liked one another. I worry about John, who is worse. Finds walking a great effort. E. leads him by the arm, making encouraging noises as one would to a recalcitrant horse. He has both sleeves of his shirt, without links, hanging over his hands. This, and his staggering gait, make him seem drunk after dinner. I felt sad. A. and I drove away, having put John in his car, and leaving Michael on the pavement.

---

[*] Diana Lister, daughter of 4th and last Baron Ribblesdale, m. (3rd) 14th Earl of Westmorland (d. 1948); her daughter June Capel m. (1966) Jeremy Hutchinson, QC, cr. Lord Hutchinson of Lullington, 1978.

[†] Sir John Betjeman (1906–84); poet, broadcaster and writer on architecture; succeeded Cecil Day-Lewis as Poet Laureate, 1972.

[‡] Lady Elizabeth ('Feeble') Cavendish (b. 1926); dau. of 10th Duke of Devonshire; Lady-in-Waiting to HRH Princess Margaret; long-standing friend of Sir John.

Thursday, 26th July

M. came to Brooks's at 12.45, to be joined by Michael Colefax.* I gave them luncheon. M. is respectful to the old. He deferred to what M.C. said, and he said a lot. Is a nice, decent man, modest and well-intentioned. At the end of the meal he told M. he would sort through his mother's papers and get in touch with him in the New Year. I gathered he was in favour of M., but one cannot be sure. When he left M. stayed behind and begged me help him correct the proofs of his excellent article for *History Today* on Guedalla and the Duke of Windsor. He took me to Earl's Court to the Royal Tournament. I had never been to one before. The historic beauty of the Peninsular uniforms, the gun-carriages, the astonishing drill moved me much. We bought and ate ice-creams during the performance. After it was over we walked to Hyde Park Square through back streets, stopping as Jamesey and I used to do at pubs. I told him that I feel alien in pubs. Perhaps due to Papa, who when Dick and I were young men, strictly forbade us entering the Sandys Arms in the village at home.

Friday, 27th July

Terrible drive to Nymans, boiling hot day, London for forty miles without a break, it seemed. Harold Acton† staying with Anne. As an old friend he feels desperately for her. Anne very brave during lunch, but oh dear, her sorrow wrings the heart. She took us round the garden. Not a sympathetic garden; still the stockbroker's, with too much colour, great clumps of herbaceous pink, and those metallic blue hydrangeas in the woods. In memory of Michael, Anne gave me a pottery vase, early Georgian. Very sweet of her.

After a glass of lemonade at 4.30 I proceeded to Sissinghurst. Only Nigel and his charming Adam, aged twenty-one, sympathetic, sensitive. Nigel hospitable and kind. Took us to dine at a pub, excellently. Made me read long letter he has written me about the book; full of undeserved praise, which I am sure is sincere. Criticism that there are not enough judgements, assessments of H.N. True enough. Does not think it much too long, and agrees that Ian Parsons' cutting far too

---

* Son of the society hostess Lady (Sibyl) Colefax (1874–1950), who was seeking a biographer for his mother.
† Sir Harold Acton (1904–94); author and aesthete; owner of Villa La Pietra, Florence.

drastic. Is prepared to accompany me to Chatto's and face them. Will be my ally. And says that, if Chatto's demur, there is always Weidenfeld & Nicolson, who, he indicated, would surely take it on his recommendation. Greatly cheered.

Saturday, 28th July

Awoke early at Sissinghurst. Walked in the garden in the cool of the morning, like God. And surely God never walked in a more beautiful garden. Once again I was overcome by its perfection, above all the layout, which is the work of a genius, H.N.

Sunday, 5th August

On Friday Tony Scotland* and Julian Berkeley† called on me in Bath after luncheon. I gave them coffee and peaches, and we talked. Object of the visit to discuss Tony's predicament at Radio Three. He tells me that the new supervisor McIntyre‡ is a fiend, who is upsetting the whole staff of announcers. Tells Tony that he dislikes his voice, which gives the impression of a man too pleased with himself who is admiring his face in the glass. Also threatens to stop the programme which he, Tony, has invented, *The Arts Worldwide*, which has proved such a success. It seems that the man McIntyre is a sort of Reith, who loathes homosexuals and dislikes gents. Tony's voice, which is soft, persuasive and totally without camp or show-off, is in fact one of the best of the announcers'. I said there was little I could do beyond writing to a BBC Governor, if I knew one. Then found in Whitaker that George Howard§ is a Governor, and have written to him. Tony is handsome and charming.

---

* Author, broadcaster and journalist; on staff of BBC Radio, 1970–91; editor of *The Arts Worldwide*, 1972–80 (b. 1945).
† Second son of Sir Lennox and Lady Berkeley; musician, founder of Berkeleyguard Automatic Security Systems, and defender (like his father) of the traditional liturgy of the Catholic Church (b. 1950).
‡ Ian McIntyre (b. 1931); worked for BBC from 1957; Controller of Radio Three, 1978–87; author of *The Expense of Glory: A Life of John Reith* (1993).
§ Of Castle Howard, York (1920–84); sometime N.T. Historic Buildings representative for Yorkshire; Governor of BBC from 1972 and Chairman, 1980–3; cr. Lord Howard of Henderskelfe, 1983; Chairman of Museum and Galleries Commission, 1984.

Tuesday, 7th August

Took late train to London and met John [Kenworthy-Browne] at Vaudeville Theatre for T.S. Eliot's *The Family Reunion*, the production in which poor Beatrix Lehmann originally played the tyrannical mother. Well acted, well spoken, beautiful phrases, sharp characters, but what it is all about I can't for the life of me make out. Neither could J. Edward Fox in the principal part still acts as though the Duke of Windsor.* Indeed, this part is one of abdication. These pseudo-psychological plays of Eliot, like those of Christopher Fry, make me query whether they are a lot of bunkum. Stayed with J. for the night.

Saturday, 11th August

I can honestly say that one of the chief distresses of my long life has been my baldness. Old men can look perfectly respectable provided they have all their hair, and snow-white hair, if abundant, palliates the ravages of age. But my late youth, when I managed otherwise to keep my looks, and my middle age, when I managed to keep my figure, were marred by baldness. And the efforts I have been put to in endeavouring first to disguise the incipient patches, then to train the hair over the developed patches, the combing, the avoidance of wind, have amounted to a constant irritation and nag.

Saturday, 18th August

Unduly depressed all this week. In endeavouring to improve Harold MS am finding difficulty in adding assessments and judgements, as advised by Nigel. Richard Shone,† when I saw him at Eardley's, advised don't. So much contrary advice. Yet I feel I must try to oblige Nigel, of all people.

On Monday the 13th I gave a party at Hanbury Hall‡ for Alvilde's seventieth birthday. A foul day, grey and ending in rain before we left. About thirty guests. Curiously, they all seemed to enjoy themselves, for

I never got over it !!

---

* Fox had played King Edward VIII in the television series *Edward and Mrs Simpson*, shown the previous autumn.

† Art historian; author of *Bloomsbury Portraits* (1976); associate editor of *Burlington Magazine* from 1979 (b. 1949).

‡ William and Mary house in Worcestershire, formerly belonging to the Vernon family, which came to N.T. through J.L.-M's efforts, as described by him in *People and Places*.

we have had numerous letters and cards of thanks. Delicious food and enough drink. Diana Cooper* stayed Sunday night for the party. She is not happy, but does not allow her unhappiness to impinge on others. Curiosity as alert as ever. Sent me dashing in middle of luncheon to fetch *Webster's Dictionary* and look up Salic Law, its derivation. Did we have it in England? No, we don't. Is there a word – phallocrat? No.

Monday, 20th August

Peter Quennell has asked me to send him any letters from Jamesey I might have.† I have sent what I kept, which amounts to a mere twenty. He is delighted with them; thinks them more interesting than any he has read. Says the *dégringolade* of Jamesey's life is evident in the later correspondence.

We lunched with Penelope Betjeman‡ yesterday. Wonderful country when one leaves the new main road after Abergavenny, through narrow, twisting lanes, shoulder high in wild flowers, brambles and hedges of nut. Reminds me of Ribbesford walks – the remoteness, the calm, the already autumnal sweet-sourness in the air. And on our left side going, the range of the Black Mountains, lowering, menacing and calm like sleeping giants that are ready to rise and assault, at the first whim of God. P's house is sparse, uncomfortable, yet cosy-kitcheny in a farmhouse way. She sat us down at the kitchen table for a fragrant farmy luncheon, all cooked by her. But she was never still for an instant; kept up a running conversation, demanding answers, while she darted from the room into the backyard to see to the pony which was having its nose scratched by the cat, or to the manure-heap to turn it. Talked of John as if he was still hers. Deplored his addiction to drugs; he takes every medicine which is going, and they conflict with one another. While A. went for a drive in her pony trap I motored downhill into Hay and looked around Booth's shop. Bought Lord Redesdale's two volumes of memoirs, which Nancy

---

* Lady Diana Manners (1892–1986), officially dau. of 8th Duke of Rutland (though later admitting to the likelihood of a different paternity); m. 1919 Alfred Duff Cooper (1890–1954), cr. Viscount Norwich 1953, diplomatist, politician, writer; mother of writer and broadcaster John Julius Norwich, 2nd Viscount.
† He was editing a volume of James Pope-Hennessy's letters, diaries and essays: see entries for 28–29 March 1981.
‡ Dau. of Field Marshal Lord Chetwode; m. (1933) John Betjeman.

always exhorted me to read, Lord Ronald Gower's diaries, which I thought might be fun, but which are discreet to the *n*th degree, about royalty and country house visits, and Guedalla's Life of Wellington, which I don't suppose M. wants.

Thursday, 23rd August

A. telephoned at one o'clock that Billy Henderson[*] had brought Cecil Beaton[†] to call before lunching with Diana Westmorland, and they wished to have tea with me in Bath. This fussed me unduly and I could not work properly. Ran to open the door and help in Cecil, who walks painfully with stick in left hand, supported by Billy on right, his poor legs sticking out sideways like a crab's. Fretfully feels his way. Wearing the wide-brimmed straw hat which becomes him. White face but wicked twinkle in his eye still. Very interested in Beckford's library and asked sensible questions. While sitting on sofa with A., he asked me to remove two photographs of Harold on mantelpiece. He hated poor Harold.

Friday, 24th August

Have arranged with Nigel and Norah that we three are to meet at Chatto's on afternoon of 12th next to discuss book. Nigel says he does not need to see MS again, but Norah says she must have it beforehand to assess length and costs – always costs. I foresee a battle. But I am delighted that Nigel is accompanying me.

Friday, 31st August

On Tuesday afternoon to London. Was met at Paddington by M., whose train from Plymouth arrived before mine. Together we went to Chatto's where I delivered MS for second time, accompanied by letter to Norah. Then to Buck's, Brooks's being shut, for cup of tea. London mysteriously empty. We went on to Liverpool Street and caught train for Cambridge. M. has a new room in corner of a court at top of tower above the Library of St John's. Charming, romantic, isolated little room. We dined at Chinese restaurant.

---

[*] Painter (1903–93); ADC to Lord Linlithgow when Viceroy of India and stayed on as Comptroller to Lord Wavell until 1946.
[†] Sir Cecil Beaton (1904–80); artist, stage designer and photographer.

The following day – my Mama's birthday – too beautiful for words.
M. worked till tea time while I wandered, and sat in St John's garden,
and visited Fitzwilliam Museum, where ate in canteen. Joined M. in
his rooms for tea. He took me to a drink in the college bar with a don
called Godfrey Tanner* and a fellow postgraduate, Hywel Williams.†
Then took me to see *Lady Windermere's Fan*. Both evenings we sat in
his rooms talking to 2 a.m. He is touchingly candid. After the play he
took me for a walk in the gardens in the dark, and along the roof of
the new block. He has an engaging air of innocence, a questioning
look in the large brown eyes. Greets one with a deadpan expression,
observing everything, followed by that disconcerting silence. I left
Thursday morning by train. He insisted on accompanying me to the
station in bus, put me on train, gave me a look of goodbye, turned on
heel and sauntered off. *Abschiedstimmung*.

In London J. lunched with me at Buck's. Again in a sadly melan-
cholic state. He is over-sensitive. Doesn't seem in the least cheered by
the success his book is having, and the excellent sales.‡ A. not particularly agreeable to me on my return. She says things like 'It is hurting
for me, and makes me feel that I am inadequate and can't give you
everything you want in your life.' Well, the truth is that no one person
can give anyone all he needs. Why do we look for extraneous interest in books, the arts, music, poetry or the company and conversation
of others?

Monday, 3rd September

On Saturday we had to get away from Badminton because of the annual
clay pigeon shooting, which upsets the dogs and gets on our nerves.
Lunched with Sylvia Chancellor and her son John, Christopher being
away.§ Then went to tea with Tony and Violet Powell at Chantry. I
enjoyed this visit, for I sat on a sofa with Tony and was able to talk

---

* Former Fellow of St John's College; Professor of Greek at University of Newcastle,
NSW.
† Later on staff of Rugby School and *Sunday Telegraph*; political adviser to John Redwood
as Secretary of State for Wales, 1993–5 (b. 1955).
‡ Robin Fedden and John Kenworthy-Browne, *The Country House Guide*, Jonathan
Cape, 1979.
§ Sir Christopher Chancellor (1904–89); on staff of Reuters, 1930–59; subsequently
chairman of various companies and charities, including Bath Preservation Trust; m.
(1926) Sylvia Paget.

with him alone, an opportunity rarely vouchsafed. He lent me two letters which H.N. wrote him in the early Thirties congratulating him on his first novels. Tony said he never was at ease with Harold, who conveyed impression of not liking him. I said this is just what Christopher Sykes* said he felt. I suppose – though I did not say so – it is because neither of these two is the least queer; and H.N. did not feel cosy with hundred-per-cent heteros. Tony also said H.N. never escaped from being the civil servant, which made him not understand people who were not civil servants. I think this a trifle exaggerated. Tony also said he could not like Ivy [Compton-Burnett]'s novels, any more than he liked Jane Austen's. But one could admire without liking another's writing.

Thursday, 6th September

On 4th A. and I motored to Boughton [Northamptonshire], 240 miles there and back. First time either of us had been there since Mollie [Buccleuch] was reigning in full fig. Now house open to the public. Being a weekday there were few people. Not that people matter, but the sad thing is that the magic of this highly romantic, lost-in-the-wood palace has vanished. Every small, homely object has been removed. Ropes everywhere, and bareness. Mollie living in the south-east corner. Nice apartment, but inconvenient: one has to enter it through her bedroom. Not, we gathered, treated well by present Duchess,† who clearly has ghastly taste; has put a small pool in the grass court outside the great hall, with raised cement curb. Mollie waited on by her sole person, the 'lady' chauffeur. So strange to see Mollie, nearly eighty, the grandest of the grand, stack between courses and wheel a trolley into the kitchenette. How are the mighty fallen! She sweet and affectionate, with that drawly, exaggerated Twentyish voice. Walked in the garden afterwards, and visited the David Scotts.‡ He ninety-two, a great charmer in fullest possession. Showed us his collection of pictures, all bought by him for a song. Includes Edward

---

* Author, journalist and broadcaster (1907–86).
† Jane McNeill, m. 1953 Earl of Dalkeith, who succeeded as 9th Duke of Buccleuch, 1973.
‡ Sir David Montagu Douglas Scott, KCMG (1887–1986); diplomatist; cousin of 7th Duke of Buccleuch; m., 1st, 1918, Dorothy Drummond (d. 1965); 2nd, 1970, Valerie Finnis, VMH, horticulturist and writer.

Lears, Rembrandt etchings. She a well-known garden lady with whom A. at once clicked.

Yesterday Eardley and I walked about seventeen miles along the Ridgeway, me carrying a full knapsack in practice for Mount Athos. Wonderful September day, golden sun and not too hot. A. asked me what E. and I talk about. I said, what *do* oldest friends talk about on walks? Everything. Non-stop. Politics, the world, friends, his painting, my writing, our loves, sex, God.

Friday, 7th September

I took A. to Heathrow and saw her off. Terrible queues, crowds, muddle at Terminal 3. A hell on earth. I kissed her fondly and left for home and the dogs.

Sunday, 9th September

Am terribly lonely here without A. The house is empty of life, and thick with coffee cups. The dogs wander around like lost souls, as though they had slipped their leash from their God, the all-provider, in a miasma of bewilderment. The telephone never rings. It is her house, not mine; I am a lodger here. I do not share her life. She said sadly at Boughton about the Scotts, 'I can think of nothing lovelier than a husband and wife sharing the same interest' – i.e., the garden. I have not been nice to her lately. I am in deepest depression. I have a conviction that my life will end shortly, and just as well, too. I would rather be dead.

Is it not miraculous that tears are given only to humans? Surely there is something divine in them, expressing as they do compassion, sorrow, love, anxiety and all feelings that associate us with the angels. I am not sure whether dogs shed tears. I rather hope they do, for they have as much of the divine in their souls as humans.

Yesterday I lunched with my great-nephews at Moor Wood. I have sacked Derry Moore from being my executor, putting Nick in his place. And I have made M. my literary executor.

Tuesday, 11th September

M. came to Bath for the day. He had a cold but was delightful. Enchanted with beauty of Bath and bought paper and pencils to draw

– not very well – various views that inspired him. We talked and dined al fresco in the flat. He loved the dogs and played with them like a dog himself on the floor. He decided not to stay the night, for his cold had become worse.

This month's issue of *Gloucestershire Life* has an article on me by Charles Lines. It is not bad by any means, and is kind. But the heading calls me 'Scholar and Gentleman'. Now, these are two attributes I can make no claim to.

Wednesday, 12th September

Motored to London in afternoon, arriving at Chatto's at 4.30 where met Nigel, already there discussing his next Virginia Woolf volume with Norah. 'Well,' Norah began, 'you asked for this interview. What is it you wish to say?' I said, 'You will have received my letter, which explains that I cannot reduce the book further than I have now done.' Nigel absolutely splendid and backed me up, praising the book as he had done in his letter to me and assuming that I had now met his suggestions. Result that Norah reluctantly agreed to take the first vol. on Nigel's recommendation, but warned that they would print few copies and sell them at a high price. I said I would rather the book had a *succès d'estime* and was a valuable work, than a popular but indifferent best-seller. Then went to Oxford and Cambridge Club to see M. for a few minutes and tell him result of interview. He accompanied me to Brooks's but did not come in: thought the sight of me retreating into my club was like a mole diving into its hole.

J.L.-M's diary of his visit to Mount Athos with Derek Hill* in September 1979 is reproduced as Appendix I.

Thursday, 27th September

A long day in pouring rain from Salonika to Florence. Flew from Salonika to Athens; changed for flight to Rome; train from Rome to Florence. Reached La Pietra at six. Half an hour later we were joined by John Sutro† without his wife. A lovely visit with these two such old friends. Harold [Acton] wonderful host and John as amusing as

---

* Landscape and portrait artist (1916–2000).
† (1904–85); founder of Oxford Railway Club.

ever in ebullient form despite bronchial trouble and weak heart and looking a million [years old]. He is still play-acting half the time, but withal so well-read, well-informed, quoting from the classics and modern literature, and so devoted to Harold [Nicolson]'s and Michael [Rosse]'s memory that time passed nostalgically and beautifully. Gave me a splendid nostalgic poem he wrote after reading my diaries, about Desmond, Tom, Hamish,* etc. Lunched one day with Hugh and John† at Lucca. I spent another morning in Florence, so crowded I could hardly move. Accademia so full that I barely saw Michelangelo prisoners, but Bargello better. Paid respects to Brutus.

Received while with Harold three letters from M. who went to France on 26th. Alvilde met me at Heathrow on 28th with bad attack of bronchitis.

Monday, 1st October

Came into Chesterfield Hospital‡ at five last night, brought by A. At 7.15 a.m. given injection in right thigh. Felt dizzy, but conscious. Was determined to concentrate on M., to see if I could carry him into unconsciousness. Was wheeled downstairs into anteroom to operating theatre. Looked around, observed things, said a word to nice anaesthetist I had met previous evening; thereafter remember absolutely nothing. Do not remember being given another jab. Was it the first one, administered three-quarters of an hour previously, that worked magically at the prescribed moment? Was plunged into total darkness and oblivion. *Nox est perpetua una dormienda.*§ M. did not accompany me. Woke up feeling well in bed upstairs and dozed all morning. By afternoon was reading *War and Peace*, and Rupert [Hart-Davis]'s¶ new book about his mother.

Next day came out and taken back to Badminton. Received an urgent telegram from M. in Paris begging to see me when he gets back, anywhere, any time.

---

* Hon. Hamish St Clair-Erskine, MC (1909–74): like Tom Mitford and Desmond Parsons, an Eton contemporary of J.L.-M.
† Hugh Honour (b. 1927) and John Fleming (1919–2001); writers, separately and together, on art and architecture.
‡ For a long-planned minor operation.
§ Catullus, *Carmina*.
¶ Sir Rupert Hart-Davis (1907–99); publisher, editor, writer; Eton contemporary of J.L.-M.

Friday, 5th October

Last night we dined with Caroline [Somerset] to meet a boring old Spanish marquesa who has published a book on gardens. Horticultural expert she may well be, but has verbal diarrhoea like so many educated female foreigners of the upper class. Also present were Charlie and Amanda Hornby.* Charlie effusive in his greetings, but a silly young man with a weak face. Appearance changed since I saw him last, before imprisonment. When we were left alone, I wondered if he was going to refer to the extremely sympathetic letter I wrote him when he was in jail, but no reference at all. I of course made none; but if I had been he, I would have done so. Possibly he was not allowed by the Governor to receive it.

This morning, while resuming Vol. II of Harold, i.e., preparing the notes for the actual writing, I await call from M. Punctually at eleven he telephones. The matter he wishes to discuss is most exciting. He has been invited to write the authorised life of the Duke of Windsor. He cannot believe it is true. Must discuss it with me instantly, and whether he should chuck his career as a barrister at the Temple, due to begin on Monday. I must say it does call for immediate and serious discussion. Is coming down tomorrow for the day, but is anxious to know if I am really well. I say I am, and seem to be. But are you really, he repeats?

Saturday, 6th October

M. comes down to Bath, arriving 10.30. Met by me at station. With burning zeal he tells me of the offer received from Maître Blum† to write the Duke of Windsor's life from the Abdication onwards, based on his papers, dealing with his ill-treatment and grievances. I hope it arouses the interest he is confident it will. We discuss how he must not chuck his Bar apprenticeship, which is to start on Monday, for that would upset his father. He taps away in his shirtsleeves at typewriter on my desk, extracts of letters from H.N. to Tommy Lascelles – highly indiscreet of me to let him, for Maître Blum believes Lascelles was the villain who engineered the Abdication.

---

* Second son of Michael and Nicole Hornby, of Pusey House, Faringdon, Oxfordshire.
† Maître Suzanne Blum (1898–1994), the fashionable and formidable Paris lawyer of the Duchess of Windsor, whom Michael Bloch had befriended in 1978.

M. full of his Paris visit, relating some things which disturbed me, but I do not want him to refrain from telling me everything. He said that Vera [Traill], whom he saw in Paris on her return from Russia, where she stayed with her relations, asserts that the moral condition of Russians is very bad indeed. Whereas on her last visit ten years ago some Russians still spoke of the regime with approval, now not a soul does. All are disillusioned. I asked if therefore the majority were behind the dissidents. No, he said, apathy, indolence and corruption were the prevailing characteristics. On the death of Brezhnev there will be a fight for power in the Kremlin which may lead people to break loose and express their true feelings, if they still have any.

Wednesday, 10th October

A. and I drove up to London for the [Noel] Blakistons'* golden wedding party. Everyone there who is not dead. Quite enjoyed it, and would more had it not been so hot and the noise so deafening. Talked to Caroline Chandos about the refusal of her father [Tommy Lascelles] to see me [to talk about Harold Nicolson, of whom he had been a close friend]. Asked her point-blank whether he disliked me, or the reason was his dislike of Nigel's book.† She thought the latter. Advised to me to write if I had any specific questions.

Thursday, 11th October

At Heywood Hill this morning, John Saumarez Smith spoke of Helen Dashwood.‡ She came into the shop with the book I had sent her, David Cecil's *Jane Austen*, saying she was returning it and asking if John would give her money back. John said flatly he would do no such thing. Either she exchanged it for another book or he took back the one I gave her. No letter of thanks from her.

---

* Noel Blakiston (1905–84); scholar, short-story writer and sometime Assistant Keeper of Public Records; m. 1929 Georgiana Russell; published his early correspondence with his Eton contemporary Cyril Connolly (*A Romantic Friendship*), 1975.
† Nigel Nicolson's controversial *Portrait of a Marriage* (1973), dealing candidly with his parents' homosexuality.
‡ Widow of Sir John Dashwood, 10th Bt (1896–1966), of West Wycombe Park, Buckinghamshire, wartime headquarters of N.T.

At 12.30 I went to the Temple to lunch with M. in Inner Temple Hall. Totally rebuilt since destruction of Victorian Gothick one during War. Good plain luncheon, potted shrimps and mutton. Surrounded by correctly dressed young men of the Establishment. M. finds it quite fun, but is convinced that in a few months he will be released and committed to work on Duke of Windsor book. Maître Blum telephones him every morning. She and he are convinced it is the book for which the world is waiting. I pray it will be so, but query whether there are not too many books on the subject coming out. M. said that under a new scheme he can apprentice himself to a lawyer of any Common Market country, and thinks he might do so to Maître Blum. This would mean living in Paris, which idea delights him. I am of course depressed by this information. We walked into 4 King's Bench Walk,* my first entry since Harold left it in 1945. Unchanged except that it is being redecorated, and an opening has been made into No. 3 next door. We sat on a bench in the sun in the garden. These short meetings, in public, so to speak, are not the most satisfactory.

Saturday, 13th October

Nan Bernays† took a party of us after lunching with the Somersets to see the eighteenth-century grotto at Goldney House, Clifton. Perhaps the best English grotto I have ever seen, and in splendid order. Done about 1730–60, of felspar, like amethysts, and huge shells brought from the East by the Bristol merchantmen. A stream of water pours down a rill from a figure of Neptune holding an urn. A really splendid and little-known treasure, this.

Monday, 15th October

I was writing a poem to M. at Brooks's when he appeared at six. Delicious talk for an hour until we parted, for I was to receive J.K.-B. J. very sweet. We ate at Brooks's and went back to his house where I stayed the night. He is not a cheerful companion, whereas M. bubbles with enthusiasms. The latter so taken up with Maître

---

* From 1931 to 1945 Harold Nicolson kept a ground floor set of residential chambers on this staircase, where J.L.-M. often stayed with him.
† Nancy Britton, m. 1942 Robert Bernays, MP, who was killed in action, 1945.

Blum and the Duke of Windsor that he can hardly concentrate on anything else.

Tuesday, 16th October

Mark Norman* last night at Brooks's asked whether I would rather the Trust accepted houses which it could not afford to maintain and went bust, or declined them and kept its independence of government interference. I replied that I would rather we risked acceptance of an important building which might be demolished if we refused it; and that even if the Trust were taken over by the Government, it would not be interfered with, any more than the National Gallery was, for the Government realised that such bodies had to be run by experts. Mark said that had the Trust been a government body during my time I would not have been kept longer than a week, for I was far too independent.

Thursday, 18th October

M. writes that he would probably spend four months of the winter in Paris as *stagiaire* to Maître Blum. Sweetly added that I must often come over, and if I couldn't he would have to think again. I replied that I would of course mind horribly but that must not prevent him going. I must stop waiting for letters, telephone calls, meetings as if they are the breath of life. But how does one control one's emotions?

Saturday, 20th October

The Vereys† gave a party at Barnsley to celebrate their ruby wedding. About thirty ate at separate tables arranged in the long room, each with a ruby table-cloth, too pretty for words. A. gave them a red Victorian work-box and I a magnum of cherry brandy, chosen by A. A county affair but none the worse for that, cosy, decent and enjoyable. I sat next to Henriette Abel Smith whom I like, direct, quick, informed and well-read.

---

* Eton near-contemporary of J.L.-M. (1910–94); banker; Deputy Chairman of N.T., 1977–80.
† David Verey (1913–84), architectural historian, of Barnsley House near Cirencester; m. 1939 Rosemary Sandilands (1918–2001), garden designer, who was then editing *The Englishwoman's Garden* with A.L.-M.

Thursday, 25th October

Motored A. to Heathrow as she is going to stay with the Beits for the Wexford Festival. We had an uneasy drive, for she would interrogate me as to where I was staying tonight, making repeated innuendos. Went on to J.K.-B. where I left him Vol. I of my Red Book* since he is doing Essex for Burke's *Country Houses*. Motored on to 1 Hyde Park Gardens.† Joined by M. to hear lecture by Kathleen Nott.‡ As M. and I agreed, it would have been far more profitable to read this lecture than listen to it, a state of affairs which I find with the vast majority of lecturers who are not Kenneth Clarks or Harold Nicolsons. We left in pouring rain, bought snacks at a delicatessen and ate them in M's flat. Then motored to Curzon Cinema to see *The Europeans*.§ Pretty scenes of puritanical American life in clapboard houses, but too obvious, too American, and not to be compared with the subtlety of a Visconti or a Zefferelli. M. came to breakfast at Brooks's next morning, whence he left for his Chambers. All such fun. I begged to be told if I had become a bore.

Saturday, 27th October

A. being away I motored, with dogs kindly invited, to stay with my dear Eardley at The Slade.¶ Mattei** and Dadie Rylands†† staying. Enjoyed visit enormously. Mattei I find extremely cosy and sympathetic. He is a gentle character, radiates charm, is singularly detached from cares of the world yet wise in his judgements. Talked about English working-men, whom he knows through his business far better than I do. Assured me they were not idle, but badly led. It is absolutely essential to destroy the stranglehold of the unions. Dadie much aged since last seen. Also very deaf. In other respects unchanged. Alert as ever, and delightful; stimulating and fun. We all talked for hours, ate

---

* J.L.-M's notes about houses were kept in a series of red-covered books.
† Headquarters of the Royal Society of Literature, formerly the residence of General Sir Ian Hamilton, married to J.L.-M's great-aunt Jean (d. 1941).
‡ Poet, novelist, and author of works on philosophy; FRSL.
§ Based on Henry James's novel.
¶ Eardley Knollys' house near Petersfield, Hampshire.
** Mattei Radev (b. 1927); picture-framer and gilder; friend of Eardley Knollys.
†† George Rylands (1902–1999), Shakespearean scholar and Fellow of King's College, Cambridge.

excellent food cooked by Bach [Eardley] and Mattei. Dogs good too, and we walked down footpaths happily.

Monday, 29th October

Left Slade at midday. Drove to Chawton and went over Jane Austen's house. Quite a few relics of hers, and some furniture which she owned, or so the visitor is led to believe. Some vagueness as to whether a writing desk belonged to Jane, or *might* have done. Picked up A. at Heathrow and motored home.

Wednesday, 31st October

Up to London again, to dinner party at Café Royal in farewell to Peter Quennell after thirty years' editorship of *History Today*. Didn't enjoy it at all. Long table in upstairs room, low ceiling, extremely hot and airless, though cold out-of-doors. Thought I should faint. Sat next to one Charles Lloyd, who turned out to be grandson of Zachary Lloyd, neighbour and friend of my grandmother at Ribbesford, the Lloyds of Areley near Stourport. Fact that we must have played together as children brought no sentimental memories. Garrett Drogheda in chair made amusing, mischievous speech in the style of vague talk, but cunningly contrived. Then Veronica Wedgwood a dull but adequate speech in praise of P. and *History Today*. Before dinner I talked to K. Clark's new wife who confronted me and spoke of Corsham and the Methuens, her aunt and uncle, where we met hitherto. A chattering female. Talked too to Michael Crowder* the new editor, and friend of M. He said, 'You are M's mentor, I believe.' No, I said, I cannot claim that honour. Rather he is mine. We both spoke warmly of his abilities. I left before the last speeches.

Thursday, 1st November

Took train for Headcorn, walking from station through the dear little town to Sutton Chart where Mrs Lamont lives. She eighty-three, clearly once handsome, now very lame with bad hip and swollen ankles. She was Vita's last love, who looked after her during her final illness and was with her when she died. I was not sure how much I

---

* Historian of Africa; d. 1988.

liked her. She cordially disliked Harold and both boys. Thought H. dishonest. Why, I asked? Because his political views were not genuine. That is all. Thinks Nigel a cold fish.

She told me that the moment Vita died, she climbed up to her tower room. Harold was pacing the lawn in anguish. She rifled Vita's files and extracted all her own letters to V. I asked if she still had them. No, destroyed them, and destroyed all V's to her, save the few poems enclosed. Saw no reason why others should ever read them. She said that V. loved her very much and that my A[lvilde] was jealous of her because she, Mrs Lamont, received everything from V. that she could desire. I was extremely guarded about A. and said I knew nothing of her true relations with V., never thinking it my business to enquire. All I knew – this a back-hander, perhaps – was that letters from V. to A. arrived almost daily for several years.

Tuesday, 6th November

Janet Stone for the night. She is in a bad way, poor thing, suffering from the shock of Reynolds' death. Says she is so miserable alone at home that she cries all the time. Every corner, every chair reminds her of R., for he *lived* in the house, rarely leaving it and the garden. Seldom went for walks, hated going away for the night, and preferred wet to fine days. Reason, that when he was a boy at school wet days meant that he was allowed to draw; fine days meant beastly games out-of-doors.

Saturday, 10th November

A. has invited M. for the weekend of the 24th. Eardley says I am mad to allow it.

Thursday, 15th November

I am reading Vol. 5 of Virginia Woolf's letters. It is entitled *The Sickle Side of the Moon*. I think these titles a silliness. Why not simply *Vol. 5*? It is interesting to compare the letters to the diaries. The letters are far freer, which is at first surprising. But the truth is that one is never freer than when addressing the perfect recipient, with whom one feels totally in accord; whereas in a diary one is addressing oneself, not an inspiring or reciprocating individual. It is a masturbatory exercise.

Different recipients provoke one to adopt different styles of writing –
facetious, self-pitying, too clever by half, guarded – depending on
one's relations with him or her.

Went today to Michael Rosse's Memorial in Guards' Chapel. Was
asked to be an usher but declined because I no longer have a morning
coat, since giving my father's away, and being so short-sighted would
never recognise anyone I ought to recognise. It was a very grand,
correct affair. Queen Mother, Princess Margaret and little Lord Linley.
Harold Acton read a moving piece, but not well. He halted and left
out a line and turned a negative into a positive sentence. Pat Gibson*
gave an orthodox eulogy, not bad. I would have given a better, more
personal one, I feel.

Saturday, 17th November

Never has a scandal caused more stir than the Anthony Blunt revelations.† No one seems sure what really happened. Why, if he was exon-
erated fifteen years ago, should he now be stripped of his knighthood,
a thing unprecedented since the Middle Ages, and disgraced? Did he
spy after receiving the knighthood? What did the spying since the War
amount to? And if it happened during the War when he was working
at MI5, why was it spying, seeing the beastly Russians were our allies?
I cannot get out of my head that shy, courteous, withdrawn figure.
Although I deprecate more than most people anyone giving information to those bloody Russians, yet I cannot help feeling sorry for
Anthony being hunted, persecuted all these years later, at his age too,
and in his indifferent state of health. I last saw him when I went to
Wimpole in July. It was then that in talking to him I mentioned that
I had come across many letters to H.N. from Guy [Burgess] in
Moscow. He drew himself in, but I persisted in talking about Guy,
unaware of the terrible secret and fear he must be bearing. I told him
the letters showed Guy's intense home-sickness and longing to see his
mother again. Then Anthony waxed angry. Said what a terrible man

---

* Richard Patrick Tallentyre Gibson (b. 1916); director of companies; Life Peer, 1975;
Chairman of N.T., 1977–86.
† Blunt (1907–83), art historian and Surveyor of the Royal Pictures 1945–72, had just
been officially disgraced and stripped of his knighthood following the exposure of his
former career as a Soviet agent (known for some years to British intelligence) in Andrew
Boyle's book *The Climate of Treason*.

the stepfather was. He loathed Guy and said pestilential things about him, trying to turn the mother against him. I could not help saying, 'But Anthony, one must remember that he was a simple colonel, in whose eyes Guy had brought disgrace to family and friends. After all, he was a spy.' No response to this. Yet I hate the idea of his being persecuted. Irrational? Am I not a little unsound about patriotism, loyalties, the last refuge of the scoundrel, and so forth?

Ghastly dinner party at Berkeley Castle on Friday. Some twenty relations present, all dreadfully boring and conventional. A hired chef for the occasion providing six courses of pretentious, messy *cordon bleu* food. This definitely not the environment to suit me. I thought of The Slade, Eardley, Mattei and Dadie, our free talk, outrageous statements and ceaseless mirth. That is my sort of society.

Saturday, 24th November

To London for the day on Tuesday, to give a short talk on my Harold book to a group of Chatto's salesmen, at Norah's request. It really was quite a success. I had notes in front of me, and improvised. Dear Nick present. Vol. I to come out next September, and they suggest Vol. II should come out not more than twelve months after that.

Fanny Partridge* and M. came to stay last night for the weekend. Agony for me. There is a tense suspicion, and a shyness on M's part which does not make hostmanship easy. I wonder if sensitive and highly-intelligent Fanny is aware.† And I hear him saying casually, 'I shall be working under Maître Blum for three months soon.' 'How interesting,' the others reply. I sit mum, nursing my own feelings.

Monday, 26th November

Weekend been and gone. Fanny's presence a great help. Also other guests well chosen – Elspeth Huxley to luncheon on Saturday; tea with Diana Westmorland; Tony and Violet Powell to luncheon Sunday. M. pleased to meet all these celebrities. Delighted with everything. Takes out his notebook and jots down what people tell him. He was sweet to A. and I have yet to hear what she really

---

* Frances Marshall (b. 1900); diarist and critic; m. 1933 Ralph Partridge (d. 1960).
† She was.

thinks. There was a good deal of 'Don't tell me you want to sit up late.' The second night, when Fanny went up to bed and I said to A. that I was going to have a drink with M., she stayed up too, in defiance. I was determined to out-sit, and did by twenty minutes. During which epilogue I talked severely to M. about the pressure of demands from friends, books, uncompleted doctoral thesis and reviews, and his absolute need to straighten these demands out. I did not enjoy this weekend and do not want him and A. to meet often, because I have a nasty suspicion that she wishes to break up the relationship by any means.

Saturday, 1st December

J. [Kenworthy-Browne] lunched with me at a humble restaurant in Bury Street. He in good form. Has made a certain amount out of his country house book, though no fortune. Went to Eardley's where M. joined me at 6.30, wearing chic new double-breasted suit with stripes. Proceeded to the Omar Khayyám dining club as his guest.* Did not disenjoy it as much as I feared. Placed between M. and a strange ex-naval commander. Many speeches, some quite funny, particularly one delivered by a youngish member directed against the guests. When he came to me he satirised the titles of my books. M. whispered that I had got off lightly. We walked away into the cool night and talked for half an hour at Brooks's. Having explained the situation to him, I left him happy. It is interesting, the gradually descending scale, like a watch which runs down and needs constant winding. I returned to Eardley's where I was staying the night, and found Richard Shone. He is having a swimgloat† with Post-Impressionist book which has already sold in thousands, and is quite rich. Told me that Rupert Brooke once slept with James Strachey but it was a great failure, so it is nonsense for John Lehmann to claim that Brooke had homosexual tendencies.‡

---

* Literary dining club founded in 1890s in memory of Edward Fitzgerald, which then met twice yearly at Kettner's Restaurant, Soho. (It still continues in 2000, meeting at the Savile Club.)
† In *Caves of Ice*, J.L.-M. notes of 'swimgloat' that it was 'an expression [meaning a state of joy experienced by someone who has had a success] used by The Souls and taught me by Logan Pearsall Smith'.
‡ The most recent biography of Brooke, by Nigel Jones (1999), suggests that he did.

Tuesday, 4th December

The Donaldsons* lunched on Saturday. Jack has taken a *coup de vieux*. He explained how he had become a Socialist in 1931 when he discovered the National Government had reduced the dole below a living wage and unemployed men were starving. He doesn't care a damn for the Labour Party *per se*, not having come from working-class stock. Men like Roy Jenkins, whose father was a miner, have passionate loyalty to the party of their class.† Frankie told me she had refused three requests to review *The Windsor Story*,‡ because it is a vile book. In her biography of Edward VIII she refrained from mentioning that the Windsors' only English friends towards the end were the Mosleys, because she thought it would do them harm. Frankie is now writing the biog. of P.G. Wodehouse. Says she has too little data, the opposite of my case. But what there is is so scintillating she feels ashamed of her own text. I said that was just how I felt about H.N., whose quotes are brilliant and my writing comparatively pedestrian.

Sunday, 9th December

Derek [Hill] who is staying the weekend at the Cottage to paint Anne Somerset,§ lunched to meet, look at and assess nephew Nick [Robinson]. Also Mary Beaufort came. She is vaguer than ever and takes little in. It is better to have her alone, or just with Caroline whom she knows and loves. Derek was tired and would not do a sketch of Nick there and then, which I had rather hoped, but is going to get in touch with him. Told me he admired his appearance, which reminded him of Rosamond Lehmann's. I can understand, but only just. Derek full of complaints of the Somersets. Caroline makes no sense and is in bed most of the day, David out hunting, and the chil-

---

* John G.S. (Jack) Donaldson (1907–98); Eton contemporary of J.L.-M.; cr. Baron Donaldson of Kingsbridge (Life Peer), 1967; Minister for the Arts, 1976–9; m. 1935 Frances (Frankie) (1907–94), daughter of the playwright Freddie Lonsdale; authoress.
† Jenkins resigned from the Labour Party a year later to found and lead the Social Democrat Party, which Donaldson joined.
‡ A recently-published scandal-sheet about the Duke and Duchess of Windsor by their former ghostwriters.
§ Only daughter of David and Lady Caroline Somerset (b. 1955); pursued a literary career; m. 1988 Matthew Carr.

dren listening to television full blast while sprawling all over the room like oafs. Derek likes attention, is sulky when deprived.

Monday, 10th December

A letter this morning from M. I droop when I am out of contact like a lily yellowing at the edges. No wonder A., who misses nothing, resents these moods which are beyond my control. I wish I could snap out of them, for it is ridiculous. At my age they may signify that I am still alive, while before he came on the scene I considered myself pretty well dead. And better dead than moribund.

Wednesday, 12th December

In the morning took the dogs for a walk in the Slates and was overcome by angst. What was the cause? I was about to see M., which I was looking forward to. My angst is so constant, so fearful that I can hardly bear it. Did it originate in fear of my father, which led me to become deceitful, timorous and dishonest as a child? I am all these things now in different degrees. In a funny way my fear of him has transmitted to fear of A. It is mixed up with appalling guilt – that I treat her badly, inconsiderately, selfishly. How I envy those friends who are unaffected by this disease (for it is nothing less), those friends who never repine, never feel guilty, always see the best side of life.

Sunday, 16th December

Such a Trollopean scene today. Sally Westminster* asked us to luncheon to meet the Beauforts and the Weinstocks. The first idea, that we should make it up with the Duke and be friends again. Second idea, that it would be an uplift for the Weinstocks to meet the Duke and Duchess and learn what real aristocrats were like. Sir Arnold W.† sat on the Duchess of Westminster's right, the Duke of Beaufort on her left. In the middle of luncheon, Master said to Sir Arnold, 'Nice coverts you have got in the place you've just bought', i.e., the large

---

* Sally Perry (1911–91); half-sister of the writer Joseph Ackerley; widow of Gerald Grosvenor, 4th Duke of Westminster.
† Born 1924; knighted, 1970; cr. Life Peer (of Bowden in Wilts), 1980; Managing Director, GEC, since 1963; m. 1949 Netta, dau. of Sir Michael Sobell.

house near Lacock which belonged to Sir Geoffrey Parsons. Sir Arnold replied, 'I refuse to let the hunt come near me. They make such a mess. And they are so rude. You as doyenne [*sic*] of the hunting world ought to teach them manners is all I can say.' Master went scarlet in the face and didn't say a word more. The peccadillo of our dogs chasing his vixen last May paled beside this enormity. Lady Weinstock who was sitting between me and Master then turned to me and said, 'And what is your view of hunting?' I whispered in her ear that I preferred not to discuss the subject in present company. 'But I don't see that it matters who knows what we think about hunting,' she expostulated. Dextrously I shut her up.

Sir A. is a brash, quick-witted, well-informed, pushing little man; also very ugly. The occasion was like Sir Leicester Dedlock meeting the manufacturer son of his housekeeper who had bought an estate next to Chesney Wold in *Bleak House*; or the Duke of Omnium keeping his temper in the company of an insolent *arriviste* at Gatherum Castle. Well-meaning Sally behaved with commendable calm and changed the conversation.

Tuesday, 18th December

Had tea with Rosamond [Lehmann]. She said that Goronwy Rees,[*] lately deceased, told her in 1930s that Guy Burgess was a Comintern agent. After Guy fled she went to MI5 and told them. Had a gruelling reception. After Russia allied with Germany at the beginning of the last war Guy pretended he had ceased to be a Communist, which was not true. I said I considered Guy had been evil. She disagreed strongly. Thought him a tragic figure; that he had one of the most acute brains she had come across, and all who knew him well thought the same.

Saturday, 29th December

Christmas with the Droghedas at Parkside again. Three nights. The Joseph Coopers[†] staying. He a jovial, entertaining extrovert. Christmas Day we went to St George's Chapel. We sat in the Garter Stalls; mine had been Winston Churchill's, which I found unendearing.

---

[*] Morgan Goronwy Rees (1909–79); author, journalist and businessman; Principal of University College of Wales, 1953–7.
[†] Pianist and broadcaster (1912–2001); m. (2nd, 1975) Carol Borg.

Lovely service. All the Royals present, including new Princess Michael, too much dolled up with that large hat and larger feather. Patricia Hambleden[*] told me 'they' all hate her like rat poison. We lunched with Patricia on way home. David Herbert[†] and Michael Duff[‡] staying. Michael incredibly thin and beautiful like a ghost. David confided in A. that he is dying. This little party which should have been such fun – when the same five of us last lunched here we laughed immoderately – was *morne*. On leaving I embraced Michael on both cheeks.

I find that septuagenarians all speak with horror about the fatal ailments of their contemporaries, as though each case is a tragedy which somehow ought to be avoided. But it's just death, let's face it. We are dying, all of us over seventy, and some of us are not yet in the terminal stage. That's all there is to it. Bad news of Raymond [Mortimer][§] again; he is bedridden, and said to be sinking.

At Parkside watched film of Leslie Hartley's *The Go-Between*, one of the most beautiful films I have seen. Lovely setting at Melton Constable. Takes place at height of summer, cloudless skies, burning sun high in heavens. The boy most poignant. Of *Death in Venice* standard. I remember Leslie telling me that the story was autobiographical. The experience had a devastating effect upon him, and turned him away from women.

This film has given me the idea for a novel.[¶] Its setting the First World War. Unsympathetic father away at the Front. Young, pretty mother and beautiful young son, same age as *Go-Between* boy, left at home. German prisoners-of-war working on the estate, kept at arm's length by guards. One, an educated Count, with English mother and speaking perfect English, is befriended by boy. Sex-starved count starts affair with boy. Mother somehow finds out. She takes Count away from her son. Father returns on leave, discovers the affair, or affairs. Then what?

---

[*] Lady Patricia Herbert, dau. of 15th Earl of Pembroke; m. 1928 3rd Viscount Hambleden; Lady-in-Waiting to HM The Queen Mother; d. 1994.

[†] Hon. David Herbert (1908–95), yr s. of 15th Earl of Pembroke; Eton contemporary of J.L.-M.; resident of Tangier.

[‡] Sir Michael Duff, 3rd Bt (1907–80); another Eton contemporary of J.L.-M.; Welsh landowner and Lord-Lieutenant of Carnarvonshire.

[§] Literary reviewer (1895–1980); co-tenant of Long Crichel (see note to entry for 17 September 1981).

[¶] Published by J.L.-M's gt-nephew Nicholas Robinson in 1990 as *The Fool of Love*.

1980

On Wednesday went to London for the night. Telephoned J. [Kenworthy-Browne] who said I might stay with him. Did some shopping and visited London Library; went to Post-Impressionist Exhibition, but such crowds it was like being on a conveyor belt and I could not study a single picture with ease. After one hour left, walking in the rain, to visit Freda [Berkeley] in King Edward VII Hospital. She told me how unhappy A. was being made by me. I told Freda how unhappy this was making me, but asked her next time A. consulted her to impress on A. what little cause she had for unhappiness on my account. I could not help being in love, but my love was platonic and surely no harm to anyone but myself.

Walked on to Hyde Park Square and joined M. in his flat. We had sandwiches and cake and tea before going to Sadler's Wells to see *The Pirates of Penzance*. Great fun. M. told me he is leaving for Paris on 12 February. This makes me mournful. But he says he will frequently be over, and asks me to stay in Paris. He said his father dissatisfied that he had not finished his thesis, and I said I did not wonder, for he had paid for his education. He sent me some of it, which reads brilliantly. Silly ass he is.

Yesterday motored Audrey* to lunch with Harry Ashwin at Bretforton.† Harry very inaudible; had to strain to hear him. Is extremely thin, walks painfully with a stick, is irritable and wretched. Said, 'I have nothing to look forward to, nothing.' After lunching we retired to the library and talked. At once the church bell tolled three times. His gaze lit up. 'That will mean £30,000 for me,' he said. I enquired what he meant. He replied that every time one of the villagers dies and a cottage is vacated, he sells it. He gets only a few shillings a week rent. Immediately the bells broke into a loud, prolonged

---

* J.L.-M's sister (1905–90), m. 1st Matthew Arthur, later 3rd Baron Glenarthur; 2nd Anthony Stevens.
† The Worcestershire estate neighbouring Wickhamford where J.L.-M. had been brought up, of which the Ashwins were squires from the sixteenth to the twentieth century.

carillon. 'Damn!' said Harry. 'It's not a death, just the bell-ringers practising.' The din continued for the rest of our visit, and Harry relapsed into intense gloom. We could hardly hear ourselves speak for the din. It reminded Audrey and me of the tennis tournaments at Bretforton on Saturdays when we were children. The Bretforton church bells – the church is at the end of the garden – always did this for hours on end. But oh the mournfulness of this funny old Victorian house, with its musty smell of black treacly oak panelling, and stuffy bewhiskered ancestors!

Sunday, 12th January

Dear old Raymond [Mortimer] died this week. Expected and not to be mourned for: he was eighty-five and exceedingly unhappy. The last day he did not speak at all, and the following morning he was found dead in his bed. I grew very attached to him. There was something paternal about him, and sweet. At first I was scared of him for he was censorious and picked one up, demanding explanations of one's idiotic remarks. He was solely a critic and not creative, with a lynx eye for the syntactical faults of other writers better than himself, as I have discovered from H.N's papers. He quite properly held my writing in contempt and latterly would not even review my books. This made A. cross, and hurt me a bit. But I bear no resentment whatever. There is to be no memorial service, at his request. In a way this makes me sad, for he seems to disappear in a puff of wind. Will he be remembered by posterity? Only by specialising scholars. Yet for fifty years and more he was a famous and feared reviewer. He knew every literary person of his own and the ensuing generation. He was received at every party of note, and was revered and respected by everyone with aspirations, either social or literary.

Knowing that he was going to die, I inserted [into the Harold Nicolson biography] last week a few things about him which I would not have included had he lived. I felt a cad doing this, but when I last spoke to him about his relationship with H.N. he said he did not the least mind what I published provided he was dead.

Saturday, 19th January

The price of gold has risen to unprecedented heights, and the result is that queues of people take their old trinkets to Hatton Gardens to be sold and melted down. Watched on TV Victorian and even Georgian salt cellars being hammered into pulp and thrown into furnaces. Had to turn my head away. It is the old world disintegrating before one's eyes.

Went to London on Monday, staying with Eardley for two nights. I took him to the funniest French film, *La Cage aux Folles*, at Gate Cinema. About transvestites, a subject I normally find embarrassing, but it was not treated seriously. On Tuesday I had my lower front teeth out. A disagreeable, almost traumatic experience. Notwithstanding the local anaesthetic, the digging, hacking, wrenching, drilling upset me so much that I was near to tears. Left for Brooks's and looking at a shoe shop window in Bond Street heard a voice behind me say, 'Would you like me to buy you a pair of those £120 reduced sale shoes?' It was Loelia [Lindsay],* laughing. I was just able to make her understand that I had come from the dentist and could not speak. M. dined at Brooks's. He gave me a Japanese handwarmer, a velvet-clad case into which you insert a burning stick of charcoal which lasts for seven hours. It is heavenly. I shall see him once more before he departs.

A. telephoned me yesterday in Bath to say that Cecil [Beaton] died early that morning. Billy [Henderson] was with him the previous afternoon reading to him and he said he did not feel well. I never knew Cecil intimately, and used to be frightened of his tongue, which used to be vitriolic. He was the most observant man I have ever met. Nothing escaped his beady or quizzical eye. The smallest blemish of face or hand was noticed. Consequently he was extremely sensitive of people's appearance. He could not stand people, like Harold and Derek Hill, who would say waspish things about him. He was an exceedingly amusing talker, the King of Sophistication. He was more sophisticated than intellectual. There was a meretricious side to him, all that stagey scenery side. Chi-chi rather than real. But in old age he became very distinguished looking, almost beautiful. Always splendidly dressed. His voice almost as affected as Raymond's, very Twentyish and not euphonious, cracked. With his intimates he lost all his spikiness and was almost simple. No, he was never simple. Since he was nice to me I liked him very much. And occasionally I could make him laugh. Surprising the columns of obituary given him by all

---

* Hon. Loelia Ponsonby (1902–93), dau. of 1st Baron Sysonby, Treasurer to HM King George V; m. 1930–47 to 2nd Duke of Westminster ('Bendor'); m. 1969 Sir Martin Lindsay of Downhill, Bt (1905–81).

the papers. He was a personality right enough, and with him passes an age, and the Twenties have gone for good. And a good thing too.

Tuesday, 22nd January

I telephoned Dr King to say that the new sleeping pills he has given me don't agree with me at all and asking if I might go back to the old ones.* He explained that the old ones leave traces in the system which take a long time to work out and counsels me to persevere with the new ones until the end of the week. I explained that they only allowed me to sleep until about 3.30, then I woke up and did not just lie awake but had headaches and nightmares. He said it was the symptom which all drug addicts suffered from when cut off from their mixture at first. So I am faced with some nasty nights ahead. Nearest analogy to these waking nightmares I can find is being on the Wembley Giant Racer in 1926, which terrified me, or looping-the-loop, which I also did as a child, in Captain Burgess's Moth over Broadway Hill in 1925, tumbling over and over with giddiness and headache.

Gloria Gibson, the Vicar's wife, told me that the burglars who stole all their jewellery and silver left two things untouched. One was her silver cross and chain, which she had left on her dressing-table in full view, the other the Vicar's silver chalice in a case. Just shows that *hoi polloi* ought to be brought up with a healthy dread of hell's flames.

Sunday, 3rd February

Bad nights persist – headaches and throbbing in the ear, and during the day I feel giddy. Dr King asks A. whether it is not due to her going to India. A. replied, 'Don't you believe it. He doesn't mind my going in the least', which in fact is not the case, for I do mind. Lately I have wondered if I am not seriously ill.

Strange goings-on with the Guinnesses in the village. She in taking to the bottle has attacked her husband with a knife and slashed him about the face. Rushes wildly about the village street, swearing and making dreadful scenes. The Vicar and his wife are Samaritans, even sleeping in her house. They got her into a home in Bristol but she

---

* In *Another Self*, J.L.-M. writes that he had been addicted to sleeping pills since suffering from a neurological illness during the War.

absented herself. Why has this nice, dull woman turned into a sot? I suppose because she has nothing whatever to do.

Monday, 7th February

I went to London for the day just to see M. who leaves for Paris on Wednesday. Felt rotten. When I got to Piccadilly Circus I could not remember where the London Library was and had to enter a shop, lean against the counter and reflect. At Brooks's was again so overwhelmed with giddiness that I had a neat whisky, a drink I seldom touch. When M. came and we went into the Coffee Room I could barely concentrate and at one moment wondered if I would not have to ask him to leave. Then recovered. He accompanied me to the Privy Council Office, where I retrieved my MS* from Norman St John Stevas. No word of thanks in the parcel. Then talked at M's flat. He will not be away more than four weeks before returning here, so the gulf will not be too long. Feel very happy indeed about this relationship, free of passion and deep-seated on both sides. He saw me off at the station.

Next morning I telephoned the doctor and said I could not continue like this. Did I have a tumour of the brain? Or diabetes? He said No. I don't understand how he knows without my undergoing examination. He told me to go back to my old pills – Dalmane – for a week and report to him next Tuesday. Since I returned to the old pills, which has been for two nights now, I have been quite well again. All dizziness, all illness gone. Furthermore, I am now able to write with renewed vigour.

Today Stuart Preston† came down to Bath for luncheon. Alvilde came over and the three of us ate at La Vendange. He and I talked in the library afterwards. He told me Guy Burgess was endowed with an asset which had to be seen to be believed. It was the secret weapon of his charm. Anyone so endowed could get away with murder, and he did. Yes, I said, but surely not with every sort of man. 'Every sort of man,' S. said. He was surely very grubby, I said. 'Very,' he said.

---

* Of J.L.-M's history of the later Jacobites, 'The Countess and the Cardinal', written in the early 1970s but not published until 1983, under the title *The Last Stuarts*. St John Stevas, who had asked to see the MS, was Lord President of the Council and Minister for the Arts, 1979–81.

† American bibliophile, resident in Paris; friend of J.L.-M. since 1938 (b. 1915).

Friday, 15th February

Have felt so much better over the past week that I have at last been
able to write fairly well. Have received two letters from Paris and on
Wednesday M. rang to remind me (I needed no reminding) that it was
a year since we first met. A short conversation, but how heavenly it
was.

Have just returned from taking A. to Heathrow. She flies to India
tonight and will be away a month. She has left a myriad of notes and
instructions, and has bought me piles of food with directions how to
cook it. At the airport she found a porter in a flash, and after a prolonged embrace, we parted. When I lost sight of her dear, grey head
and upright little figure, I wept.

Mary Beaufort asked herself to luncheon with A. yesterday. It was
at eleven o'clock, which meant that A., who was busy packing, had
to make an effort to entertain one elderly Duchess. Mary said to her,
'I only like the Royal Family. No one else interests me in the least.'
A. asked her why the Queen looked so sad these days. Mary said she
was sad; it was the times.

Sunday 17th February

Yesterday I took Diana Westmorland to luncheon with Nan Bernays.
Nan is a dear, kind woman; must have been pretty. Teeth now old
ivory. Her brother Jack Britton lunching, but left early to see his wife
who is dying of cancer. Nan told us he was so rich – from shoes – that
he had set up twenty different trusts for charitable purposes, but he
would not give her sons, and he has none of his own and no nearer
relations, one penny.

Today I lunched with Billy Henderson and Frank Tait[*] at Tisbury.
Dickie Buckle present. He lives all alone in a small cottage in a valley
surrounded by woods and fields. Sees hardly anybody but is not lonely.
He is delivering a dissertation at Cecil Beaton's memorial service in
March. Brought a tape of it and played it, asking us for criticisms. I
told him he should pause more before sentences. Enjoyable day. I took
Dickie back to his cottage and had a cup of tea.

Frank who is a great friend of the Sutherlands says poor Graham is

---

[*] Australian child psychiatrist (b. 1923).

dying of cancer of the kidneys. Ten days ago he went for a check-up.
They told him something seemed to be the matter. Now he hasn't got
more than a few days to live, Frank says. Then, on the midnight news,
announcer said that Graham had died.

Monday, 18th February

Papers all publish hideous photographs of Graham in old age, face collapsed, whereas he was a singularly handsome man until he was sixty.
Why does one have to be recorded for posterity in one's hideous
decline if in one's heyday one has been good-looking? There was a
time when A. and I saw a lot of the Sutherlands at Roquebrune. In
fact she found their house above Mentone for them. Then came a
coolness. Cathy, a very mischievous little woman, made trouble
between us and the Kenneth Clarks by repeating something we had
allegedly said about one of the Clark children. I was made by A. to
tackle them about this one day when we went to San Remo together.
I said to Cathy that she must have known that what she repeated was
not true. Graham flew to her defence and got extremely red and huffy.
Our relations were never the same after that. My impression of
Graham is that he was a clever but not an intellectual man. He talked
a good deal of hot air. Had theories which he propounded as though
he were a sage. But intellect and artistic genius do not always go
together; and I believe G. did have genius. He is certainly one of the
best British artists of the mid twentieth century. Socially he was very
unsure of himself – small blame.

Tuesday, 19th February

Went to London for night. Peter Quennell lunched at Brooks's.
Talked about Jamesey Pope-Hennessy and the letters he is editing.
Says his visits to royalties when he was writing *Queen Mary* are
brilliant and funny. Is publishing visit to the Windsors, but not to
Balmoral to see present Queen, or to Gloucesters (uproarious) because the Duchess is still alive. Peter is then going to write a book
about certain characters he himself has known, stringing them
together in some sort of sequence. Misses *History Today*, but likes
the new editor, Crowder. Very kindly said he would read through
my Vol. II of H.N. Went to Maggs and bought a pretty drawing of

Rupert Brooke, having first taken it to National Portrait Gallery where I ascertained it is the copy of a photograph taken of Brooke by Cherrill Schell, a German who took a series in about 1913. Still it is nice to have. Went to see Diana Mosley. We talked about Maître Blum whom she thought rather mad. She wants to meet Misha and warn him. She spoke of the films they are making about the Mitfords, three of them coming. One features me in the incident where Lord Redesdale turned me out of the house. Diana very beautiful, tall and straight.

Then I dined with John Betjeman and Elizabeth Cavendish and their new doctor, a charming woman whose husband is Chairman of British Rail.* Much hilarity and laughter. John read us part of a poem which he is composing about Magdalen, his contribution to the Fabric Fund. Elizabeth and he had stayed last weekend at Royal Lodge – surely a change in the tradition of royalty never to countenance domestic irregularities. John was given a bedroom next to the Queen Mother's and not next to E's. Nevertheless she went to say goodnight to him and tuck him up. She told the policeman on duty, who apparently sits all night on a chair outside the QM's bedroom, to see if John needed anything during the night, which this kind man did. The doctor motored me to J.K.-B's where I stayed the night.

Boring Properties Committee meeting at National Trust all next morning. Lunched with dear old Ralph Dutton† and Geoffrey Houghton-Brown‡ at Grosvenor Hotel. Ralph is extremely blind; cannot read more than headlines of newspapers, yet will not try to get a really potent magnifying glass. Went to Osbert Lancaster's exhibition at Redfern Gallery. Very good, and how varied his styles. Some like Lears without the romance, and many caricatures. Nearly all sold and I did not bother to ask price of few unsold as I didn't like them well enough.

Apparently poor Cathy [Sutherland] told Frank Tait today that she intended to commit suicide. Frank very sensibly said she couldn't for at least six weeks, for there was too much for her to do, and only she could carry out Graham's wishes and the directions of his will. At the end of that time they could discuss the subject again.

---

* Jill, wife of Sir Peter Parker, of Minster Lovell, Oxon; also a keen gardener.
† Architectural historian and writer (1898–1985); s. cousin as 8th Baron Sherborne, 1982.
‡ Dilettante and painter (1903–93), in whose house in South Kensington J.L.-M. kept a flat from 1946 to 1961.

Sunday, 2nd March

M. is back. I wrote proposing that I should meet him on his arrival, but he parried this. I went to lunch with the Michael Colefaxes on his behalf last Wednesday, M.C. wanting me to identify some of the houses which Sibyl stayed in during her early years and photographed. I have never met a man who listened less to what one was trying to say. He kept interrupting, kept on hugging the albums so that I could not see the snapshots. By 4.30 I was so tired that all I wanted was to get away. M. will have a devil of a time working with him, nice though he be. But by then he will have had some practice with another diffi-cult customer, Maître Blum. Anne Colefax kept asking whether he was going to be too partisan in the Windsor book. I of course upheld M. as much as I dared without showing my feelings for him. Anne C., who is German, loathes the French and loathes the Windsors.

Monday, 3rd March

This diary is becoming an obituary column. Now Michael Astor has died.[*] A very nice jolly man but underneath both neurotic and sad I suspect. He had many wives and a not very happy life. A great friend of Robin Fedden.[†] I last saw him during the summer expedition to Cornwall last year. We talked for hours in the train on the way back, about the Astor family. He was very candid, no barriers. In fact a most candid man, with pronounced sense of humour, looking upon the world with gentle, cynical eyes. No base behaviour surprised him; on the contrary, it amused him. Suffered from no illusions. Drank too much I would say. Was indolent, with a good brain. Much the most sensitive of the Astor family. Saturnine beneath the jollity. A dear man. Tough physically. Belonged to the Robin, Paddy L[eigh]-F[ermor] set; not mine really, but I liked him very much.

Tuesday, 4th March

I motored to London this morning. Freda [Berkeley] received me with the news that Michael Duff's death was in *The Times* today. Not unexpected because at Christmas he looked so ill and ghost-like. Dear

---

[*] Hon. Michael Astor (1916–80); s. of 2nd Viscount and of Nancy, Viscountess Astor, MP; patron of artists, writer, and Chairman of Committee of London Library.
[†] J.L.-M's successor (1951–74) as Historic Buildings Secretary of National Trust (1909–77).

Michael, an affectionate, funny man, an anachronism, being a very rich landowner in North Wales, huge estates, living in huge Vaynol, one of the last of the bright young people of the Twenties. David Herbert will be miserable, except that he is never miserable about anything. Michael a most lovable man. I embraced him warmly when we parted because I knew I should not see him again.

Motored to Islington to lunch with Paul Hyslop.* He lent me two packets of Raymond's letters from Harold. The larger packet contained H's letters before 1930, which period I have finished. Nevertheless it is important to read of H's attitude towards that love affair. No doubt he did love R. I have never read any of Harold's letters so uninhibited. As much lust letters as love letters, and curiously not as quotable as Harold's to Vita. In fine, I wonder: could H. love anyone? These letters not as good as his diaries. So far only read half.

Met M. for tea at Oxford and Cambridge Club. He waited for me downstairs by the door. Quite unchanged. Talked of his work in Paris with enthusiasm. We went to see a bad film. I felt depressed on return to Badminton next morning. Pouring with rain; dark, empty, desolate house. Took dogs for soaking walk, then came back, drew curtains, lit fire and read Raymond's letters.

Wednesday, 5th March

Handsome David Ford came to tea and talked about his photography of the Bath prints. A nice young man indeed. Norah telephoned that galley proofs of H.N. Vol. I are ready. She is sending a set to Nigel who has asked for them. This fills me with misgiving. I told her that Paul H. had lent me a vast batch of H.N's letters to Raymond and I hoped that, if I needed to, I could add some quotations to the proofs. She asked what they amounted to. I said they were love letters. She gave a contemptuous laugh which annoyed me. Struck me as retrograde that she of all people, chairman of a great publishing firm, should find a relationship of this sort between two eminent and intelligent men a joke.

Sunday, 30th March

On Wednesday the 26th A. and I went to Michael Duff's memorial service in Chelsea Old Church. A crowd of old friends, Jimmie Smith

---

* Architect; friend and executor of Raymond Mortimer.

in front of us looking a million. A beautiful church almost wholly rebuilt after the War, owing to Richard Stewart-Jones's gallant efforts. Was reminded of this by spying in a distant aisle his memorial tablet, to the inscription of which I remember making objections which were ignored. Meanwhile I was concentrating on Michael, so very different, so rich, so sophisticated, patrician, carefree, yet badly educated. So sweet in manner, so funny if you were able to get on his exclusive wave-length. Two things struck me during this service. One was the late arrival of Jane Assheton-Smith, who slipped into a back pew near ours. She was divorced from Michael in 1937. The second was the hassock I was kneeling on. Like all the hassocks in this church, this was needleworked in memory of a past parishioner – somebody M.A. with the dates 1821–1908. I calculated that he was alive in my lifetime and in that of Keats and Shelley and Byron.

This morning A. said to me while we were at the sink, 'Would it be a nice idea if I joined you for a night or two in Paris on your return from Viviers?' Quite calmly I said no, because M. would be there then, as she knew, and I had arranged to spend a day or two with him. This caused hurtness of feeling. Silence, followed by caustic remarks. I hate being made to feel guilty when I have so little to feel guilty about. Nearly all my life I have been pursued by this guilt complex, induced first by my father, then by A. It was only for the years between 1945 and my marriage in 1951 that I was wholly free from guilt, and happy.

Tuesday, 1st April

A. went to London, and left with my luncheon packet a note to be read and digested. Such a sad note and so accusatory that I can hardly bear to refer to it. Even suggesting that it might be better if we separated. But oh dear, what cause? Not my purely socratic friendship with M. Not the charge that I, aged seventy-one, am not attentive enough. In the evening we discussed the matter calmly and affectionately, and embraced, and agreed to let it pass. I am still riddled with guilt, and yet I am guiltless – surely?

Sunday, 13th April

I have fired in the corrected galleys of H.N. Norah said in an aside that the corrections will cost either me or the firm over £800. But I refuse to take these ominous words too seriously. The correcting has occupied me for nearly a month, what with Nigel and Rupert [Hart-Davis] sending me their batches back, my coming on the Raymond correspondence and inserting extracts from it. Nigel has been a saint, producing photographs and twice meeting me at Chatto's for the purpose of selection, and helping me with captions.

Yesterday in Cirencester a huge reception given by Paul Weller the bookseller to over 150 people to celebrate Alvilde's and Rosemary Verey's garden book.* It was a best-seller in last Sunday's list. A. had to sign more than a hundred copies, and is enjoying a swimgloat which I delight in.

Tuesday, 15th April

Stayed last night with J.K.-B. who took me to an Italian film, *La Luna*. Beautiful photography of Rome. Strange story of beautiful boy of fifteen who takes to drugs. His mother, operatic singer, very pretty and young, is in love with him. There are scenes in which they go to bed together, which rather shocked me. J. says idiotic to be shocked. What is there to be shocked by? Yet I am by shots of son putting hand on mother's cunt and mother committing fellatio with son.

Lunched dear Midi [Gascoigne].† She talks much and asks questions to which I doubt whether she wants an answer. But a darling nevertheless. Happy in her soulless flat in Cranmer Court, a sort of St Andrew's Hospital for the wealthy senile. Left her to join M. who took me to meet Hugo Vickers‡ who is writing Cecil Beaton's life. A handsome youth possessing that rare ability to smile with the eyes. He met his subject only twice, but Cecil took to him and engaged him to do his biography. He says Cecil only published one-eighteenth of his diaries, assiduously kept in his own handwriting until the day of his death. After his bad, penultimate stroke, his lady friends Clarissa Avon and Anne Tree§ thought it would be safe to regale him with outrageous gossip which he would be in no condition to record. They were mistaken; he learnt to write with his left hand. Now they are trem-

---

* *The Englishwoman's Garden* (Chatto & Windus).
† Hon. Mary O'Neill, Mrs Derick Gascoigne (1905–91); mother of Bamber Gascoigne.
‡ Writer (b. 1951).
§ Lady Anne Cavendish, dau. of 10th Duke of Devonshire; m. 1949 Michael Lambert Tree, painter.

bling, because Cecil was scrupulous in attributing what he learned to its source.

Thursday, 1st May

It is May Day here in France. Shops are shut, trains stopped, workers in the cities presumably marching in demonstration against the status quo, but in Viviers in the Ardèche the inhabitants are *en vacance*. Eardley and I left London on the morning of 21 April by OAP ticket, £46 return to Montélimar, via Dover and hovercraft, which took a noisy half-hour, half risen in the air, half beating the waves, to Boulogne. Thence by train to Paris. Taxi to Hôtel Prince Albert, rue Ste-Hyacinthe where dear M. staying. There I found a sweet note of welcome from him. E. took a female friend to dine. M. and I dined with Stuart Preston in a neighbouring bistro, and went to see Stuart's new apartment under the roof of a palace in the rue de Rivoli. Admittedly a fine view across the Tuileries, corner of Louvre (as in our Max Jacob painting in Bath), Invalides, Eiffel Tower. But apartment so small as to be a dwarf's cell, and that's the only residence of a rich American. So strange. He wants to divest himself of possessions. M. is devoted to this old Henry James, this well-educated piece of time's jetsam.

Lovely journey to Montélimar on express train. I lunched in buffet car, a model for British Rail – choice of delicious salads, quiches and half-bottles of wine. At Montélimar we were met by Geoffrey Houghton-Brown's friend, Father Brian Houghton, a distant cousin. Driven to Viviers where he lives in a canon's house two doors from G's in Cathedral Close. This retired, dissident priest, follower of Archbishop Lefebvre* whom he knows well and calls saintly but foolish, has walked straight out of a novel by Ronald Firbank. Intensely affected, rather a bore, but very intelligent.

E. and I spent two nights in a clean, modern hotel just outside town but on main road. Thundering traffic all night. We were so depressed that next day I telephoned Geoffrey in London and asked if we might camp in his house. He assented. We moved into this prettily decorated (by him) No. 2 Chemin de Ronde. Very sad, this quarter of town. Large Cathedral, bare and empty. Famous tapestries which lent colour, stolen. All altar furnishings gone. All canons dead and not replaced. Fr Houghton is allowed to celebrate mass at 8.30 every day.

---

* Marcel Lefebvre (1905–91); Catholic schismatic (objecting to the modernised Catholic liturgy); excommunicated 1988 by Pope John Paul II.

I attended twice, as sole member of congregation. His gestures and delivery are markedly eccentric and melodramatic. Consequence of a break with discipline, like the Orthodox monks of that isolated monastery attended by Derek and me on Mount Athos last autumn.*

Practically every day a letter from M. and three times I have telephoned him. To my protestations of love he replies with the dignity of youth. Sent me his review of John Lehmann's *Rupert Brooke*, not yet out, which is brilliant.

Father Houghton motored me to see early churches in Drôme region across the Rhône.

La Garde Ardhemar, eleventh-century. What he calls 'Roman' architecture, not Romanesque. Façade shows recognisable traces of almost Palladian broken pediment devices (cf. S. Francisco della Vigna, Venice).

Chapelle du Val des Nymphes on old Ligurian site, in ilex grove, troglodyte caves and roughly hewn apses from rock grottoes (Ligurians did not build roofs), much running water, pools.

Les Trois Châteaux, St Paul, St Restitut. Much Roman carving it is true, quite classical brackets, egg and tongue mouldings, basilica formation and plan, timeless, Latin, more ancient than any English Christian churches. Not Byzantine Fr H. says. He says that the chisel was invented in 1180, having lapsed with Romans who knew how to heat forges to high temperature. Hitherto hammer carving.

Fr H. explained how scientists baffled by moon discoveries since landings. For example the moon did not come out of the Pacific, and is older than the earth. How did it get there? Why is it not revolving on its own axis? It is hollow, its surface a few miles thick, and of eggshell fragility. It could easily be destroyed by some foolish bombardment, involving the end of tides on earth, wind control, plant control. This could produce devastation and unknown disasters, even end of life on this planet. He also says that between galaxies there are voids without space, without time, impenetrable, unknown mysteries.

Fr Houghton is also interesting on death. As a priest he has witnessed hundreds of deaths. Says that the dying never believe they are leaving the world. The world is leaving them. People, friends are deserting them. Therefore it is so important to rally round the dying.

---

* See pp. 213–14 below.   N. B

Moreover one should never discuss them or talk of them as though they have gone, when in a coma. He has known many cases of dying persons, who for weeks have been speechless, suddenly making sensible remarks, swan-songs. His argument in favour of immortality of the soul is that every person is the centre of the universe which revolves around him. He experiences his death, therefore the fact that he experiences what an incredulous atheist would call annihilation is proof that there is no such thing as annihilation. Not altogether convincing. His experience is that humans are far less wicked than they or we think, but far more stupid.

We have suffered from five days' mistral. Bitter cold but much sun, and in the courtyard of Geoffrey's house one can sit in sun-trapped corners out of the wind. E. sketches indefatigably. I brought my rejected *Last Stuarts* MS, and have read through it making corrections. Have thought it not at all bad and so have told M. to whom I shall show it. Yesterday I thought I would go through it again and decided it was dismally boring. Since every publisher to whom David Higham submitted it thought the same, it must, I fear, be so. Its failure has caused me much chagrin and brought about loss of confidence.

Have not made progress in plan of new novel. I thought of it as I walked along the lane downstream to the new suspension bridge below Viviers. But concentration difficult. Diversions in nightingales, swallows, ravens, even butterflies encountered. Sweet-sour, sperm-like smell of May blossom. Pyramidalis orchids out, wisteria, lilac, even gorse, broom. In fact, for novel-plotting one must be at a desk with pen and paper. If one goes for a walk, notepad essential for ideas that flash into mind and must be caught like butterflies on the wing. But the planning not possible. How am I to know how German prisoners in First World War were kept in camps? Were they allowed freedom, out on their own? I remember Mama in the last War told me one accosted her, and she, delighted, protested as she supposed was only correct – 'I am old enough to be your mother' – to elicit the curt response, 'No, old enough to be grandmother.' So evidently contact was possible. But how to introduce seduction of young son by hungry, handsome prisoner, with A. looking over my shoulder?

First cuckoo heard, but even they must feel the cold.

Yesterday, Father Houghton dined with E. and me. He has a positive manner. No standing on ceremony. Sat himself down at table saying, 'I don't like watching people eat.' Reminded me of Byron, who could not bear seeing women eat. 'After all,' said Father H., 'one does not look at people going to the lavatory.' Argument ensued about symbolism in painting, E. trying to explain motives of. Fr H. said that painters must observe the basic common meanings of symbolist expressions. Even the post-impressionists did that. The moment the basic understanding or language was rejected and an artist adopted his own symbolism, confusion arose. He was painting for himself and not for others.

Friday, 2nd May

E. and I left Viviers by afternoon train for Paris. Were met by M. at Gare du Nord, apologetic that he was not able to secure the Duchess of Windsor's chauffeur to meet us. We again stayed at Hôtel Prince Albert. E. and I obliged to share a room despite fact that M. had ordered us a room each the week before. Next morning E. left for London, and I kept the room on for myself for two further nights.

Saturday, 3rd May

Walked with M. across the Tuileries, over the Pont Royal to 53 rue de Varenne. He took me upstairs to the *grenier* under the eaves where he works, where I shall be able to picture him in the weeks ahead. While I telephoned A. he discreetly withdrew, and on return said his Master would receive me. Didn't want to be received, but could see that M. considered reception by her the highest honour. We waited till she was ready. Then ushered into her library where previous day she had been photographed and knocked sideways by the charm of Lord Snowdon. Very distinguished old lady, very correct, but thinner than I had imagined, sharp features, strong eye. Talked of Duke of Windsor's '*droiture*'. Asked us to translate. Sense of duty? No. Sense of honour? Not quite. Honourableness? More like it. He was a gentleman with a strong sense of what was fitting. This formidable interview over, I slipped away.

I lunched with the Margeries[*] in rue St-Guillaume. She unchanged since 1932 or 1933 when I met her with Georges Cattaui.[†] A bluestocking, whom Harold found maddening. He a distinguished old man, tiny and owl-like. A granddaughter lunched. Could see she was

---

[*] Roland de Margerie; French diplomat; First Secretary at French Embassy in London, 1933–9.

[†] Egyptian-born author of three books on Marcel Proust, who became a Catholic priest in Switzerland.

embarrassed by her grandmother who never stopped talking.
Husband said little, but always to the point. Produced large packet of
letters to him (not her) from H.N. down the years. She said that I must
now read these, and whichever ones I liked they would copy for me.
But before I had got through the first letter she interrupted, and continued to do so. He sat quietly, merely answering the questions I put
to him. At one moment, irritated, he said to her, '*Tais-toi! Il veut lire.*'
Madame de M. took exception to a remark in H.N's published diary
that when the Margeries were coming to London she need not
suppose she would succeed in establishing a salon. It has rankled all
these years. After all, she said, salons do not happen just like that, they
happen if a woman has friends among intellectuals, poets, artists,
writers, composers. He reminded me that he was responsible for H's
successful retrieval of the Duchess of Windsor's papers left in the hotel
at Evreux. At H's request, he sent letters to those in authority asking
them to help H. 'She of course left the papers on purpose, in self-
advertisement', interjected Madame de M.

M. and I dined with the Mosleys* at the Temple de la Gloire
[Orsay]. Met at station by Irish manservant and driven to Temple. I
enjoyed the evening enormously. Besides us four, Alexander Mosley†
and pretty young wife whom I discovered to be a daughter of Mary
Anna Marten.‡ Sat next to Diana who exuded charm. She said I had
been a help in persuading the film director not to turn Lord
Redesdale into a monster. And that I was the last friend who had
stayed at Swinbrook to be alive. Tom greatly changed. Now a very
old man. Shapeless, bent, blotched cheeks, crooked nose, no moustache, and tiny eyes in place of those luminous, dilating orbs. I sat
with him after dinner on a sofa and talked for an hour. 'Let us talk
of Harold, and then of Uncles and Aunts,' he said.§ But we never got

---

* Sir Oswald Mosley (1896–1980), 6th Bt; MP, 1918–24 and 1926–31; Chancellor of
Duchy of Lancaster in Labour Government, 1929–30; founded New Party, 1930; founded
British Union of Fascists, 1932; interned under Defence Regulations, 1940–43; m., 1st,
1920, Lady Cynthia Curzon (d. 1933); 2nd, 1936, Hon. Diana Guinness (*née* Mitford, b.
1910); resident of France from 1951.
† Paris publisher; b. 1938, son of Sir Oswald and Diana Mosley; m. 1975 Charlotte
Marten.
‡ Born 1929, o.c. of 3rd and last Baron Allington; m. 1949 Commander George Marten;
owner of Crichel estate in Dorset (including Long Crichel).
§ Sir Oswald's maternal aunt, Dorothy Edwards-Heathcote, had married J.L.-M's paternal uncle, Alec Milne Lees-Milne (1878–1931).

to the Uncles and Aunts, and he had not much to say about Harold. 'He was a dear man. The most loyal of my supporters.' Sir O. has mellowed to the extent of never saying anything pejorative of anybody. I asked him what Hitler was really like. Tom replied that he was gentle and gentlemanly. He slipped shyly into a room. His bombast was reserved for the platform. Unlike Musso, who was all bombast and impossible to talk to. Not so Hitler. Had only he, Mosley, spoken German in those days he believed he could have influenced Hitler. As it was he only learnt German in prison from a fellow prisoner, a black band-leader, charming. Hitler never wanted to fight England or the British Empire, he wanted unity with us in the fight against Bolshevism. But, I said, he wanted war with other, smaller countries which he could overwhelm. Tacit agreement. I asked boldly if he thought he had made a mistake in founding New Party. He admitted it was the worst mistake of his life. The British do not like new parties. Said that if he had led the Labour Party he would have kept Edward VIII on the throne. He [the King] was eminently suited to be an intermediary between his country and the dictators. Said that the critics of both himself and the Duke of Windsor never made allowances for the fact that they detested war, having experienced the horrors of the trenches. They wanted to avoid it happening again at all costs.

We discussed Britain's present situation. He thought hopeless, so long as we did not produce and sell as much as the French and the Germans. Not all the fault of the Unions. He always got on well with them. Cook the Communist was a great friend, who made outrageous statements in public but was reasonable in private conversation. What was now needed was a great figure from the West who would go to Moscow, breakfast every day for six months with Brezhnev, and talk heart-to-heart with him about the common threats to civilisation.

On and on we went until Diana joined us from the small sitting room to say the Alexander Mosleys were going and would motor M. and me back to Paris. Tom said, but we haven't discussed the Aunts and Uncles yet, what charming people they were (when they were alive he never bothered with them at all). I helped pull him to his feet. He stands unsteadily, but assured me his head was all right. Held me by both hands and said I must come again. Why not come tomorrow? Come and stay. Charming he was. Diana seems to like M.

Thursday, 8th May

Walked the dogs in Westonbirt gardens this evening. Beautiful misty sun. Everything out in the perfect, evanescent stage of fresh green. Heard one cuckoo, not so long after my Viviers cockoo. *Prunus pendula rubra* in full blossom. Bluebells in clumps at the feet of trees. A dark blue rhododendron. Not a soul about, but we three. Cherries against the silver firs, against the deep green yews. Alvilde and Rosemary have just given an interview in the garden here. A marvellous moment. And does M. realise it? Is he aware of nature, and the spring? Apart from the rise of his own sap?

Friday, 16th May

Dined last night with the Vereys at Barnsley. David very upset because three weeks ago they were burgled. All their silver and all their good china stolen while they were sleeping upstairs. Burglars broke through the drawing room window beneath them. A Swiss banker who was also dining told me he was leaving tomorrow (Friday) for New York in Concorde and returning the same night by Jumbo, and would be playing polo at Cirencester on Saturday afternoon. This expedition will cost several thousand pounds, and for what? Some decision or indecision which could have been arrived at by letter or telephone? While I was walking dogs this morning in the Slates, Concorde passed overhead with this ridiculous man inside it. Another guest, a French banker, told me that an expression used by the French when they have sipped a mouthful of delicious wine or tasted a good pudding is *'Quel bon petit Jésus en culotte de velours!'* Would this be used by Charles de Noailles?* Must find out.

Have finished *War and Peace* at last.† This, the greatest novel ever written, is badly composed. All those accounts of battles, irrelevant to the story, and the final dissertation on the meaning of causes, make the book shapeless. But genius may be allowed these irregularities, these deficiencies of art. Shakespeare and even Keats were similarly guilty.

Incensed by the Pope's telling black Kenyans last week that contra-

---

* Vicomte de Noailles, leading member (with his wife Marie-Laure, d. 1970) of French Society, and regarded as a great arbiter of taste.
† Started on Mount Athos in September 1979.

ception a sin not to be practised, I wrote a good letter to *The Times*. They have not published it, which does not surprise me. Rees-Mogg would never tolerate any criticism of Pope or Church. Yet this is the most critical subject facing mankind. The population of Kenya has doubled within twenty-one years.

Oxford University Press have written again to me. They definitely want me to do the Country House Anthology. Then there is Bamber [Gascoigne]'s* Bath book which I am being bamboozled into. When Vol. I of Harold comes out, will I be invited to write something which really appeals to me, which these two do not?

Wednesday, 21st May

A delicious day. Alex Moulton† called for me at 8.30 and we went off in his heaven-borne Rolls for Wales. Weather broken after three weeks' sheer sunshine, but beautiful with purple storm-clouds over the Black Mountains and golden sun thrown as a backcloth. I think the country, my maternal country around Glanusk, the most beautiful probably in Wales. At Picton Castle we stopped on the creek, ate picnic brought by Alex, and had a kip in the car. We talked of sex, death and despondency. I speak pretty freely. We both agreed that we had been failures, I more so than he, for he has invented some important things which will endure – the Moulton bicycle, his motor-car suspensions. But he has not got to the top in his profession, and I suspect thinks that not being made a knight but only a CBE is a seal of his failure. I honestly seek no worldly honours, only some recognition from the public and approval from those writers who matter. But I have not achieved this. Moreover my National Trust work has received no recognition. Told him I did not attribute my failings to anyone but myself, my character.

We visited the Graham Sutherland museum at Picton Castle. What was he striving to do? These symbolisms of what? Figments of a disordered imagination? He was not a deep or clever man, rather pretentious. All nonsense – but he could paint. His colours blend and never jar. His drawing superb. Imagination, when not totally abstract, fine.

---

* Arthur Bamber Gasgoigne (b. 1935); author, broadcaster and publisher; son of Midi Gascoigne.
† Dr Alexander Moulton (b. 1920), of The Hall, Bradford-on-Avon, Wiltshire; engineer and inventor.

Walked up to the Castle. Saw Hanning Philipps* getting into a car and being driven away. We drove on to St David's. I had romantic memories of the Cathedral, not seen for years. Outside by no means disappointing. Marvellous grey stone, licheny, and yellow pinnacles at four corners of square tower, a good, striking contrast. The steep ascent of the interior I remember, but it used to be emptier of trash and unsightly chairs. Hate chairs in Cathedrals. The east end sealed off at the rood screen, a great mistake. Best thing about the interior is the roof of the nave. Wooden, delicately carved, with pendants. Norman aisle piers and arches renewed in Victorian times.

In the course of our travels we killed two birds on the road. Now if we have done this, how many thousand birds must there not be killed by motorists each year? It is appalling thought. I loathe killing anything and it saddens me dreadfully.

The flycatcher has returned to the stone escutcheon under A's bedroom window and is building her nest again. But is it the same bird? Or the bird's progeny? This has happened every spring we have lived here, bar one.

Thursday, 29th May

To Oxford yesterday to New Bodleian Library to look at papers of Walter Monckton, who was Director-General of Ministry of Information during the time Harold was Parliamentary Under-Secretary.† Found only one reference to H.N. in seven densely packed boxes of paper. I looked carefully enough not to miss anything of consequence I think. Interesting how quickly one sizes up the character and ability of a man whose papers one looks through during but one day. He emerged from initial darkness into transparent light. A nice, good, clever man without much culture; respected by colleagues; loved by friends, certainly by the Stafford Crippses who wrote to him

---

* Hon. (Richard) Hanning Philipps (1904–2001), bro. of 2nd Baron Milford (who in 1928 as Hon. Wogan Philipps, painter, had m. Rosamond Lehmann); m. 1930 Lady Marion Dalrymple, dau. of 12th Earl of Stair; owner of Picton Castle and trustee of the Graham Sutherland Gallery which opened there in 1976.
† Sir Walter Monckton, KC (1891–1965); arch fixer who advised on Abdication of Edward VIII and other delicate matters; played extensive wartime role in fields of propaganda and security; Minister of Labour, 1951–5; Minister of Defence 1955–6; cr. Viscount Monckton of Brenchley, 1957.

most affectionately; a man of slight political convictions. Went to Blackwell's and bought book recommended by Stuart Preston on Ministry of Information. While I was writing out cheque, the cashier must have read my name printed on it, for she asked, 'Are you by any chance the author of *Ancestral Voices?*'

Saturday, 31st May

Much shocked to read in today's *Times* the obituary (excellent) of Babs Johnson, Georgina Masson.* She was terribly ill-looking when she stayed with us this time last year, and also maddening – peremptory, argumentative, verbose and contradictory. We were nearly driven mad. I took her to the station thinking I could never go through another visit from her. Did absolutely nothing about her, and from time to time felt guilty. Never heard a word from her or about her, poor dear. Now I recall her kindness to me in Rome in the days when I was always there, usually with a book in view. She was generous in helping me, and all architectural historians. She was a good woman, and achieved a position for herself in Rome in the footsteps of Mrs Ross and Mrs Strong.† Every scholar visiting Rome got in touch with her. Her knowledge of the city was phenomenal. Her photographs of Italian gardens were superb, taken with an old Box Brownie. Whenever we dined in Rome she would suggest a new restaurant, somewhere unknown to tourists where they specialised in delicious wine. Poor Babs, I salute you with affection, gratitude, respect, remorse and irritation.

Desmond Shawe-Taylor‡ to stay. He took us to a Mozart concert in the Bath Assembly Rooms, of wind instruments. As good as could be. I studied closely the faces of the musicians. Some looked agonised, some indifferent, some bored. The French horns had persistent

---

* Author of *The Companion Guide to Rome* (1965) and other books on Italian subjects.

† 'Mrs Ross' was Janet, dau. of the literary hostess, and translator of Ranke, Lucie, Lady Duff-Gordon; m. 1860 Henry Ross. of Alexandria; sometime correspondent for *The Times* in Egypt; later, until her d. in 1927, ran a working farm near Florence, and wrote about aspects of Italian life and villa architecture. Mrs Arthur Strong is described by Harold Acton (*More Memoirs of an Aesthete*) as 'the *doyenne* of the British Colony in Rome' (where she d., 1943) and sometime Assistant Director of the British School of Archaeology; she also wrote.

‡ Music critic (1907–95); original co-tenant (with Edward Sackville-West and Eardley Knollys) of Long Crichel (see note to entry for 17 September 1981).

trouble with what looked like their spittle. One kept taking a brass stop out of the mechanism and shaking drops onto the carpet whenever he had a pause. Rather unattractive.

Tuesday, 3rd June

Have been thinking of J.K.-B. since I stayed with him last week. He leads a quiet and virtuous life. I wish though that he could be happier. He has few enthusiasms. So unlike M., who is back in England and telephones me excitedly to say that Edward St George,* the new husband of Henrietta FitzRoy, is one of the most interesting men he has ever met. It is always like this. Why, I ask? Because he is so clever and amusing, a big-shot in the Bahamas, and has offered to help M. in his research into the Duke of Windsor's governorship there.

Saturday, 7th June

Desmond was shocked at breakfast when I told him I was no longer the least interested in the National Trust, or in architecture. Why, he asked? Well, I think it may be because I have given up the battle of conservation. The world is ruined, and that's that. Besides, having looked after the N.T's buildings for so many years, my interest has just evaporated, and that's all there is to it. But it shouldn't be, he said. Are you no longer interested in the buildings of Venice or Rome? You were never in charge of buildings in those two cities. I am not interested in them from a scientific point of view, I said, only from a general aesthetic one, for associative reasons. The intricacies of architecture bore me now.

At four o'clock I went to meet M. at the Oxford and Cambridge Club for tea. Hadn't seen him for over a month. He looked well, no shadows under eyes. We went to dine with his friend Charles Orwin at a French restaurant in Ebury Street. I have never met a person more attached to his friends than M.; he will hear no criticism of them. Charles Monteith, Chairman of Faber's, Fellow of All Souls, present. Old bumble bee telling rather long-winded stories, but nice enough. Made me feel young though he must be only about sixty-five.

---

* Lawyer and Chairman of Grand Bahama Port Authority; m. 1979 Lady Henrietta FitzRoy, daughter of 11th Duke of Grafton, KG.

Another handsome young man who is a schoolmaster in South London. Agreeable dinner which must have cost Charles more than he can afford. I motored M. back to Hyde Park Square, and stayed the night with Eardley.

Awkward luncheon with Anne Rosse at Overton's. Very expensive. Lady Abdy, Anita Leslie* and two young museum men working at Stafford Terrace. Conversation impossible because of Anne's gush and interruptions. No wonder Harold [Acton] does not want to come over and stay with her for long periods. She depends on his friendship more than anyone's. But as H. says, she has no education, is unread, uninterested in the arts, and is only interested in giggly tittle-tattle. Yet I am so fond of her and sorry for her.

Adam Nicolson† stayed last night with us. On a walk, pack on back, along Cotswold Way. Is writing a book on walks for the National Trust. Arrived at door having come from Bath by byways and visited Dyrham en route. Looks so young (22), fresh, fair and clean. A charming boy, intelligent, sensitive. I have absolutely no shyness with him. He has a nervous laugh, rather engaging. His looks more Vita's than Harold's; long oval face, not chubby like H's; but fair, unlike Vita. Fairness inherited from mother, all peaches and cream. Adam wants to go into Parliament, but would only stand as a Labour candidate, and fears his Eton and Castle background may make this impossible.

Wednesday, 11th June

A letter from M. this morning expressing deep affection. He has met Betty Hanley,‡ who has some Windsor letters, and who asks him to lunch at her cottage in Essex next weekend to meet Ian McCallum.§ Here the green-eyed monster enters, for Ian is a tremendous pouncer and quite unscrupulous and lecherous. I couldn't bear it if he had an affair with M. And there is A. quizzing me about M. on every pos-

---

* Writer; daughter of Sir Shane Leslie of Castle Leslie, Ireland.
† Son (b. 1957) of Nigel Nicolson; writer.
‡ Miss E.C. Hanley, American-born owner of a business in Westminster which held the Royal Warrant for the supply of lamps and lampshades. Her aunt having married the French time-and-motion tycoon Charles Bedaux, she spent much of her early life at Candé, the Bedaux property in Touraine where the Duke and Duchess of Windsor celebrated their wedding in June 1937.
§ Curator of American Museum at Claverton near Bath (1919–87).

sible occasion, making snide little remarks about young men who write books about society people in order to oil their way into society. And suggesting that M. come to stay with us again. My dependence on M. is such that I can honestly say I wish I had never met him. In some dreadful way I almost wish he would die so that I could thereby possess him totally. At times I feel I am going mad.

Thursday, 12th June

M. came down by train for the day. My heart bounds to see him emerge from Bath station, smiling softly. Spent day in flat discussing his predicament – has three books to be completed by the end of this year,* plus doctoral thesis, and has undertaken to Michael Colefax to start on the biography of Sibyl next year. Impossible I should say, but he works quickly when he does work. He is going to Ascot with the St Georges next Tuesday and hopes to see Fort Belvedere which St G. has bought.† A. came over to lunch with us in Bath. Was sweet to him. Whether from shyness or not he does not speak at first. Have noticed this on other occasions.

Strange how he is not much interested in art or artefacts. I showed him a ravishing pair of ormulu candlesticks in a shop and he did not register. Said possessions meant little to him. When I asked if there was any object in my library he would like to have, he said he did not think he would have anywhere to put it. I take it for granted that my friends are interested in the arts, but I suppose such people are a minority.

Caroline Somerset told John Wilton‡ that, at dinner last week, she had a terrible bore on her right, Lord Cowdray, and an even worse bore on her left whose identity she had forgotten. 'That was me,' said J.W. sourly. She is the vaguest girl in the world.

I forgot to record that last month A. became a great-grand-mother. Chloe, Clarissa's eldest child, has produced an infant. I am appalled.

---

* The never-completed biography of Philip Guedalla; and the works eventually published as *The Duke of Windsor's War* (1982) and *The Secret File of the Duke of Windsor* (1988).
† Bought in fact by Edward St George's brother Charles, insurance tycoon and racing personality.
‡ John Egerton, 7th Earl of Wilton (1921–99).

Monday, 16th June

M. gave a dinner at his club – Betty Hanley (I couldn't hear a word), his Foreign Office friend Hugo Haig-Thomas,* dear Charles Orwin and Michael Mosley.† Latter charming with old-fashioned good manners. He was frank about his father, to whom he is devoted but whose activities he doesn't much care for. Wanted to know about his mother who died when he was two. I could not help much for I only once saw her. M. a good host, quiet, attentive, plying guests and keeping ball rolling gently.

Tuesday, 17th June

Alvilde and I lunched at Coutts' Bank in the Strand. Extravagant luncheon with cocktails, white wine, red wine, port and brandy for those who wanted. Those who seemed to want were our hosts, the manager of our branch and his associates. Painfully suburban lot, so unlike our hosts of last visit, John Smith and Tim Egerton. Conversation kept going by A. I dried up, absolutely no lien of sympathy or interest. They want to get hold of our, or rather A's, money for investment. We agreed merely to let them do our taxes for us.

The Manager told us that one day Baroness Burdett-Coutts was shocked to see crumbs on the beard of one of the staff. On making enquiries she discovered that the man had been eating sandwiches prepared by his wife. She at once gave orders that henceforth no member of staff might wear a beard or moustache; and further, that the Bank must supply every member of staff with a proper midday meal. Ever since, the male staff have had to be beardless and moustacheless, and have been given free luncheon. They still of course wear frock coats.

Wednesday, 18th June

I went to Hampstead to see Derek and the portrait he has done of Nick. Awful visit. D. in dreadful mood, saying everything had gone wrong that morning and he had just returned to find a flood in the bathroom. Showed the picture with pride and expectancy of approval. I looked at it long and carefully. Could not say a word, for the por-

---

* Then *en poste* in Yemen Arab Republic (b. 1947).
† Son (b. 1932) of Sir Oswald Mosley by his first wife Lady Cynthia Curzon.

trait was not of Nick. Hardly recognisable. D. dreadfully hurt and upset. I took away the sketch to look at it with A. who quickly found several things wrong. He is asking Nick to sit again. Meanwhile I felt so guilty that I agreed to buy for £250 a little picture of a monk on the quay of Karakolou Monastery, Mount Athos. It turned out when fetched not to be the one I had seen and liked. Took it anyway and must give D. the money in cash. Admired a glazed, painted plate he had. He said it was by Ann Stokes, widow of Adrian,* who lives in Church Row. Went to her house and bought one fresh from the kiln, warm still like a hot-cross bun. Took it to Mulberry Walk as a seventieth birthday present for Diana Mosley.

Collected page proofs from Chatto's. Learned a new word. The lady who handed them to me referred to 'signatures': 'We must put the illustrations between the signatures.' 'But I see no signature,' I said, peering for an autograph. She explained that a signature is a batch of pages.

I am reading Barbara Cartland's life of her brother Ronnie. Was impelled to get this book having read a mention in Harold's diary that he, Tommy Lascelles, Ronnie Cartland and I dined together and had a splendid evening and conversation. I can only remember Ronnie's suave, rather handsome, hair-plastered head, and the aroma of goodness and nobility emanating therefrom. The book reveals what an extraordinary young man he was. So earnest, sincere, patriotic, religious. He was killed fighting in 1941. There is no indication whatever whether he loved or sinned fleshwisely. He was like my Uncle Robert.†

Saturday, 21st June

John Codrington‡ who is staying told us that at a dinner party in India in the 1930s he met the Maharajah of Patiala who was wearing a *rivière* of diamonds, with one immense and sparkling diamond in the centre.

---

* Writer on artistic/architectural subjects and sometime Trustee of Tate Gallery (b. 1902); m. 1947 Ann, dau. of Revd David Mellis.
† J.L.-M's maternal uncle Robert Bailey (1882–1917), a Clerk to the House of Commons who was killed fighting in France.
‡ Lieut-Col. John Codrington (1899–1991) was a regular soldier for 26 years, then worked in films and for BOAC before, at the age of 59, returning to a childhood enthusiasm and becoming a landscape gardener.

Codrington admired it so much that he begged the Maharajah to tell him its history. Diamond bought in Elizabethan times by English merchants in India. Came into Queen Elizabeth's possession; part of Crown Jewels. James II on his escape to France in 1688 smuggled it across. Sold it to Louis XIV. At time of French Revolution, Louis XVI entrusted it to his faithful servant Sans-Souci to give to the Comte de Provence. Sans-Souci captured by revolutionaries and swallowed the diamond. Was guillotined and buried. When the Comte succeeded as Louis XVIII he had Sans-Souci's corpse exhumed. Diamond recovered from stomach. Appropriated by Napoleon III. His widow Eugénie sold it at the end of her life in 1920 to Patiala. Is known as the Sans-Souci Diamond. Where is it now?

Created by Porter. their longest commission ever

Wednesday, 25th June

Dined with the Garnetts* at Bradley Court. Tony Snowdon staying. He and his troupe spent day trying to photograph Keith Steadman's garden.† What with pouring rain and this garden having no shape, no architectural features, and being a tangled muddle, he failed utterly. He greeted me with warm hugs. Very sweet and charming as usual. How small he is, almost a dwarf, but large hands I noticed, which suggest potency. After dinner he sat at my feet by the sofa and talked about Anne and the family. Complains that she doesn't 'play straight' and is alienating the children who are ready to be as kind to her as they can. She has already driven off young Tom Messel who was her slave. She refuses to meet or speak to Tony's new wife Lucy.‡ He invites his mother to luncheon, asks others to meet her, cooks delicious meal (has no servant), and Anne chucks at last moment on spurious grounds that she does not feel well, though he later finds she entertained sixty to drinks that evening.

He spoke lovingly of Michael [Rosse] who never in all the years he knew him treated him as other than a beloved son. Tony said the

---

* Andrew Garnett, entrepreneur; husband of Polly Devlin, journalist and author.
† The garden made by Keith Steadman at Wickwar in Gloucestershire over thirty years was indeed rather outside the mainstream, but highly regarded by *cognoscenti*; like John Codrington's in Rutland and Sir David Scott's in Northamptonshire, Keith Steadman's was among those featured in the new book A.L.-M. was editing with Rosemary Verey, *The Englishman's Garden* (1982).
‡ In 1978 Lord Snowdon had m. Lucy Lindsay-Hogg (*née* Davies).

only two happy marriages he knew of were those of his mother and Michael, and of Oliver [Messel] and Van the Great Dane.* Talked of his photography. Said he could modestly claim to have revolutionised photography in the late Fifties and Sixties by getting away from the Cecil Beaton technique, which was to make women's faces look like masks with gashes for lips. Whereas he emphasises lines and crows' feet, without being unkind like some photographers. A sweet little man to meet, but I suppose, being a Messel, he is a bundle of insincerity.

Saturday, 28th June

Have finished correcting page proofs of H.N. Vol. I. A specialist index compiler, who works at London Library, has been engaged, thank God. I could not face this task. The subdivision of subjects under Harold's and Vita's names alone was too daunting.

Last night we dined with the Loewensteins.† Colin Tennants staying.‡ She is a real beauty, with deep eyes and regular features. Wearing a pearl choker, most becoming. Colin extremely friendly, yet there is something about him which causes the shivers. Slightly pansy mannerisms. He is completely bald like his father. Was interesting about his father, who married his mother in order to do down his younger brother David, the parents' favourite, to whom Pamela§ had been contracted. Strange that even as recently as the 1920s such behaviour was current. Told me he thought the future of this country was assured, for when our oil came in faster we would become very prosperous. The world has confidence in Britain as shown by the strength of the £ and the stock exchange boom. This is difficult to understand with unemployment rising and the closure of businesses.

Colin is determined at the end of the century, when he will be seventy-two or -three, to retire from the world to a cave in a

---

* Van Ries-Hansen, Danish theatrical producer; close friend of Oliver Messel.
† Prince Rupert zu Loewenstein (b. 1930), financial adviser; his wife, Josephine Lowry-Corry.
‡ Hon. Colin Tennant (b. 1926); m. 1956 Lady Anne Coke, d. of 5th Earl of Leicester; businessman; succeeded father as 3rd Baron Glenconner, 1983.
§ Pamela Paget, dau. of Sir Richard Paget, 2nd Bt, m. 1925 Christopher, 2nd Baron Glenconner; m. diss. 1935.

monastic settlement in Siam. Has booked his cave. There he will celebrate the entry into the new millennium and devote his life to prayer.
I said I doubted whether he would do it when the time came, for here
was I, now at that very age, writing books and reviews, married, and
quite unable to retire even if I still had the inclination to do so.

Friday, 4th July

The most dismal July on record. Never a ray of sun; and cold, cold. I
wear winter underclothes and pullovers. Still my blue *Geranium pratense*
thrives on the roadside: it provides the deep, deep blue which one
misses in the sky. Drifts and drifts of it.

Monday, 7th July

A. and I stayed at Deene Park with the Brudenells for one night. I met
them with Derek Hill. A. had never met them. Liked them
immensely. The house is splendid, large and grand, but with no out-
standing feature. No, I am wrong – the early sixteenth-century great
hall with hammer-beam roof. Cardigan of Balaclava fame dominates
the house, and his widow, the nymphomaniac beauty.* Beautiful she
certainly was, her portraits reminding me of Anne Rosse, but more
regular features. Those of her as a young woman show her with raven
black hair; in middle age with red tresses. On Saturday afternoon a
horticultural symposium held in great hall, on which A. served and
acquitted herself very well. Lane Fox† held forth too much and was
too pleased with himself. Anne Lancaster‡ and Fred Whitsey§ the

---

* Edmund Brudenell (b. 1924), of Deene Park, Northants; m. 1955 Hon. Cynthia
Manningham-Buller, dau. of 1st Viscount Dilhorne. His grandfather was Lord Robert
Thomas Brudenell-Bruce, grandson of the 1st Marquess of Ailesbury; his father had
abandoned the 'Bruce' on inheriting Deene Park from his brother in 1917. Lord Cardigan
was a cousin of the 1st Marquess of Ailesbury and Deene Park belonged to his 2nd wife,
Adeline Louisa Maria, dau. of Spencer Horsey de Horsey (she m., 2nd, Antonio, Comte
de Lancastre, and d. 1915); they had no children, and the 7th Earl of Cardigan's titles
devolved to his kinsman, 2nd Marquess of Ailesbury.
† Robin Lane Fox, Fellow of New College, Oxford and Lecturer in Ancient History (b.
1946); his *Alexander the Great* (publ. 1973) won numerous prizes; gardening correspondent of the *Financial Times* since 1970.
‡ Anne Scott-James (b. 1913); journalist and writer about gardens; m., 2nd, 1967, Sir
Osbert Lancaster (1908–86), cartoonist, painter, writer, and friend of J.L.-M.
§ Editor of *Popular Gardening*.

others. Edmund Brudenell, Levantine, quick, with perfect manners. She very capable and quite handsome, suggesting to me what Harriet Baring or Caroline Norton must have looked like. Two dark sons, twins, address their father as Squire. I went to Communion Sunday morning in ugly church in park, about to be declared redundant. One twin read the lesson, the other took round the alms bag. Was impressed by the earnestness of both; the taciturnity, expressing hidden turmoil beneath. Splendid family. Enormous dining table covered with great white linen cloth and bedecked with silver.

On Sunday we called at the Sitwells* at Weston. Georgia reclining on a chair from which she did not move. Her legs like matchsticks, shoulders like those of a starving Vietnamese, grey face, large luminous eyes. Clearly doomed. Sachie blooming but very bent. Both pleased to see us.

Friday, 11th July

Last night before dinner I watched for ten minutes the flycatcher, which has laid a second brood of eggs in the customary nest in the escutcheon under A's bedroom window. It perched on the back of a white garden chair on the terrace. With a zigzag movement, it darted into the air, paused, and flitted back to its seat. This it did eight or ten times before A. came from the garden and disturbed it. Not once could I see a fly or the bird's beak open, the whole operation was so quick. No wonder the moment the weather becomes cold – and it is not hot yet – the flycatcher leaves for the South and the Mediterranean climes.

While we were dining, telephone rang. It was Gerda Barlow† asking us both to dine on Friday week. I said I was going to London that day and did not think I would be back in time. This provoked a storm of nagging from A. Why was I going? Michael, she supposed. But he was coming here to stay next weekend. I didn't say that I wanted to see him alone. I just said, 'Yes, it is Michael, and I don't yet know whether I shall be seeing him in the evening or afternoon.' Hurt feelings. Then she said, 'I was upset when you said last week that you did not mind when I and Vita corresponded.' 'No,' I said, 'I was not jealous.' 'No, you are never jealous, you don't know the meaning of the word.' God in

---

* Sir Sacheverell Sitwell, 6th Bt (1897–1988); m. 1925 Georgia Doble.
† Wife of Basil Barlow of Stancombe Park, Gloucestershire.

heaven, thought I, I am wracked with jealousy, but I said, 'It is always the greatest mistake to show it, however much you feel it.' And so it went on. There are times when I wish I lived alone, and was free.

Thursday, 17th July

They all came on Saturday morning at midday, Burnet [Pavitt]* motoring Diana Cooper and M. I told M. that I felt an invisible string attached to him, which might grow taut, might grow lax, but was there when others were about. It is also there when we are apart, wherever we may be. It tugs at my heart. The weekend was success-ful in that he was delighted to meet Diana. He thought her ravishing, and was fascinated. We dined at Sally [Westminster]'s, where he stayed the night, being brought over by Sally on Sunday morning, when she joins the procession round Badminton estate with David [Somerset] and Master. I can't pretend I enjoyed his being here.

I motored him to Chippenham station late Sunday afternoon, returning in time to change for the Hollands' annual concert, enchanting performance by girl and guitar. Pouring rain, never seen the like, and cold, eating in the cloister with wind blowing. I wore my cloak throughout. Diana Cooper cannot taste any food or smell any flower. On the ball, perfectly. Her talk always pointful, her reading, her knowledge complete. Really an amazing personality. And still a beauty, as M. says.

Monday, 21st July

Motored to London, though feeling tired and irritable. Full of traffic, summer sales. In despair where I should park car. Thought of Burlington House. Went straight there and got permit from Society of Antiquaries. The only use I ever make of this ridiculous Society. Walked to Air Street to deliver A's gold watch to little shop kept by two old, nice Jews. They in a dreadful state because two nights ago burglars broke into the manager's house in the suburbs at dead of night, forced him to give them the keys of shop and safe, and went straight to Air Street where they cleared the shop of their goods and clients' clocks and watches. The hell of it. Then to dentist. Walked down Bond Street. Called at d'Offay's Gallery where Bloomsbury pic-tures on display. Those by Carrington far the best in my opinion. To

---

* Businessman and musician (b. 1908); trustee of Royal Opera House.

London Library. I congratulated [Douglas] Matthews, the Librarian
Designate, on the splendid index to my H.N. which he has done.
Eardley lunched with me at Brooks's which was about to shut for
summer vacation. We had a filthy luncheon and were unable to eat
the treacle tart which I refused to pay for. Bill came to £11 as it was.
At 2.30 to Chatto's. Audience with Norah handing over Index and
Corrections. Norah sat there huddled and aged, going off at tangents
about irrelevant subjects. This again irritated me. At 4.30 to Oxford
and Cambridge Club to tea with M. who had invited Caroline
Blackwood* who had asked to meet me to talk about her father.†
Chain-smoking, churchyard cough, beautiful blue staring eyes,
raddled complexion. Attractive. I spoke of her father when I knew
him best at our prep. school and Eton. A difficult girl. No come-back,
no return of the ball.
    Got car from Burlington House and drove to Radnor Walk for
drink with Betj[eman] and Eliz. The darlings. She left us to go to a
meeting across the street. I told J. I had just seen Caroline B. for the
first time. He told me he once saw her twenty years ago and was so
moved by her resemblance to Ava, and so attracted to her, that he
decided he could never meet her again. Then told me that he was
more in love with Ava than with any human being he had ever met
in the world. His Oxford career was ruined by this unrequited love
for 'Little Bloody'. He loved his gutter-snipe looks, his big, brown,
sensual eyes, sensual lips, dirtiness generally. Never received so much
as a touch of a hand on the shoulder. He then said that in after-life no
loves ever reached the heights of schoolboy loves. I told him about
Tom Mitford and myself at Eton, and how on Sunday eves before
Chapel at five, when the toll of the bell betokened that all boys must
be in their pews, he and I would, standing on the last landing of the
entrance steps, out of sight of the masters in the ante-chapel and all
the boys inside, passionately embrace, lips to lips, body pressed to
body, each feeling the opposite fibre of the other. J.'s eyes stood out
with excitement. And then? he asked. And then, I said, when Tom
left Eton it was all over. He never again had any truck with me, and
turned exclusively to women. J's eyes filled with tears.
    At last Vol. I is really finished. I have nothing further to do. Very

---

* Novelist (1931–96).
† Basil, 4th Marquess of Dufferin and Ava, killed on active service in Burma, 1945; an
exact contemporary of J.L.-M. at preparatory school, Eton and Oxford.

disappointed that Chatto's have had refusals from America. Nevertheless, I showed with pride to Norah a letter I received this morning from Anne Hill,* who writes that John Saumarez-Smith raves about the book which he has read in page proofs. Anne says she has never known him to 'go on' about any book as he did about this. J.S.S. is very censorious and hard to please, so this is gratifying.

Extraordinary to think on J.B's last words to me today; that he, aged seventy-four, suffering from Parkinson's Disease, crippled so that he can barely move without help, still has the desires of a youth of twenty. That is little satisfaction to him, poor old boy.

Friday, 1st August

Droghedas to stay last weekend. Not relaxing. Like the full operatic orchestra, with temperament. Garrett looking pale, drawn and much aged. Is very restless; has to be on the go. Has to visit gardens. Joan fusses. Is hurt if left alone for more than five minutes. Their last evening, very sweet. But what with his insistence on being entertained and her refusal to sit and read, we found them a tiring couple.

Met the Beits again staying with Loewensteins. A protracted argument with Clementine about the Mosleys. I told her I found Diana adorable and Tom 'sweet'. Absurdly wrong adjective, of course, for he is not sweet; I meant charming. Clem insists that if Hitler had invaded, Tom Mosley would have been a Gauleiter. I said next time I met him I would ask him outright what action he would have taken. Can't believe that a man who fought throughout the First War as he did would have actively collaborated with the Germans.

Was much grieved to see announcement of Elspeth Baldwin's death. I became very fond of her. She had beauty with those keen blue eyes, and that transparent skin of the very frail. Heart, I suppose. When I saw her last year and helped her pack her books it was evident that she was packing up. Received a letter from Joan Arbuthnot† lamenting. Nice to hear from mutual friends on the death of those one mourns and can share a modicum of sorrow with.

---

* Lady Anne Gathorne-Hardy (b. 1911), o. dau. of 3rd Earl of Cranbrook; she was betrothed to J.L.-M. in 1935–6 and remained a lifelong friend and correspondent, but m. 1938 the bookseller Heywood Hill (he d. 1986).
† Friend of J.L.-M's correspondent over many years, Monica Baldwin (d. 1975), cousin of Stanley Baldwin, 1st Earl.

On Tuesday, Colin McMordie* came down for the day from London to Bath. I was touched that he thought it worth while making the long expedition. Much improved. Less affected. Still extremely handsome. About the most handsome young man I know. Now about thirty. Has matured. Shares an exclusive gallery with a 'friend'. Specialises in early nineteenth-century French romantic landscapes. Sensible choice. Says he adores Paris and would not live anywhere else. Has achieved his ambitions. Wants nothing more. Looks radiantly content, which is nice to see. Made him walk in the Park with the dogs. Nice boy.

Dined that evening with Alex Moulton. Had his new friend, young GP from Bristol, Stuart something. I liked him. An engaging smile. He talked about the Trades Unions wrecking the economy. How the clever young (he is thirty-four) loathe them as the destroyers of Britain. I thought Alex talked too much in pontifical style. Friend may become bored. At present is amused.

On Wednesday was driven by Bruce Chatwin† in an old rattletrap to Nymans. On way there and back we talked very freely. He asked if he might come with Derek and me to Mount Athos. No, I said, you can't. Was I fear rather bossy. Would not let him open roof of car. Bruce asked if I had known Robert Byron. Able to say yes. Told him of R's love for Desmond [Parsons], transferred after D's death to me, to my discomfiture. He admires Robert's writing but says the strained jokiness of that generation embarrasses him. Also finds Waugh's facetiousness embarrassing. Found myself lecturing him about treatment of his wife, but good-naturedly. He asked me frankly if I was glad I had married. Was able to say Yes. I don't think he is at all. Is going off for three months, writing, and will not tell wife where he is going. I said that was cruel. He agreed. Is convinced that he has made the grade and is now a literary man. Has two more books coming out. He has yet to grow up; laughs far too much when telling his own stories.

Stayed Wednesday night with M., he having taken me to theatre, *Dr Faustus*, strange and haunting play. We talked for hours into the night, and night became morning.

* Former Oxford art history student; friend of J.L.-M. since 1973.
† Travel writer and novelist (1940–89); he and his wife Elizabeth lived not far from the L.-Ms.

Tuesday, 5th August

A. and I motored to Chatsworth for two nights. Met Pam* at Moreton-in-Marsh and had picnic luncheon sitting on public park seat in lime avenue planted by Lord Redesdale, P's grandfather. We all took dogs. E. Winn† and Tim Bailey‡ staying, and Betty Farquhar,§ cross old woman of eighty-one who hadn't a good word to say of anyone. Debo absolutely divine. I know no châtelaine to compare with her. Tim Bailey reminded me of an incident forgotten by me. Years ago when staying at Maugersbury with the Baileys, Uncle Percy decided to make us all spend the day building a dry wall. The four Bailey boys and Tom Mitford, also staying, felt obliged to comply. Apparently I said I hated that sort of thing and sloped off for a long walk of my own. Came back hours later, approached the wall which had assumed impressive proportions and length, when wall instantly collapsed. Fury of Uncle Percy; and the boys believed that I was cause of collapse.

Sunday evening after dinner we sat in the 6th Duke's Library, looking at Rembrandt drawings and climbing into the gallery. Apropos of which Debo said that Lord Salisbury staying there as Prime Minister with Harty-Tarty¶ asked how one got into the gallery. The Duke who owned the place replied, 'Damned if I know.' Evening ended with the women singing old music-hall songs in these august surroundings.

Sunday, 17th August

Last week spent visiting three lots of friends in East Anglia. First Nicholas Guppy and young wife of twenty-five, he being fifty-four, handsome still but with greying hair and a stomach. Then Heywood Hills at Snape where I used to stay throughout my engagement to Anne when her mother was living at the Priory. Then two nights with Billa Harrod,** who is bent but otherwise little changed. Horrible

---

* Mrs Derek Jackson, *née* Mitford, sister of Duchess of Devonshire.
† Dau. of Hon. Reginald Winn and his wife Alice Perkins, sister of Nancy (Tree) Lancaster, professional decorator.
‡ Cousin of Mitfords whose brother Dick was an Eton contemporary of J.L.-M.
§ Irish racing personality.
¶ 8th Duke of Devonshire (1833–1903); Liberal (later Liberal Unionist) statesman.
** Wilhelmina Cresswell (b. 1911), Norfolk conservationist; widow of Sir Roy Harrod (1900–79), Oxford economist and biographer of Keynes.

experience at the Hills'. In the field next door was a bird-scaring gun
which started at 6 a.m. and went on to sunset. Honey is gun-shy and
behaved with hysteria, poor thing. When I put her out of doors to pee
in the morning she took fright and bolted. We notified police and
neighbouring farmers and searched in vain. Finally police telephoned
that an errand boy of fifteen saw her nearing the main road, took compassion, induced her to follow him and allow herself to be shut up.
Retrieved Honey with much rejoicing. Oh the misery of those hours!

We had a picnic at Stowe [School] in front of the house. Were
shocked by the new laboratory, a hideous building set to the right of
the entrance front, at right-angles but detached. Incredible that the
Governors could allow so shoddy a job totally out of keeping with the
augustan façade.

Freddy Ashton* lives in a charming Regency Gothic white house
on the very edge of Eye village behind a crinkly brick garden wall.
There is an element of Cecil Beaton about the house, which is
extremely pretty, verging on the stagey. Very pretty garden layout of
box hedges, few flowers. He is a most sympathetic man, but looking
older than when we last saw him at Firle; exhausted by the success of
his new ballet at Covent Garden for the Queen Mother. He had a
youngish man with a moustache living with him, who appeared to be
a permanent affair.

We also lunched with the Gladwyns† at Bramfield, nice old
Georgian house on the edge of the village of that name. Most hospitable. They hired a cook specially for us and gave us champagne and
Mouton Rothschild 1976. It was A's birthday, so she was pleased.
Gladwyn quiet, morose and yet humorous. Cynthia a great gossip
about friends' *moeurs*. Heywood Hills say she has a passion for vulgar
seaside postcards, the broader the better. She showed me a portrait of
herself by Jacques-Émile Blanche, dated 1911 and giving the sitter's
age as thirteen. She must therefore be 82. Incredible.

Billa took us to see extraordinary garden made by two brothers in
a mill at Corpusty, by name Last.‡ Profuse in plants and flowing with

---

* Sir Frederick Ashton (1906–88; Kt 1962); choreographer; Director of the Royal Ballet
until 1970.
† Hubert Gladwyn Jebb, 1st Baron Gladwyn (1900–97), diplomatist, and his wife
Cynthia.
‡ John and Roger Last's garden at The Mill House, Corpusty was included in *The
Englishman's Garden*.

water. Not unpretty but too many grottos, follies and busts. One brother is a poet. She also took us to Sheringham [Park]. Tom Upcher very decrepit and looks ghastly ill. Friend with flaxen hair deceived me into taking him for forty, until he told me he was seventy-three. Whisked me upstairs to listen to old phonograph records in which he specialises; contrives trumpets and amplifiers which eliminate all scratchy sounds habitual to ancient records. But he kept me from seeing over house which I wanted to do. It is dreadful that the N.T. has been unable to accept this important house and park by Repton.*

Unfortunate thing happened on last morning at Billa's. Letter arrived from M. which I was expecting. A. came down before me and saw it at my place. She was cross, said it was insensitive of me to have M. write to me there. All the way home in the car she would hardly speak, except to say that she thought she would not do another gardening book because she had so much on her mind which made her unhappy. Now this does not seem to me to be reasonable behaviour. On return home managed to telephone M., who was leaving for France next morning to stay in the country with Maître Blum.

Wednesday, 27th August

The Times has agreed to publish an extract of H.N. in September. I looked to see yesterday what extract they had chosen. Discovered that it was the bit about Harold's affair with Raymond. Telephoned Norah to say I would not agree. She urged me to reconsider. Said it would be good publicity. I replied that I would have to consult both Paul Hyslop who had lent me the letters and Eardley, with whom I was going to stay last night. Paul said he didn't mind in the least. E. read the offending pages and thought they would pass. So I told Norah I would agree after all.

Sally Westminster had a lunch party in Gloucester in Canon's Chambers for concert in memory of her late espoused saint, Duke Gerald.† I talked to Mary Elgar who somehow was invited. She told

---

* John Adey Repton designed Sheringham Hall for Abbot Upcher 1813–19 (H. Colvin, *Dictionary of British Architects*); his father Humphry Repton designed the landscape park, now indeed held by the N.T.
† Her husband, the 4th Duke of Westminster (d. 1967).

me she was the great-niece of the composer, whom she remembers well. Said that his wife did much harm; was a tiresome lady with social ambitions who made Elgar dress and behave like a colonel in the Indian Army whereas he hated society and wanted to be left alone with his old cronies among the organists in Worcester.

Books & Bookmen telephoned yesterday to say they were closing down and I need not review the books sent last week. The disappearance of this mag. is a tragedy. Theirs were the best book reviews in existence. Nothing to touch them. Diana [Mosley] will be upset for she wrote for them every month without fail. Most strange behaviour, for a month ago Foyle's gave a luncheon to celebrate their 25th anniversary and got distinguished contributors to make speeches. There was no hint of closure.

The diary of J.L.-M's tour of Normandy with A.L.-M. and David and Rosemary Verey, 1–8 September 1980, is reproduced as Appendix II.

Saturday, 13th September

The remainder of this week has been spent in Bath typing out Chapter 5 [of second Harold Nicolson volume]. Much distracted by builders from No. 20 sawing stones on pavement, young men of radiant beauty. Then distracted by the filming of house on the other side, No. 18, a film called *Nanny*. Film people very jolly and friendly. Much walking up and down pavement, and I'm sure I shall be detected peeping from behind my window curtains.

A disappointment is Derek's portrait of Nick my nephew. He has made alterations but there is still no likeness. Curious thing is that Derek sent me a photograph which he took of the boy before painting him and he, D., claims that the portrait is identical. So it is in attitude, pose, shape of head and hair, yet that elusive thing, the personality, is totally unidentifiable. Nevertheless I have paid Derek £450, he having asked me to settle a bill for a new carpet rather than give him a cheque.

I am guilty of a reckless piece of extravagance. I have bought a sketch by Daniel Gardner of what purports to be William Beckford, and I think it is he. Cost me £800. Picture was sold at Christie's in 1977 and in their catalogue attributed 'traditionally' as being of Beckford. I wrote 'to the vendor' but have not received a reply. Am pleased to have the thing; but if it turns out not to be Beckford, shall re-sell.

Sally o Henry Clive

Sunday, 14th September

A. who is undecided whether to write another gardening book, which I am encouraging her to do, suddenly thought she would like to see George Clive's garden at Whitfield, Herefordshire. So I accompanied her on a sudden whim. Whitfield is a delightful, 'dim' later Georgian house, unpretentious with nice rounded window bays extending from ground floor to roof-line, and little about it of architectural importance. A family house set in unspoiled, remote country. Full of family portraits, a large cosy library, whole house crammed with books, old morocco and modern. George Clive, a charming boy (whom I discovered on returning home and looking up to be forty), fair, very youthful face, huge hands, a bit of a podge. Knows a great deal about trees and shrubs. A. impressed by his knowledge. He is carrying out many landscape schemes, fountains, follies, *bassins*, etc. His mother Mary Clive lives with him. Delightful, intelligent, well-read and unpretentious like all Pakenhams. Her voice reminded me of her sister Violet Powell. While A. went round the garden, she and I had long talk. She reminded me that we once met at dinner with Patrick Kinross,* and Angela to whom he was then married; Evelyn and Laura Waugh and Nancy Mitford were the other guests. Also Eleanor Smith† who, she remembered, bored us all with talk of circuses. I had totally forgotten the occasion. It must have been before George was born, before the War in fact.

The diary of J.L.-M's third visit to Mount Athos with Derek Hill, 18–26 September 1980, is reproduced as Appendix III.

Sunday, 5th October

I shall be sad never to return to Mount Athos because it is like a visit to the Middle Ages. There can be no other region left in the West where one can escape from the twentieth century.

Past week spent typing out Vol. II. But why do I bother? On Friday when about to leave Bath for home telephone rang. Hoped it might

---

* Patrick Balfour, 3rd Baron Kinross (1904–76), author and journalist; m. 1938 (as her 2nd husband, she having previously been married to J.L.-M's friend John Churchill) Angela Culme-Seymour (from whom he obtained a divorce, 1942).
† Lady Eleanor Smith (1902–45), a dau. of 1st Earl of Birkenhead (F.E. Smith); as well as circuses, she was passionate about gypsies, ballet, and Spain.

be M. It was Hugo Brunner from Chatto's to announce that the printers were in a state of anarchy and the release date of book, 28th, had to be put off. Doesn't know when book will now come out, perhaps 15th Nov. I am sickened by all this. It is the second postponement because of bloody printers. Also I fear that because of anarchical state the book, when or if it ever does appear, will be full of mistakes. Very depressed by this, and not hearing from M., who went to Paris a few days before I got back.

A. went to London during the week for one night. On her return she telephoned me in Bath. In moment of euphoria I said that at breakfast that morning the sun was shining, the day was lovely, I felt a twinge of Wanderlust. 'Why should I not come with you to Australia,' I said unguardedly. She had been thinking of going alone in November. When I got back she said, 'It will be very unkind of you if you change your mind now. You know it is what I have wanted to do for years and years.' So I have not changed my mind. We at once sent a telegram to the Downers in Australia to ask if we would be welcome. By that time I should have finished typing out Vol. II and got it off to Nigel. I shall have a break before getting down to my Anthology and Bamber's Bath book in the winter months. This morning received reply from Margaret Downer, 'All Downers will be delighted. Love. Writing.'

It is astonishing how snobbish the English gentry are. Wherever we go to lunch or dine we are placed at table according to rank. Sally Westminster will always be seated on the host's right and Caroline Somerset on his left, regardless of how many other women may be present with far greater pretensions to intellect and distinction, such as Elspeth Huxley, or even older women, or women strangers who have never been there before and therefore, according to the rules of hospitality, ought to be treated with special deference and politeness.

Sunday, 12th October

The son of old Mrs Rich, wife of one of the gardeners to the House here, came to ask A. if he might work one day a week in the garden. Naturally she was delighted. We have known this boy for his regular attendance at Communion in church, and lately for the rather surprising spectacle of him dressed in a becoming white stole, tied round the waist with a cord, and following the Vicar to the altar, where he stands and kneels like a server but without actually serving. When we told

Peggy she pursed her lips and said she must tell us something about him. He was not like other boys. His contemporaries in the village called him Queenie or some such name. He had been known to pinch cigarettes, and could not be trusted alone in the house. Now, he looks to us a very nice, quiet, sensitive young man, quite handsome, very neat and intelligent. But in a small village community the likes of him are shunned. They drift to the towns, where they feel persecuted and prostitute themselves.

On Friday we motored to Devon. Stayed the night with Anthony and Rosemary Chaplin.* Rosemary is enchanting, sensitive, very intelligent, sane, a bit of a poet. Anthony has declined greatly. He has lost all looks, has a strange, sinister line about the mouth, is grey in the face, and is argumentative and gushing by turns. In fact he is an alcoholic. Pours down brandy, three and four glasses after dinner. Starts off with elevenses of rum, continues at luncheon, ending with four liqueurs. He makes me feel sad. He has achieved nothing much in life, thrown his talent away; composed a few cadenzas perhaps for the piano, what else? Has produced no son. The title will die out. He affects not to care. Thinks only of himself and his ailments, brought on by drink. One of his daughters by Rosemary has married a Liverpool Geordie who lives on his wife and the dole. An argumentative youth who talks the hind legs off a donkey on subjects of which he knows nothing. Sounds hell to me. The other daughter lives with a man who can't marry her, also of no breeding. And then there are his and poor Alvilde's grandchildren who only like French boys from neighbouring villages. Oenone told A. the other day that her sister, the youngest granddaughter, has a French boyfriend who is over here in London with a job at Boot's Cash Chemists and taking the dole money as well. A. was furious and told Oenone she would report him if she could. Oenone merely expressed surprise at A's attitude and thinks the boy is behaving perfectly sensibly. Now if this does not come from lack of education on the part of the Luke family, I don't know what does.

To return to Rosemary Chaplin, it appears that Sir Alan Lascelles is madly in love with her at the age of ninety-four. He has handed her all his correspondence with her aunt Lady Gwendolen Cecil, with whom Sir A. was in love before the War, for her, Rosemary, to edit

---

* Alvilde L.-M's first husband Anthony, 3rd Viscount Chaplin (1906–81), father of her daughter Clarissa Luke, and his 2nd wife Rosemary, daughter of 1st Viscount Chandos.

and publish. She has also seen parts of the memoirs which the silly old man is having bowdlerised and then privately printed.

Betty Watkins the postmistress is Secretary of the Badminton Village Club. They had a disagreeable meeting the other day at which the Club Steward was sacked, quite rightly, because in a drunken brawl he had assaulted one member and then turned on the octogenarian father-in-law of another and knocked out his false teeth. As President, the Duke of Beaufort was present at the Court of Enquiry. The peccant Steward's wife, whom everyone hates, turned on the Duke and called him a 'bloody bastard'. Rather near the knuckle, with John of Gaunt and all. Don't suppose he has ever been so addressed in his life. Apparently he stared straight ahead in ducal dignity without moving a muscle in his face.

Having finished Newsome's life of A.C. Benson,* wrote to M. expressing amazement at the prevalence before the First World War of romantic friendships at Cambridge University. Seems that practically every don was in love with practically every undergraduate.

Saturday, 25th October

Yesterday I went to London for the day to meet M. for first time in five weeks. We together collected from Chatto's the first five copies of my Vol. I. Gave him the first copy. Norah spoke to me warmly about the book which has already sold 2,000 copies. About all that will be sold, I gather, for the price of £15 is exorbitant. Even Vol. I which looks nice enough is very thick and the print small. M. has got rid of his moustache, thank the Lord. Maître Blum made him go out and have it removed instantly. We spent the afternoon together happily, and had tea in Jermyn Street in a tiny tea-room. He accompanied me to Paddington.

I entered a flower shop to send a wreath to Georgia [Sitwell]'s funeral today. Sachie is the second old friend to be left a widower within a week. The first dear Roger Fulford† whose darling Sibell died aged ninety. Found difficulty in writing to Sachie, who will be bereft.

---

* David Newsome, *On the Edge of Paradise: A.C. Benson the Diarist* (John Murray, 1980); winner of Whitbread Book-of-the-Year award.
† Sir Roger Fulford (1902–83) of Barbon Manor, Carnforth, Lancs; historian; President of Liberal Party, 1964–5; m. 1937 Sibell Lyttelton (whose son by her earlier marriage succeeded as 4th Baron Shuttleworth, 1942).

Said to A. last night how odd it has been that many of the people whom I have liked, admired and felt closest rapport with have been people I met but from time to time and hardly knew, such as William Plomer,* Bloggs Baldwin, Alick Downer and Sheila Birkenhead.†

Finished last night Isabel Colegate's *The Shooting Party*. Her best novel yet, firm, balanced, well-written. Yet makes me hate Edwardians. I firmly believe I have turned against the aristocratic tradition. Their arrogance was unpardonable.

Wednesday, 29th October

Last Saturday the Johnstons motored us to Llanstephan to see the new house Nicky has built for Hugo Philipps.‡ Molly is divine, very pretty, sweet expression, intelligent as one would expect of daughter of Lord Sherfield. Hugo is not handsome and unlike Ros to look at. Large nose, harassed face, seeming over sixty whereas he must be in fifties. Not easy to communicate with but a nice man. The house they live in is hideous. Of a machine-made brick, uniform, rather dark earthy brown but not pretty. No variety in texture or shade. Building in lovely position in old park overlooking River Wye and Black Mountains, yet looks like an institute or a large lavatory. No proportions. Lacks verticality. Really a horror. Will it ever be admired? I bet not, for it is ignoble. Such a dear man, poor crippled Nicky Johnson. Our bathroom had no window and air conditioning operates when light turned on, inexcusable in the country I think. Moreover the air conditioning produces a howling draught from under the bath while one is drying oneself on the mat.

Yesterday A. and I drove to London for the day. I went to Chatto's, took away more copies of book and sent others by post as gifts. Then lunched at Simpsons with M. to meet his Australian actor friend Andrew Sharp. Certainly is a beauty, bewitching smile, charming and

---

* Writer, poet, and editor of the *Kilvert Diaries* (1903–73); J.L.-M. wrote about him in *Fourteen Friends* (John Murray, 1996).

† Hon. Sheila Berry, dau. of 1st Viscount Camrose; m. 1935 Frederick Smith, 2nd Earl of Birkenhead (1907–75).

‡ Hon. H.J.L. Philipps (b. 1929); only son of Rosamond Lehmann and Wogan Philipps, 2nd Baron Milford; m. 1959 (2nd) Mary, daughter of 1st Baron Sherfield (Roger Makins) (m. diss. 1984).

intelligent. Enchanted as I was I did not suffer from lust. The most beautiful person in the world would not make me fall out of love with M. now.

Tea with Eardley and a good talk. A. called for me and we went to party given by her children for Mollie Buccleuch's eightieth birthday. Very low rooms at top of Carlton Gardens, extremely hot and noisy. Couldn't hear a word said, although many old friends present – Billa, Alan Pryce-Jones looking puddingy but delightful and funny. Queen Mother present, radiant and not a day over fifty to look at; young Gloucesters, he unimpressive like any bank clerk, she nondescript. Everyone who knows them finds them charming. Princess Alexandra, rather aged, he boisterous and rather bounderish. Did not enjoy it one bit.

Am in a stew about Australia. Feel I ought to prepare and have done nothing, read nothing about the continent. Yet am rather excited and pleased to go, happy that I shall be seeing M. the night before we leave at dawn on Sunday the 2nd.

J.L.-M. mentions that he kept a diary of his Australian experiences in a blue notebook. This has not been found among his papers. His letters to the editor, however, convey some of his impressions of the continent.

Wednesday, 5th November

Martinsell, Williamstown, Adelaide, South Australia

Contrary to all expectations and in mockery of thinnest summer clothes brought and total lack of warm jerseys, weather here is bitterly cold. We reached this rather nice, semi-grand neo-Georgian country house last night. Today it has poured with lashing horizontal rain without recession. Impossible to set foot out of doors. Read shivering all morning before green log of gum tree in narrow grate in spacious, draughty hall and this afternoon went to bed till six o'clock. Anyway can't keep eyes open for jet lag I presume and Evelyn Waugh's Letters no inducement to do so. Having read two hundred pages am not captivated. I don't like him at all. Never did. Am repelled by aggressive allusions to women, contemptuous allusions to homos, arrogance and piety. Letters contrived I feel, and oh how lacking compassion and cosiness they are. Horrid, horrid man. But you don't want to hear me on Waugh, but on Aussieland.

Well, can't tell you much yet. Journey out was *de luxe* once the six-hour delay at Heathrow was forgotten. First-class accommodation on a Jumbo jet was like a very expensive nursing home. Attentions are unremitting and incessant: unwanted champagne and little biscuits with *foie gras*; gifts of folding toothbrushes in Qantas red boxes; delicious meals; gracious hostesses like best trained nurses hand one steamy hot rolled towelettes with which to mop the sticky brow; unwelcome screen let down to provide very out-of-date cowboy film, the talking part conveyed by earphone so that one can ignore film apart from raucous laughter coming from simple neighbours. Then the seat can be made horizontal and one sleeps, lights lowered, as if in the London Clinic, rather fitfully.

My impression of inhabitants of continent so far very favourable. Welcome and friendliness and helpfulness from everyone so far met with. Clinical cleanliness. Perth a rather nice city, wide boulevards, few people, no rush, fuss or squalor. Squalor reserved for outskirts of cities which are ghastly (like USA I imagine), shoddy shacks, adverts and cats' cradles of sagging overhead wires. Then the open spaces. Flying from Perth to Adelaide, the land below like brown linoleum squares, no buildings – then hostile bush, i.e., scrub and black rock, for mile upon mile.

Tomorrow (Thurs.) A. and I being packed off on our own in nice Mary Downer's car to 'up country' for two nights to see the kangaroos at play and the parakeets, lyre birds and flying foxes, and the wild flowers. Then Mon. to Adelaide, I to stay alone at Club to which I look forward. Otherwise never alone thereafter . . .

Monday, 10th November

The Adelaide Club

There is a strike in Aussieland of fuel-tank drivers – so every plane in the continent is grounded and no mail, damn. They say it will not be settled for at least three days, and possibly not even then. So I merely send you this brief line to tell you that I am well (except for a baddish back which causes twinges of anguish) and happy. We came here from the country (Martinsell) this morning. Suddenly weather switches from late March to mid-July temperature overnight. Agreeable but too hot to cruise about in the daytime. I am being interviewed on the ABC on Wed., lunching at Government House on Thursday, dining with a judge tonight, alone by myself tomorrow night in this divine club, more 1880 than you can imagine. Friday we go to Melbourne, if a plane flies. If not, back to Martinsell . . .

Wednesday, 12th November

The strike is over but it has become incredibly hot, far hotter than anything I have experienced. To set foot on the pavement is like entering an oven. One gasps like a stranded fish. Today it is 100 degrees. Yet it is a dry heat. One does not sweat much. London in July can be far worse. The shops and restaurants are air-conditioned, and this club is deliciously cool – atmospherically. It is the stuffiest, most Victorian establishment you ever beheld. All the members over eighty, wearing dark suits and ties. They sit downstairs all day and offer each other drinks. I escape either to my nice old-fashioned bedroom or to the silent Library.

Honestly I am only half enjoying this expedition though I do not want A. to know it. We only consort with the stuffies, people she knew when here as girl and their OK families. I have not met anyone who either interests me or makes me wish to see them again. Adelaide strikes me as a horribly conventional city . . .

I have just been interviewed on radio for twenty minutes by a famous programme compère called Philip Satchell. He had just read *Prophesying Peace* (published more than three years ago) and talked about it and the National Trust. Not a word about H.N., but I cunningly slipped in a reference to the biography when he mentioned Sissinghurst. Tonight another oh so boring dinner party. The strain of being polite to people who bore the pants off one is intense. Tomorrow luncheon with the Governor who is a salacious Methodist doctor wearing a toupee, and Friday off to Melbourne . . .

And tomorrow out comes H.N. Vol. I. No one but you will say it is too short: but you are right in sensing the cuts. For instance, I gave a lovely account of his drive from the station in a cab with tuckbox and homesickness to Wellington to start his first term. I am alarmed by your allusion to the thin bits. I am aware of them. There are many howlers. Worst of all is the lack of analysis of H's character. I do want you to read Vol. II before I go over it again.

At the bottom of the stairs here is half of an enormous stuffed fish with a nose like a sword, caught by my father-in-law (the whole of it caught, not merely the half), and under it a framed account of his gallantries in World War I. And in the Library a photograph of him,

dappled with military stars and carrying a hat enmeshed in ostrich feathers. He certainly was a handsome and splendid pro-consular figure. But
would he have liked me? No. And would I have liked him? No.*

Monday, 17th November

Union Club, Sydney

We arrived here at Sydney today, the last lap. I shall be glad when it is
all over and long to be home. The Aussies are so hospitable, so
gushing, that one is embarrassed. Last night in Melbourne Mrs Prime
Minister's mother gave a party for us. Very kind I'm sure: but twenty
strangers dressed to kill, men wearing black ties, temperature a
hundred degrees. I very nearly died of it. The further one gets from
Adelaide the more American the *train de vie* seems to be. Here
Sydneyans try to be like New Yorkers. The taxi drivers are Greeks, an
impertinent race. The tempo is rushed, the temper is frayed. They are
not as nice as the Adelaidians, or even the Melbournians.

I don't think I like Sydney. The skyscrapers are truncated and
square-topped. Un-beautiful by day. By night arresting. We have just
come in from dining by ourselves for the first time since we came out,
in the Opera House restaurant, overlooking the harbour, the bridge,
the steamers and a thousand twinkling lights. The Opera House is
astonishing. Sited on projecting peninsula into the Harbour, superb of
course. I did not realise before that it is not on the open sea but within
a narrow creek. Architecturally it is a revelation of dare-devilry and
outrage. And it succeeds. Tomorrow we are doing a cruise of the
harbour and then dining with Sydney's Queen of the Highbrows,
Dame Helen Blackland, who has sent a list of the *invités* and remarks
upon their varying celebrity and achievements. Now I simply hate all
this. I am an anti-social being with nothing to say to people I don't
know. I get tongue-tied, while A. loves the attention.

Yesterday we also went to Melba's house, some 25 miles from
Melbourne. That was thrilling. Lady Vestey† lives there. It is called
Coombe Farm. She is Melba's granddaughter and worships her

---

* Alvilde's father, Lieutenant-General Sir Tom Bridges (1871–1939), had been Governor
of South Australia, 1922–7. J.L.-M. had met him once briefly in the 1930s.
†By courtesy: Pamela, d. of George Armstrong, m. Capt. The Hon. William Vestey, o.s.
of 2nd Baron Vestey, k. in action 1944; their s. Simon succ. his grandfather in 1954 as 3rd
Baron.

memory. She motored us there for luncheon. House exactly as Melba created it. Absolutely Edwardian, crammed with her treasures, nothing changed. Pamela V. lives very simply without a single servant bar a 'weekly', and cooks, and does housework herself. And house v. large and straggling. And you know how rich the Vesteys are. Servants don't exist here. Yet the Australians are very correct. Tables groan with silver epergnes, urns, cups and a million little boxes, all of which the hostess removes before the last course, just as old-fashioned parlour maids used to do before dessert in England . . .

Either 22nd or 23rd November

Somewhere above Oman or Onan or Yemen

I write this somewhere above Arabia. Have just crossed a wild mouse-trap of corrugated mountains between oceans of sand-tinted coral by a slowly rising sun. Slow because we are chasing it, never far behind. It is the weirdest sensation being on the world's longest flight from south-east to north-west. Time has no meaning whatsoever . . . What is interesting is the inhospitality of most of the earth we have just travelled. Ocean, desert and mountains. Teeming man is confined to a fraction of the earth's surface which he has ruined aesthetically . . .

Australia for me was only a half-success. You see I was never off the rein. And only once came within sound of siren voices. There was a beautiful young architect in Sydney of thirty-three who held my hand and invited me to lunch in his charming little Victorian house the day we left. We were on the way to the airport. A. had to come too. My architect said *A. Voices* and *P. Peace* were the most candid diaries ever published (which must be nonsense) and that he had fallen into love with the author! I blushed and turned away. Too late, I replied . . .

The diaries resume.

Wednesday, 26th November

For several days after arrival and return we both suffered from jet lag, feeling very tired but unable to sleep when one should. Time meant nothing during the journey. Very peculiar sensation, time like a maniac scattering dust.

During our absence my book came out. To my intense joy M.

telephoned me from London while I was in my room at the Adelaide Club, to say there were two very favourable reviews in *The Times* and *Daily Telegraph*. On the whole, I am told, the reviews are good and the book has been taken notice of. Came back to a pile of letters but only one was from a comparative stranger to whom I had not given a copy, Sir David Scott.* I always maintain that thank-you letters containing praise of a book don't mean much.

Thursday, 4th December

I went to London yesterday. Attended meeting of Palladian Trust. Clear that X was a knave. He urged a client of his to donate £500,000 to the Trust on condition that they buy four or five pictures with the money as an investment. I always tried to see these pictures but was fobbed off. Now it appears they are fakes and worth little.

Having sought in vain in the Mellon Foundation for evidence that my sketch by Gardner is of Beckford, I went to the National Portrait Gallery. Was received by the young man I met at Anne Rosse's over the summer. He was unable to provide any proof beyond showing me a photograph of another Gardner head purporting to be of Beckford.

Tom Mosley has died. Talked about this to Philip Magnus† at Brooks's. He told me that Mosley was a knave. I asked why. He said that in the Thirties Tom asked PM's cousin Lionel Cohen how much he would give his [Mosley's] party to call off the persecution of the Jews. Hard to believe. Then in the evening they put out a film on the British Movement, the most disgusting exhibition of sheer ignorance and bestiality I have seen for a long while. Inarticulate thugs and skin-heads, lusting for violence and blood, crooning anti-Jewish and anti-black slogans. I cannot believe that Tom would have approved, or that these ghastly toughs from the overcrowded cities are his disciples. But I am ignorant of his recent activities over here. Did he have an office, and was he still the head of a 'movement'?

At Paddington having bought my single fare ticket to Chippenham for £1, special British Rail Christmas concession to OAPs, a little man ahead of me asked the price of a ticket to Taunton. 'Oh dear,' he said, 'I'm £4 short.' As he wandered disconsolately on the platform I offered

---

* See entry for 6 September 1979.
† Sir Philip Magnus-Allcroft, 2nd Bt (1906–88); biographer; m. 1943 Jewell Allcroft of Stokesay Court, Shropshire.

to lend him a fiver. He gratefully accepted and wrote me out a cheque. Said he had mislaid return half of ticket and otherwise could not have returned and did not know where he would have spent the night.

Saturday, 6th December

M. writes that I do not seem to be pleased by the reception my book has had. Well, of course I am pleased that it has been recognised and received some good notices, but it is difficult to explain my attitude. Is it the dog's reluctance to return to its own vomit? Is it shyness? Is it fear of adverse comment? I think it is embarrassment.

Below Tom Mosley's obituary in *The Times* was one of Romain Gary, who has killed himself. I remember him in Roquebrune days when he was married to Lesley Blanch.* He used to wander down to our little house at midday. Would protest that he could not stay to luncheon. Often A. had just enough for her and my slender midday needs. Then he would stay. Having protested that he ate nothing but special biscuits which he would produce from his pocket and munch, would invariably accept our food and eat it. Very gloomy, morose, eccentric, tied-up little man. He would wander in the hills behind the village apparently aimlessly, apparently in despair, and thinking about his book. I was doing the same, I suppose, but I walked purposefully for miles. Was also unhappy for I hated Roquebrune, the isolation, the pent-upness of our doll-like house and the claustrophobia of the village on a steep precipice betwixt mountain and deep blue sea. Never felt any affinity with Romain, who was too abstracted, and distracted.

Melissa Wyndham

Saturday, 13th December

Last Sunday my book was listed among the best-sellers. This is pleasing but means nothing because only the select few booksellers, like Hatchards, Sandoe, Truslove and Hanson, are approached. On the other hand, in the *Sunday Times* books-of-the-year no one mentioned it, which is a disappointment. How sensitive one is.

---

* Romain Gary Kacew (1914–80); b. Tiflis, Georgia; served with French Air Force, RAF and Free French, 1937–45, then joined French Foreign Service; author; m. 1945 as her 2nd husband Lesley Blanch (b. 1907), writer of travel and biography (m. diss. 1962); he m. 2nd Jean Seberg, actress.

Last weekend Dick and Elaine* stayed with us. Had not seen them for nearly two years. Was much shocked and saddened by their appearance. Dick has developed a large paunch for he can't take exercise or walk more than a yard or two, owing to asthma. Puffs after leaving the car and walking into the house and has to squirt stuff into his nose. Elaine is worse. Very haggard, has continuous pains in stomach and eats nothing. Goes to bed at 9.30, stays in bed in morning and rests after tea. My heart yearned for them. Went to see Diana Westmorland on Thursday evening. She has had a *coup de vieux*. Does not seem to take in much unless one speaks slowly. One must not change subjects too swiftly with the old. She said to me, 'I ought of course to die. In a way I want to for I hate being alive. And yet, I don't want to.' She said sweet old age was a damnable lie. There was nothing whatsoever to be said in its favour. Every day she noticed some deterioration.

Tuesday, 16th December

Last week I stayed the night with John [Kenworthy-Browne]. We dined at Brooks's and went at my request to the cinema, *Caligula*. Roman orgies. So boring that we left in the interval. Then Stuart [Preston] came down from Paris. Somehow I cannot recapture with the Sarge† the easy intimacy of yore. It is a bit of a strain. Talk does not flow. Then yesterday M. came down for the day to Bath. We lunched and chatted with oh what ease and affection. He presented me with the copy of *King George V* which Harold presented to the Duke of Windsor and the Duke had bound in red calf, together with a letter from Maître Blum which exculpates me if anyone questions how I came by this book. My first sight of M. for six weeks.

Saturday, 20th December

On Thursday I finally faced up to reading all the press reviews of Vol. I sent by Chatto's. In the last batch Norah included a note of warning that some of them were rather rude. So they are. Chief complaint that H.N. an insignificant figure not deserving two volumes. A point in

---

* Richard Crompton Lees-Milne (1910–84) and his wife (*née* Brigstocke), J.L.-M's brother and sister-in-law, residents of Cyprus.
† Stuart Preston was known as 'The Sarge' from his days in London with the US Army during the Second World War, when he was a sergeant 'attached to HQ'.

this of course. Another that I am too verbose, too laudatory, and that my vocabulary and punctuation are faulty. Don't like this one much. On the whole I consider the book has had a mild *succès d'estime*. Have given MS of Vol. II to M. to read. He is taking such immense pains with written notes and suggestions that I feel guilty taking him away from his own pressing work.

To London on Thursday. Stayed with Eardley. Dined with Betty Hanley in her Ebury Street house, other guests M. and Charles Orwin. Betty is a dear, rotund, plain, good-natured, understanding, intelligent, darling woman with a voice like a corncrake. She talked of her war experiences in France. She was left alone in her aunt's country château while her aunt and mother, both Americans married to Frenchmen (Betty being American by her mother's first husband), remained in Paris. Says that she kept the retreating Germans out of the château by inviting all their officers to dinner and saying she expected them to wear full-dress uniform. They came and were strictly polite. By playing the gracious *grande dame* she kept them at bay.

Sunday, 28th December

We stayed at Parkside with the Droghedas. Besides us only Burnet [Pavitt] staying. Perhaps the most enjoyable Christmas spent there. Joan having had a bad fall on her face was slightly disfigured. Not so tense; both Ds calmer. Sweet to us. Christmas morning to St George's Chapel service. Sitting with Garrett – Joan did not attend – in Garter stalls on north side. Had close view of Queen and royals opposite. Princess Alexandra thin and frail like a medieval saint in a niche. Queen puts money in collection bag. Boxing Day evening went to Charterises* in Provost's Lodgings at Eton. Warmly embraced by Gay on staircase on arrival. Splendid long room upstairs painted strong curry (excellent background) and covered with portraits of Eton boys by Reynolds, Romney, etc. Martin Charteris took me to see an Eton boy's Montem† dress of circa 1820 just bought for the school museum.

---

* Lord Charteris of Amisfield (1913–1999); courtier; Private Secretary to HM The Queen 1972–77; Provost of Eton, 1978; m. 1944 Gay, dau. of 1st Viscount Margesson.
† For Montem, see e.g. *Brewer's Dictionary* (1897): 'A custom formerly observed every three years by the boys of Eton School, who proceeded on Whit Monday *ad montem* (to a mound called Salt Hill), near the Bath Road, and exacted a gratuity called *Salt* from all who passed by. Sometimes as much as £1,000 was thus collected. The custom was abolished in 1847.'

Slashed hose, funny little Byronic cap with feather. He is Chairman of Heritage Fund. Was able to talk to him quite frankly about objectives of the Fund. He defended his purchase of the Altdorfer from Luton Hoo. I begged him to concentrate on English objects and the most perishable, viz. buildings. He reminded us that he had contributed £1½ million to Canons Ashby.* I said I thought a lot more was needed. He said we would get it, we need not fear. A lovely, peaceful atmosphere in this house. The poor son said he felt far happier there than in their Windsor lodgings when Martin was Private Secretary to the Queen. Said that one sensed that evil things had happened in the Castle in former times, whereas there was nothing evil in the Provost's House.

Gervais J. Stops

---

* Unspoiled 17th-century house in Northamptonshire belonging to Dryden family, saved for the nation with much of its original contents, 1980–1, through joint endeavours of N.T., Landmark Trust, Historic Buildings Council, several private benefactors – and The National Heritage Memorial Fund, which contributed £1.5 m. by way of an endowment.

1981

No New Year celebrations. I went to bed early on the eve and read. A. went to a New Year's drinks party at the Loewensteins. I motored to London for the night and stayed with J.K.-B. who is worried about his brother's separation from his wife. London strangely deserted. I met M. at the Paddington Hotel at 7.15. We went to his flat to listen to a repeat of Vita's 1950s broadcast on Walter de la Mare. Vita's mellow, fruity, southern, Keatsian voice has a shrillness in the top notes which I do not remember, possibly the fault of M's wireless set. At nine we decided we must dine. Paddington Hotel said their restaurant was shut but advised us to try Italian restaurant in Praed Street opposite exit ramp from station, where we had an excellent dinner.* Next morning went to Colindale† and read several broadcast talks in old *Listeners* given by Henry Green‡ about whom I have to write something for the American *Twentieth Century Writing* mag.

This past year A. and I have both enjoyed the distinction of being on the best-seller list, she several times, I only once that I know of.

Anne Rosse telephoned me from Womersley. Tells me that every day she and Lady de Vesci eat luncheon together in silence. 'For she hates me,' Anne said. So extraordinary after these forty-five years. One would suppose that Lady de V., now ninety-seven, would forgive and forget.

Last Sat. Pam [Jackson] brought Diana Mosley over to lunch with us. Diana very gaunt, thin and sad. Pam told me that the hour and a quarter wait in the extreme cold in the chapel of the crematorium in Paris, waiting for the ashes to cool, was a mournful proceeding. The sons read Tom's favourite passages from Swinburne between the music. Diana said that she and the sons would have to close down

---

* This was Caprini's, a survival from the 1950s with old-fashioned waitresses; it eventually gave way to an Aberdeen Steak House.
† The British Newspaper Library in North London.
‡ Pseudonym of Henry Yorke (1905–74), novelist, a friend of J.L.-M. in the 1930s. J.L.-M's essay on him is included in *Fourteen Friends*.

Tom's office which he had kept all these years in Victoria Street. Could no longer afford the rent, £4,000 p.a. for two rooms. I should have asked her what the office was for. Still don't know whether he supported the National Front, or what. Greatly enjoyed seeing Diana. Always so much to talk about. Said she had been asked to edit Nancy's correspondence, but couldn't possibly undertake it because of the terrible things N. wrote about her loved ones.*

Tuesday, 13th January

Have finished titivating Vol. II of Harold and am taking typescript to London this afternoon. M. has been the greatest help, reading through the whole thing and making suggestions. I know it is an indifferent volume. And Vol. I has not caused the repercussions I in my self-magnifying way thought it would. Have received few letters from strangers and not many from friends.

Sent off two days ago the article on Henry Green for the American mag. Didn't know what I could say about him, then wrote more than I meant. It is weird how many people I have known are now historical personages. We watched a programme about Willy Maugham. Were glad he was not shown as the cad which recent books about him have made him out to be. Robin Maugham[†] asserted that Willy was not an unhappy man at the end of his life, that he enjoyed his riches and travels. Then the other night saw the end of a programme about Fothergill, the proprietor of the Spread Eagle at Thame, which I frequented when at Oxford.[‡] Wish I had seen the beginning. Went there, I remember, with John Gielgud[§] during that short-lived affair. Fothergill was a left-over from the 1890s, being a friend of Bosie, Oscar Wilde, etc., and a disagreeable fellow too, very rude to customers whom he disliked. Would send them packing before they had finished eating and not bother to ask for payment. Just hoofed them out if he got into arguments with them, for he was always roaming around

---

* A volume of Nancy's letters was later edited by Diana Mosley's daughter-in-law Charlotte.
† Robin, 2nd Viscount Maugham (1916–81); author; nephew of W. Somerset Maugham.
‡ John Rowland Fothergill (1876–1957) had also collaborated in forming the Boston Museum Fine Arts collection of Classical Antiquities; his book *An Innkeeper's Diary* deals with his years at the Spread Eagle (republished 2000 by The Folio Society).
§ Sir John Gielgud, actor (1904–2000).

the tables. Excellent food of course. I thought him a million in those days when he was probably in his fifties, the 1890s being closer to me then than the 1930s are now.

David Ford came round with 250 photographs he has taken of Bath prints and engravings, with message from Bamber that he expects me to begin the Bath book now. Am in a fix for am also being persecuted by OUP for the Country House Anthology. Think I must tackle Bath first.

Wednesday, 14th January

Went to London last night, mistakenly thinking it was the day Sheila Birkenhead had asked me to meet the Queen Mother. Also took typescript up to Chatto and dined with M. who leaves for Paris today. He showed me a review of H.N. he has written for *History Today*, by which I was delighted. Norah says Vol. II should be out next November or even October. She told me that Compton Mackenzie's widow had just telephoned to say how much she was enjoying Vol. I. Coming out of Brooks's, ran into Alan Clark.* He stopped to say how much he enjoyed my diaries, which he kept beside his bed and read and re-read. Now, how can people like them to this extent?

This morning called at Brooks's. Saw to my surprise Sachie sitting disconsolately on the morning room sofa. His first visit to London alone. Said he was lonely and miserable and would welcome a visit from us. I did not think his mind was as bad as I had been led to believe. Talked perfectly rationally, but assured me he was extremely forgetful. Attributed it to the shock resulting from Georgia's death. I asked if he was going to have Francis [his younger son] and family to live with him at Weston. He said he could not bear having F's wife to live there, so he had told them he contemplated marrying again. Said this with the old mischievous smile.

John Jolliffe† told me that he received a large cheque from Diana Mosley for his memorial which is to be erected on triangle facing V&A Museum to Polish nationals sent by Eden to their deaths in

---

* Son of Kenneth Clark; author and politician (1928–99); at this time a backbench Conservative MP. He later achieved celebrity as a diarist, expressing the view that J.L.-M. was the greatest twentieth-century master of this art.
† Author, editor, reviewer (b. 1935).

Russia. John wrote to Diana pointing out that she had already sent a cheque a year ago. She replied that she had not forgotten but wanted to contribute again.

I asked Alan Clark how his father was. Said that he was well physically, except that he was inclined to shuffle. Mentally not so alert. Was forgetful, but when concentrating on a subject and able to give undivided attention his mind was as clear as ever. I am getting like that. Interruptions disturb one's concentration so that one cannot quickly return to the subject one is working on.

Thursday, 22nd January

Rupert Loewenstein tells me that the Trees have a collection of drawings by Cecil Beaton of Vita and Violet.* Says I really ought to see them. They are far more vicious than those of Anne Rosse which the Trees now own and I have seen.† But I don't think I could bear to see Vita made fun of – fun hardly being the word, for they are appalling and brutal. Cecil was a bitch really.

Saturday, 31st January

I have begun work on Bamber Gascoigne's *Images of Bath*. Have now sorted out photographs of all the prints which I intend to discuss in the text. David Ford is my collaborator and in the process I have got to know this charming, handsome, rather pathetic young man. He has told me his story. He is thirty-four. Grew up with anti-Vietnam generation of students. Says I have no idea how that war divided America down the middle. He had begun a lucrative job on Wall Street but found colleagues so unsympathetic that he left, much to his conventional parents' chagrin. Crossed the Atlantic, determined to work in England. Has remained ever since. Yet has no proper job. Prospects bleak. Started doing social work, meals on wheels, helping the aged and stricken in London. Liked it. Then got bored. Wanted something more cerebral. Attached himself to Bamber and Christina who are his protectors, I think. Something vulnerable about him. He told me he hated being young. When I expressed amazement, assuring him he

---

* Violet Trefusis (1894–1972), dau. of Colonel the Hon. George Keppel and his wife Alice; novelist; lover of Vita Sackville-West.
† See entry for 20 June 1974, *Ancient as the Hills*.

was at the peak of life, he solemnly avowed that he wanted to be old. I have not pressed him to tell me about his love life, although I already know he had a serious affair which broke down and upset him deeply. He is, I think, very serious, probably romantic, and not promiscuous. I carefully refrained from plying him with indiscreet questions or appearing to be inquisitive. But when he packed up his files yesterday and said goodbye, I said, 'Let me give you a chaste embrace', and did so. Far from there being any resistance he warmly reciprocated, and made as if to kiss me on the mouth. Perhaps all the young kiss on the mouth these days without implying emotion. When I was their age it meant only one thing, that both were in love or intended to go to bed together there and then. Alas for those halcyon days. I have grown fond of David and shall miss him.

Saturday, 7th February

Have read Isaiah Berlin's *Personal Impressions*. He writes excellently like a man of culture. How English is he? Brought up in Russia. The essays mostly about distinguished Fellows of All Souls whose names mean little to me. I realise how out of touch I am with the intellectuals of this world. I like to think my friends are intellectuals, but very few are compared with all these clever people from the Universities. Very impressed by the nice things Berlin says about his colleagues. Never bitchy, inclined to see the good points and ignore the bad.

On Tuesday evening motored to London for Rosamond [Lehmann]'s eightieth birthday party given by her granddaughter, Anna Woodhouse. Held in a large and charming Victorian house at Clapham. All R's family assembled, charming young grandchildren, yet I thought none of them looked as beautiful as some of the oldies had looked when they were in their twenties – Ros herself, Alvilde, Dadie, Eardley, all real beauties. Many old friends but I had much difficulty in hearing. John Lehmann present. He is a wreck of the former self, large, puffy, white-haired, badly dressed, very crippled, moving with a stick. He sat on the upright fender seat. He is polite, but one senses that if he knew one better he would not be. He clearly shuns talk about cerebral things except with his intimates. Jack [Rathbone]* sitting next to me at one moment on sofa said in a loud

---

* John Francis Warre Rathbone (1909–95); Secretary of N.T., 1949–68; President, London Centre of N.T. from 1968.

voice as John walked away from party, 'There goes a really horrible man.' Nick Ridley's new wife was introduced to me.* Said something about a new book, how much she liked it. I vainly supposed she was referred to H.N. and thanked her. Turned out she was referring to A's book.

Next morning at breakfast I told Eardley that Norah wanted me to cut out a reference to Vita's amusing remark when she learnt of Angelica Bell's engagement to David Garnett, 'It's a case of adding incest to sodomy.' He said, 'Ring up Fanny Partridge immediately', she living in the flat below. Did so, and she said certainly don't cut out. Garnett was her brother-in-law and also the father of her daughter-in-law. I was delighted to tell Norah this during morning session with her, going through typescript of Vol. II.

Tuesday, 10th February

Motored to London for Sheila Birkenhead's party in Wilton Crescent for the Queen Mother. Invited at 6 for 6.15. Walked into house at 6.05. Ushered into room upstairs. Before I could embrace Sheila I was seized, no other word for it, by that predator Rosalie Mander,[†] wearing a horrible pink knitted dress and grey felt hat covered with stains and dust. She transfixes one like a butterfly on a board. Did however say that my books got better and better. Bill De L'Isle[‡] like-wise rather a bore, dribbles while he talks and keeps wiping the wet off his chin, drove me relentlessly into the fireplace until I had to say I was burning the seat of my trousers. He said that Shelley from whom he is descended, he now being the Shelley baronet, was a silly man.[§] I agreed. But would you have liked him, I asked? To my surprise he said he would because he liked arisocrats to be radicals, no matter how

---

* Hon. Nicholas Ridley (1929–93), yr s. of 3rd Viscount Ridley; Conservative MP for Cirencester and Tewkesbury; m. 1st, 1950. Hon. Clayre Campbell, dau. of 4th Baron Stratheden and Campbell (m. diss. 1974); 2nd, 1979, Judy Kendall.
† Rosalie Glynn Grylls (1905–88); author of works on nineteenth-century literary figures; m. 1930 Sir Geoffrey Mander (1882–1962), sometime MP for Wolverhampton; during 1930s they donated their house, Wightwick Manor, Staffordshire to the N.T.
‡ William Sidney, 1st Viscount and 6th Baron De L'Isle, VC (1909–91); soldier and politician; Governor-General of Australia, 1961–5; Eton contemporary of J.L.-M.
§ The ostensible purpose of the gathering was to present HM The Queen Mother with a copy of Shelley's poems, obtained by J.L.-M., which had belonged to the poet's daughter Ianthe Esdaile.

silly they were. Talked to Quentin Crewe in his chair. He unable to shake my hand. But said he was about to write a book about the Sahara, necessitating his going there, camping in tents. Courageous for a man so crippled and immobile as he.*

Dear Sheila has dreadful teeth but I love the woman. She took groups of people up to Queen Elizabeth. Then watched to see if the encounters were successful, and when it was time to remove them. She edged her way towards me. Out of the corner of my eye I saw her coming. Tried to hide behind the Leigh Hunt family. But she caught me. Made me stand expectant while Q.E. talked to a group of three. Sheila kept saying, 'Push your way in.' 'I can't,' I said, 'it's not in my nature.' Then the Q. turned from the others towards me, and they took the hint and dissolved themselves. We confronted one another. Was I to speak first? She smiled awkwardly. Then Sheila said, 'He wrote a book about Rome.' 'Oh, how interesting,' she said. 'Yes,' I said, 'but a long time ago. It is full of mistakes and luckily now out of print.' Q.E.: 'Do you like your books when you have done with them?' J: 'No, I rather hate them. I used to hate them only when they were finished. Now I hate them before they are finished. I would', I continued, 'make a bad parent if I treated my children like my books, which are said to be the brain's children. I would dislike them before they were grown up.' 'You certainly would make a bad parent,' she answered. That was a pretty silly introductory exchange. A glazed look came across her eyes. She said desperately, 'Where do you live?' I told her Badminton. Eyes lit up for there was a subject for conversation. How much she liked the place and village. Asked which house ours was. I explained, by the lodge to the gates. She asked after Master and Mary Beaufort. Said how sad that Mary was becoming so vague. I said she often did not know who we were. 'She can be quite funny,' she said. 'And sharp,' I added. Where did we live before? Explained Alderley, which we loved; which became too big; had to move. 'Do you go back there?' 'Not unless I have to,' I said, 'although the new owners are charming friends of ours and love the place.' I said one ought never to return to places one loved. She agreed. Became wistful. Said she adored her two old homes. I said feebly, 'But one must preserve the magic of beloved houses in one's head, and not allow the images to get misted. If one refrains from re-visiting, which merely

---

* Author and gastronome (1926–99); *In Search of the Sahara* was published in 1983.

causes confusion in the memory, they remain as one knew them.'
She liked this, and said, 'You have said something which I shall
think over.' Then turned to the next guest. I can't pretend it was
very satisfactory, but then I always find these royal encounters
unnatural, artificial and profitless. I had the opportunity of looking
at her close to. Her teeth, which are her own, are bad. She has little
finger nails upturned at the ends – not pretty. Her hair straight,
wispy, stringy. Nevertheless she has dignity and charm – how often
has that been said? – however evanescent; and stamina. For 1½
hours she stood – never once sat – talking to total strangers and
making herself agreeable.

I had an enjoyable conversation with the Lady-in-Waiting, Lady
Elizabeth Basset.* Told her my story of Edmund Esdaile refusing to
have name of his ancestor Shelley mentioned in his presence, and how
he had the line on the gravestone of Shelley's daughter Ianthe in
Cothelstone churchyard recording her as daughter of P.B. Shelley cut
out and a plain slot inserted.

Trevor Leigh Hunt talked to me afterwards. Told me that the Q.
Mother had said this and that to him when he was presented. I was
standing behind him and heard every word said. The words did not
coincide with his report of them. Poor man, what pleasure he derived
from his fabrication.

Could not get away till nearly eight. Dashed to Covent Garden to
join A. I missed the first ballet but was just in time for Freddy Ashton's
Month in the Country. Very pretty but ought to have been longer.
Seemed like one evening in the country.

Friday, 13th February

In afternoon did some shopping in Bath and looked at the medieval
East Gate squeezed between the Market and Empire Hotel. Returned
to library thinking of M. whom I first met two years ago today. Had
sent him a cable to Nassau this morning. As I entered, telephone rang.
It was M., ringing from New York which he has not yet left. I
reminded him of the occasion. He said, Yes, that was why he was telephoning. Overjoyed.

---

* Lady Elizabeth Legge, dau, of 7th Earl of Dartmouth, m. 1931 Ronald Basset.

Saturday, 14th February

We motored to Weston, to lunch with Sachie. He is greatly recovered, though refers constantly to 'poor darling Georgia'. The wonderful Gertrude, who has been with them for fifty-two years, looks forty and has the manners of a duchess, told A. that Sachie cannot be left alone for longer than half an hour, and must talk. He said he was dreadfully lonely and would like to stay a weekend with us. Full of stories and reminiscences as of old. He said there was a hole in the garden wall at Weston which had always been known as Pug's Hole, into which betrothed girls put their fingers (and boys I dare say something else) to ensure begetting children. Sachie has discovered that it is a corruption of Puck's Hole, fertility rites, pre-Christian derivation. He has been staying with Reresby at Renishaw and seems quite reconciled to him and wife. I always suspected that Georgia fostered that little trouble. He found the house as haunted as it used to be when he was a child. One of the haunts is a ghostly kiss which is not only heard but felt by the recipient. Once, while Sir George Sitwell was leading a woman guest into dinner, she asked her host if it was true that Renishaw was haunted. 'Of course not,' Sir George replied, whereupon he received a slap in the face from an unseen hand. Sachie said that Osbert was in the same regiment as Master, who got into trouble for absenting himself without permission. When asked why, he said the first thing that came into his head, and replied that he had gone to get a bunch of violets for his commanding officer. He talked about his mother which I had never known him to do before. She was eighteen when she married Sir George, who was over forty and wrapped up in medieval genealogy and folklore. She was bored stiff with him from the start.

Sachie is the great-nephew of Master's grandfather, whichever Duke that was. That Duke had a mistress who left him. He was dreadfully upset. He made the Vicar pray in the church at Badminton for her return. She did return within a few days. While on the subject of Dukes he said that Westminster (Bendor)* was the kindest of men. I had always understood him to be a brute. He, Bendor, would sit up all night at a casino trying to lose the enormous sums of money which

---

* Hugh Grosvenor, 2nd Duke of Westminster (1879–1953); his nickname Bendor is said to be derived from his grandfather's horse Bend Or, who won the Derby in 1879; Hon. Loelia Ponsonby (later Lady Lindsay) was his 3rd wife (m. 1930).

his high stakes had brought him, in order not to break the bank. It was quite a difficult operation, losing, but he managed if he set his mind to it.

Monday, 23rd February

A. drove me up to the Preeces' lodge on Sunday at the bottom of the Newark drive, and I walked up to the house with the dogs. Bob Parsons' grounds a mass of snowdrops and aconites, which were closed, it being a grey and cold day. Some daffodils were already in bud. Honey bolted before I had got round the first corner. Searched for her in vain and went home. Had not been in the house five minutes when Bob telephoned to say the Preeces had found her. I went to fetch her and talked to Preeces. A nice family. Asked him how his job was going – he was a printer. Said he had been made redundant, not by his firm but his union. Then six months later was asked if he would care to return. As he is nearing retirement age, and his redundancy had given him a shock from which he had only just recovered, he naturally declined. Then their child Katherine, whom I used to give children's books to, obviously a clever girl, told me she could not get a job. The parents said she had a far better education than they ever had. Father said she was facing the same situation as they faced in the Thirties. Felt sorry for these decent people. It is depressing and demoralising for them.

Percy Perks, A's old occasional gardener and a dear, told her yesterday that he had experienced what he called a second vision. She asked him what he meant. He explained that in the middle of the night his dead wife appeared to him, begging to be allowed to come back to him. He said to her, 'Go away and stay where you are.' 'Wasn't that rather unkind?' A. asked. He said, no, she could not return and he would soon be joining her. He was very upset by these experiences.

Tuesday, 24th February

It is rather weird and dreadful how firms close down overnight. I had a letter this morning from a garage asking for my patronage and saying that of course I knew that Benter Motors where I have my car serviced has closed. I knew nothing of the sort. Then Caters, that nice, old-fashioned grocers in Margaret's Buildings, which has been going for a hundred years, is closing at the end of the week. There I get my cider, for I can park close to the shop. Damn.

Friday, 27th February–Monday, 2nd March

On Friday morning Alvilde, Caroline Somerset and I flew to Prague. Weather was intensely cold, so cold that wearing several jerseys and a greatcoat I was perished. It was impossible to take notes out of doors, the fingers were frozen stiff. We stayed at a hideous new building, the Intercontinental Hotel on the river. Drove there from airport (good and clean) in taxi through new suburbs, ugly, drab and grey. Newly built, yet cement peeling. Hotel comfortable and warm. Food, not representative of what the natives eat, tolerable without being good. Only once we dined out, at Moscow Restaurant, all restaurants being shut during weekend. The unreality of our hotel made me feel uncomfortable, because the city inhabitants clearly very hard up. Dressed in subfusc, cheap plastic clothes. Not a single shop in the whole city in which one would buy a thing. This comes of national-isation; no competition and catering only for the meanest tastes. Inhabitants seemed nice and inclined to be friendly, but woebegone. Quiet people; little applause in the Opera House where we saw a goodish performance of *Eugene Onegin*. I have seen this opera in Moscow and Covent Garden. Was not much moved this time. It lacked fire and passion.

Most beautiful city seen. Castle on its heights over the river dom-inates the town. A number of Rococo palaces and houses, and churches legion. Spires and towers in profusion. But the condition of all buildings poor. Much repair work being undertaken, slowly. Why so long a time since end of the War? On Sunday we visited several churches. Those which function well-maintained and full of worship-pers. Noticed many young, which is always moving. They, like the Poles, may identify their acute sense of nationalism with the Catholic Church. The guide books do their best to emphasise the heroism of Jan Huss as someone who in the Middle Ages defied authority and feudalism, but eighty per cent of Czechs are Catholic. Evidently no fear of worshipping. These Baroque and Rococo churches the only places, apart from the Opera House, which provide glitter and romance and escape from the appalling drabness of their lives.

All the Czechs we met were ready to accept tips. First morning we motored round city in a bus, guided by nice young man, the only handsome Czech I saw. He told me he conducted tours during week-ends when free from his work as a biochemist in order 'to increase my budget'. We duly tipped him equivalent of £2.

Unfortunately the Tyn Church or Cathedral in Old Town was shut for repairs. Those places which left most impression on me are: the Library, Rococo, brown mahogany and gold shelves with white vellum books; St James's Church, perhaps finest of all, Rococo over Gothic very long nave, and long sanctuary, with boxes high up, each with urn and putto sitting on it, splendid painted ceiling by Reiner I think. Also very high marks to St Nicholas in New Town across Charles Bridge, itself a fine thing with Rococo groups of statuary, which has deteriorated so badly through pollution during past twenty years that each group is being replaced with a copy and originals taken into Museum. St Giles Church, also Rococo. St Vitus Church in Castle complex, Gothic and aspirant.

A. observed that every window was dirty and every doorstep unswept. Certainly every public garden and footpath was worn down by feet, and the litter was dreadful. This unlike Russia where none is allowed. We did not of course go inside any apartment, but the glimpses we had of what must go on inside were depressing. The most favourable things to be had are the *slivovice*, a sort of schnapps which warms the cold cockles, and the red wine, a delicious plonk.

Saturday, 7th March

On Thursday lunched at Hole-in-the-Wall* with Julian Mitchell,† Tony's playwright brother. He wanted to talk about a play or novel he is writing – not yet sure which – on the theme that the Cambridge traitors, Burgess, Blunt, etc., were chiefly actuated by the inhibitions imposed on them regarding their homosexuality. Wants to know from those who lived through the Thirties how circumspect they were obliged to be. I assured him that they had to act covertly and could never let their tastes be known. Only the most bold and rash did so. Julian believes their pro-Sovietism was a getting their own back on England. Interesting. Yesterday he spent day with John Gielgud who sent me affectionate messages. I told him how inti-mately I knew John in 1931 when I was an undergraduate at Oxford.

---

* Bath restaurant, famous for excellence at this time.
† Also novelist and biographer (b. 1935). The play was *Another Country*.

For six weeks I was infatuated with him. Then it passed like a cloud. I like Julian Mitchell. He is unattractive, with the sort of beard which continues down his open neck, but sensitive. I talked to him about my *Heretics in Love* which I knew was a poor novel but thought might make a good film. Gave him a copy which he took away, and he will let me know his opinion.

Tuesday, 10th March

Embarrassing thing happened last Saturday. A. bought expensive tickets for an evening at Longleat in aid of Cheshire Homes. On arrival, each guest given a card with a list of fourteen treasures which were displayed on a large table, mostly silver objects and Fabergé boxes. We had to guess and write down the date and country of origin of each object and the value. Then we dined at odd tables, having filled and handed in the cards. After dinner the winners' names read out. I headed the list and was awarded a magnum of champagne. Then there was a draw of raffle tickets. A. won that, receiving a huge salmon as a prize. We were conducted round the house by Christopher Thynne. Some of the state rooms only illuminated by searchlights from outside. Nearly all the interior of Longleat is nine-teenth-century, of very best quality – inlaid marquetry doors, painted ceilings by Walter Crane. Most rooms very pretty. Huge and palatial house. Caroline says Badminton a cottage by comparison.

Saturday, 14th March

Malcolm Muggeridge* has become a good old trooper; after years of travels by deviant ways he has come to the straight and narrow. I have pondered much on the wise things he has been saying on the telly lately. When asked about the outcome of the last War he said he knew all along that only Communism or Nazism could be the victor. Now I always felt this way, though believed that Nazism would be defeated in the long run. That the War would be a blow for democracy I always foresaw, just as I saw Communism as the greater evil because more lasting and insidious. Nazism, terrible thought it was, was ephemeral by nature. It could only flourish with trumpets, while the other works slowly, underground, in silence. I shall never forget learning, in hos-

---

* Author, journalist and broadcaster (1903–1990).

pital in Birmingham, that Russia had become our ally. To me it meant
the end of all things, our compromise with evil.

Lunched yesterday with Peter Tew,* retired architect, in his nice little
house on Richmond Hill. Outlook over Bath shaded from nastiness.
Quiet air of genteel well-being, *Gemütlichkeit*. Rather tiresome, jaggering
wife, who would say, 'Now, I have another question to put to you.
Did you know Nancy Mitford? Yes, I thought so', and without listening to anything I might have to say about her, continued, 'And what
did you think of Evelyn Waugh? Good, I thought so', I having said
nothing. 'And now Harold Acton.' Then, 'I have something to show
you which will, I hope, give you pleasure.' And she rushed to fetch my
Harold book. I began to express pleasure that she had bought it. 'Oh
no,' she said, 'I couldn't afford to do that. I have got it from the Library.'

Peter Tew lent me a lecture he gave on Bath chapels and told me
much I wanted to know. He told me that at seventy-six he had
become wholly superfluous; that it was extraordinary to reflect, while
one's mind was still sound, that one was cast on the dust heap,
unwanted, unused. He has nothing whatever to do; gets up late, takes
dog for walk, retires to his study (which he calls his 'dog hole') and
rearranges papers. Quite cheerful and says he doesn't have a care in the
world. Doesn't mind a fig what anybody says or thinks about him. Yet
something piteous and terrible in this.

Tuesday, 17th March

Julian Mitchell turned up waving *Heretics* in the air and asking me to
sign it as if it was a gift. Then casually told me that it would be unsuitable for a film because the principal characters are portrayed at
different ages. He quite understood how Visconti was attracted to it,
but it would not do for television. So that is that. I took him to Hole-
in-the-Wall, very expensive, and on parting he said we must lunch
again soon. But have said to him all I have to say.

Thursday, 19th March

To London to meet M., who returned yesterday after several weeks
in New York and the Bahamas. He came to Brooks's from Trumpers

---

* 'The hearty old architect who worked for Paul Methuen at Corsham' (*Ancient as the
Hills*, 16 October 1974).

where he had all his long hair cut off and looked like a skinned guinea-pig. Was in good form until the end of dinner when I noticed his large eyes turning into slits and said he was dog-tired and ought to go home to bed. He admitted it. He is like a child, falling from one mood into another. I drove him back to Hyde Park Square and told him he must work like a daemon at his book and finish it as soon as he can.

Made plans with Eardley for our jaunt to Calabria in May, and fetched pile of remaindered novels from Chatto's – a humiliation.

The Times is hell. Again they have refused to publish my letter on the subject of over-population. They just ignore this, the most pressing issue in the world. I really think that if they offer to take extract of H.N. Vol. II this autumn I shall say No. The Peter Hayman case revolts me. The appalling hypocrisy of the British. Bloody Tory MP called Dickens* insisted on publicising in Commons name of ex-diplomat Hayman† for indulging in admittedly rather sordid fantasies, but not culpable in law. Today he [Dickens] tells press that he is leaving his own wife, after which he goes to telephone wife to this effect. If that isn't double shittiness, what is?

Saturday, 28th March

Terrible spring depression during past week. Bloody spring. Depression is not relieved by left eye having blown up. Don't know what is the matter but woke up on Tuesday with sharp pain seemingly behind eyeball. After two days went to Dr King who looked through a telescope and said I should apply some grease four times a day and I would be all right. But I am not all right and discomfort persists. Last night I discovered I could hardly see with this eye, certainly not to read, even with spectacles.

Motored to Oxford for interview with Oxford University Press, whom I have been treating very cavalierly. It was over two years ago when I agreed to do Country House Anthology for them, and have not started yet. Anyway nice girl, Judith Chamberlain, has let me off and gives me further grace. I promised that as soon as I had polished off the Bath book for Bamber which is nearing end, and entries for

---

* Geoffrey Dickens, MP for Huddersfield West, 1979–83; m. 1956 Norma Boothby.
† Sir Peter Hayman (b. 1914); UK High Commissioner in Canada, 1970–4.

DNB (also OUP) on Nancy and Jamesey, I would begin, hopefully in June. Then picked up Derek Hill at New College where he had been painting the Warden, Cook. Saw portrait, quarter-length in grey. Rather good likeness of dreary face which I met on staircase as we walked out to a good luncheon at French restaurant in High Street. Made plans with Derek for yet another visit to Mount Athos in early September when weather will be stiflingly hot, but we must go then if we are to visit the Grand Lavra. This really must be my last excursion to Holy Mountain. I will always forgive Derek whatever tiresomeness he displays, for he is the most affectionate and loyal of friends.

Miss Chamberlain of OUP handed me a book called *Places* in which she pointed out there was a contribution by me. Had forgotten all about it, so long ago did I write the rather shaming piece about the church at Wickhamford, and had no idea OUP were the publishers. Don't think much of the other contributions but the book nicely produced. Clearly people find difficulty in conveying to others what the secret cherished places of their heart mean to them. They see magic in what to others may be a very ordinary house, or wood, or piece of downland. I have also been sent by Weidenfeld's Peter Quennell's book on Jamesey* which I am avidly reading. Disappointed there are only four letters to me, one of which is embarrassing about some love affair I was immersed in in 1938. Letter, without mentioning sex of object, makes clear what it was. But James's letters to Clarissa [Churchill, later Avon] are the best. Really very remarkable, full of sharp observations, and abounding in affection. Boy called Vinson, American, whom he dearly loved, I never met or knew about. Indeed, as soon as the War was over my intimacy with James practically ceased.

Poor little Folly had to be operated on three days ago for a cyst on her neck. She is very sorry for herself, has huge gash and is still wobbly on her legs. Her bewilderment at what *we* have done to her is poignant. She was so well when we took her to the vet but the swelling was increasing, and the operation had to be done.

Have been ruminating upon possibility of becoming totally blind. What would I do? For I write or read most of the sixteen hours of the day. And use eyes ceaselessly. Would I go into monastery and pray?

---

* *A Lonely Business: A Self-Portrait of James Pope-Hennessy*, ed. Peter Quennell.

Would I commit suicide? What would poor A. do? I would be the heaviest burden upon her, heavier than I am already.

Sunday, 29th March

It is Sunday. For once we have no engagement of any kind. It rains all day relentlessly. In the evening, for the days are longer now the clock has changed, I walked with Honey on her lead down the Luckington Road. The landscape is grey, dank and dripping. A sour mist of damp hovers over the fields. The horses look shaggy and saturated. The ducks in the farmyard I pass shake their wings as though they have emerged from a pond, whereas there is merely ubiquitous wetness. I think about Jamesey Pope-Hennessy, the book about whom by Peter Quennell I am reading with sorrow. I find a chord of sadness throughout. There was something wrong with the way of life which caught up with him. The fascination of *la boue* became a fixation, and surely he wasted too much time with empty heads like Len. Or am I being snobbish and limited? He would have said so. I know I irritated him increasingly. Few letters to me have been included by Peter, whereas I thought there were some very entertaining ones he omitted. It is so long since I read them, and it required a little courage to read the few in this book.

Tuesday, 31st March

Went to London for the day to see Pat Trevor-Roper.[*] He said I definitely had a cyst behind the eye. Gave me some different drops and told me, if eye not better in a fortnight, he would have to scrape the cyst away by local anaesthetic. I did not dare ask if this meant taking the eye out of its socket. Very idea makes me feel sick. I am not as brave as St Agatha, and more squeamish.

Went to William Strang exhibition at National Portrait Gallery. Vita's portrait there, the *Lady in the Red Hat*. Very good likeness and a charming composition, with her straight upright back. A. asked me if I thought Derek as good a portrait painter. Answer No, not quite. But Strang is very obvious and realistic, not subtle. Strange that a painter of this century should in doing nudes cover the male pudenda

---

[*] Ophthalmic surgeon (b. 1916); co-tenant with Desmond Shawe-Taylor of Long Crichel (see note to entry for 17 September 1981).

with ivy leaves and omit pubic hair. Self-portraits of Strang made him look like a civil servant. No romance.

Monday, 6th April

Lunched with the Guy Hollands in their barn. She asked me to write a *dédicace* in H.N. Vol. I. So I put, 'To Joan Holland, Euterpe* of the Cotswolds'. Neither she nor the Reresby Sitwells had heard of Euterpe and didn't know what I meant. But a clever young man from Oxford called Terence Rodrigues, of Portuguese extraction, explained. Silly woman thought I was insulting her. Penelope Sitwell told A. that their relations with Sachie were now perfectly affectionate. It was Georgia who had made the trouble. P. said she had been an evil woman and on her death-bed her expression was wholly evil. A nasty thing to say about one's mother-in-law, but I think Georgia made a great mistake in being so beastly to this girl.

Today A. went to London to see Anthony [Chaplin] in hospital. She returned greatly shocked and distressed. Says poor Anthony in last extremity of illness. Is bright yellow, hair snow white, face fallen in, speaks in inaudible whisper. Is to be operated on on Wednesday. We must hope and pray he dies under the operation, for if he comes through he can only last a short time in great distress, without a pancreas and with half his liver removed.

The Times has published today my appreciation of Alick Downer. I don't think it is very good, and the mistake I made was to write it before the obituary appeared, because my piece is repetitive. Wrote a difficult letter to Mary Downer and sent her the two *Times* extracts.

M. telephoned from Paris this afternoon. There was a piercing screeching noise while he talked which I thought came from the wires. He explained that Maître Blum had bought a parrot and installed it in his room, possibly to prevent him telephoning so much. I said I was glad that this plan was evidently not succeeding.

Monday, 20th April

It is Easter Monday. We have had Heywood and Anne Hill staying since Friday. The perfect guests whom we treat as we do each other. No effort required, no making of conversation. One can wash up the

---

* The muse of lyrical poetry, commonly represented with the double flute.

breakfast things while they are finishing eating at the table and talking. Whereas last weekend we had two strangers, a couple A. had met in India. Oh the strain!

Went on Wednesday to Bath University to hear that great man Bernard Lovell* give a lecture on William Herschel. Delivered in a deliciously casual, ruminative way. Lovell holds him in immense esteem for becoming an astronomer when over the age of forty, at which time in a man's life he has normally passed the climacteric and the mind is on the descent. Lovell much admires Herschel's musical compositions and the Cholmondeley girl† played a few of his pieces on a bad, harsh piano. They were like Mozart, though written earlier, and none of Herschel's scores has been published yet. A field day for BBC Third Programme?

Have finished writing my *Images of Bath* and begun typing out. Shall not be able to finish it before leaving for Italy with Eardley on 29th, and on return shall be faced with galleys of H.N. Vol. II. My MS boring and factual I fear, containing no fantasy. I am not an imaginative writer. Am contemplating a biography of Gosse and have got the Evan Charteris biog. out of London Library. Pros are that G. knew a large circle of literary people over many years; was mixed up in T.J. Wise forgeries; may have been queer without knowing it; had a most eccentric father. All depends whether there are Gosse papers in existence. And whether Chatto's consider him a publishable proposition.

Heywood is as round as a tub and brick red in the face. When I think how pretty – the just word – he was in youth, and desired by all. He is like a dormouse which uncurls itself in order to make a sly remark and giggle, immediately curling up again. Very sweet, still very perceptive and intelligent. But very quiet and slow in movement.

Thursday, 23rd April

Forgot to take a sleeping pill last night. Turned out light at midnight. At 2.30 promptly woke up. Remembered pill. Too late to take one now, I thought mistakenly. Had terrible night of 'mares and headache. Result that today I feel just ill. It is not insomnia but drug addiction. And tonight we go to Derry Moore's dinner party. There are times

---

* Sir Bernard Lovell (b. 1913), astronomer.
† Lady Rose Cholmondeley (b. 1948); eldest dau. of 6th Marquess of Cholmondeley; concert pianist and secretary of Chopin Society.

when I feel I cannot travel as far as London, that I shall break with tiredness. This is how Midi has felt for years. News that she has had a heart attack and is in hospital. Telephoned Bamber who takes grave view. Also news that John Betj. has had a stroke. Oh God.

Sunday, 26th April

Today, Sunday, we are without light or heat. Terrible storm during the night. Woke up to thick snow, and spent morning shaking what we could off the cedar trees, box hedges, hollies. Several plants destroyed, like roses torn from walls, honeysuckle. The poor Acloques* telephoned to say that at Alderley the large amelanchier blown down, the birch tree by gate, one of the largest in the country, torn down, also fir bearing 'Kiftsgate' rose. During the day snow has melted but not entirely gone. Freak weather for April. Telephones also out of order. Good thing I returned from London last night in time.

Went up on Thursday evening for party given by Moores. Derry and Alexandra excellent hosts, plying us with delicious food. I did not know many people, though at dinner sat with Joan Drogheda. We reanimated flagging conversation with handholds and protestations how lovely it was to be together. Next day, Friday, I spent at exhibitions. Adrian Daintrey in Motcomb Street, variable. Then to Queen's Gallery to see her collection of Canalettos. Some forty paintings and a hundred drawings. Extraordinary collection, much to credit of George III through Consul Smith I suppose. Particularly struck with draperies – the flags from campanile, sails, tents, booths, clothes, feathers and waves. A rare artist whose drawings for once inferior to finished paintings. Then to Westminster Cathedral. Looked again at Blessed Sacrament Chapel, wonderful vaulting and walls covered with Boris Anrep's mosaics. Great artist he was. Wandered into the desolate Chapel of St Andrew in which I was received by drunken priest, Father Napier-Hemy, in 1934, and supposed I was at the time sincere in my fervour. All so cold and empty to me now, I mean the Catholic faith, to which I am hostile. Then walked to restaurant Como Lario in Holbein Place where Rosemary Chaplin joined me. She looks dreadfully tired and dusty. But was calm and resigned about Anthony. Said he might live for three weeks or four. It was awful telling him that the operation was a failure and the surgeon

---

* The Guy Acloques, who purchased Alderley Grange, Glos. from A.L.-M. in 1974 and maintained the famous garden she had created there.

could not remove the tumour on his pancreas. But she said, 'I am grateful for thirty happy years'. I looked away.

Then trained to Sissinghurst. Nigel met me and daughter Juliet
who was also on train. The cold at Sissinghurst intense although no
snow yet. Enjoyable visit to meet Victoria Glendinning.* Not what I
expected, which was a blonde divinity à la Diana Mitford for some
reason. She is in fact slight, with dark hair and clever face. I think she
will make a good and fair biography of Vita. Anyway we got on and
I gave her my address and telephone number in case she may want to
communicate when she starts writing. Nigel handed me a very laudatory review he wrote of my Harold I for Book Choice. Strange of
him to review a life of his father but he did it, as he does everything,
well. Juliet enchanting and husband James MacMillan-Scott even
more so. After dinner I sat up till two, talking with him on sofa.
Extremely handsome man of about twenty-eight, now a banker. He
told me he has to dine with many women, business acquaintances,
when he travels. Many of them expect to go to bed with him. Says it
is such a bore. Says he has no prejudices or disapproval regarding sex
and was surprised that I of this mind too. But he got bored with sex.
Was just as content with platonic love. I said Yes, that is all very fine
for you who can get the other without raising a finger. He, James, said
that age was no bar to him if he loved. Well, well.

On my return yesterday that angel Misha lunched. Left him on
pavement in Piccadilly in the rain before leaping on to a bus. We
embraced under a clash of umbrellas.

*The diary of J.L.-M's visit to Calabria with Eardley Knollys in April–May
1981 is reproduced as Appendix IV.*

Monday, 18th May

Fear I got on E's nerves [in Calabria] though he has written totally
denying this and most affectionately hoping we would go off together
on another expedition soon. I love him too but he got on *my* nerves
at times.

E. told me that he suffers from the same syndrome as I do – namely

---

* Hon. Victoria Seebohm (b. 1937), author and journalist; dau. of Baron Seebohm; m.
1st, 1958, Professor Nigel Glendinning (m. diss. 1981); 2nd, 1982, Terence de Vere White
(1912–94), writer on Irish topics.

that something impels him to walk across the bows of cars and buses in London streets. Mattei or any other young companion who may be with him is appalled by this careless behaviour. Now, Harold also used to do exactly this when he became old. In my case I barely look round, but sense there is no oncoming traffic. At other times I see a car but think I have time to cross in front of it. So far have managed, often by the skin of my teeth. Strange impulse.

Motoring to Chippenham in the early morning last Friday I saw in a flash a scene which told me so much. A young couple were standing stock still on the pavement. On his face was not triumph, because the expression was sad, but relief at having said what presumably had long been on his mind. Her expression was tragically sad, one of resignation, misery. Had he just told her that after all he could not marry her? She had a small child in a pram beside her which made the scene more poignant. This within an eye-wink.

Listened on Thursday to the programme *Books* on Radio 4 about my published diaries. Commentator and a man called Christopher Matthew. I did not like it. Spoke of them as gossipy, which they are not entirely. Spoke about the exclusive circle in which I moved during the War, as though composed of an extinct species like pterodactyls. Both men agreed that such people as Bridget Parsons, the Dashwoods and of course Emerald were confirmed good-timers, the most despicable of beings. Whereas my real friends were Harold, the Pope-Hennessys and other writers and intellectuals. Matthew took as a general theme for the diaries a remark I made when I broke down on the road and was told my car had run out of water: 'I am humiliated. I am always humiliated.' Have modern reviewers no sense of humour?

On Thursday evening, when we had the clock man from Hawkesbury Upton over to collect my gold clock and Joan Lindsay and Cynthia Llewellyn-Palmer were here for a drink, the bell rang. It was Mary Beaufort, looking so changed, so strained and sad that I barely recognised her. She said A. had told her she might come to luncheon. It was then 6.15. Her wig slipped over her forehead, just above her nose. However she stayed for a quarter of an hour and made some sense. Walked home by herself. Daphne [Fielding] appalled when she learnt this. She had escaped her nurses.

Caroline told A. that when Mary's brother* died the other day,

---

* 2nd Marquess of Cambridge (1895–1981); m. 1923 Dorothy, dau. of Hon. Osmond Hastings.

Mary told David who was with her that she must telephone the Queen. This he did, and got the Queen on the line. Handed receiver to Mary, who had already forgotten and said to the Queen, 'And who are you? What do you want?' After that conversation she said she wished to speak to her brother. David said that would be difficult and had she not better speak to her sister-in-law? 'No,' she replied, 'she is an absolutely horrid woman.' Next day Caroline took a party of distinguished American ladies to the house by appointment. Mary greeted them with kindness, mistook them for a choir, and said, 'Now tell me what you are going to sing.'

Went to see Anthony Chaplin in bed last week in flat lent him by Elizabeth Sutherland.* Looked less bad than I expected. Colour grey, but he had not been shaved for some days. Hair not white. But extremely thin, eyes glazed and sunken. Delighted to see me and held my hand for long time. Tears and laughter. When I said I heard that his children had been good to him, he sobbed; also when he spoke of Elizabeth's kindness. I asked him if he had been through any spiritual experiences during his illness. Brightened up at this. Said he had been thinking of Judas Iscariot and felt sorry for him. This reduced him to tears, which seemed an odd cause of grief. Poor Anthony, full of jokes just the same. I cannot see that he will live very long. Said he had written an anthem while in hospital which he was sending to the Bishop of Lincoln. A. says this not possible, as he has been incapable of writing a score or thinking consecutively.

Tuesday, 19th May

Looked at *Panorama* last night, about American rearmament. Very disturbing. On my way to Bath this morning with the dogs – A. being in London – I felt sure that before many years have passed, Russia will deliver an ultimatum to the West demanding complete capitulation within a week. If she does not receive it she will fire the first nuclear bomb, which will cause appalling devastation. There will be no need to launch two. Yet she does not want to take over a devastated West.

With these thoughts in mind I went into No. 19. There was a heavenly letter from M. written before he left for Florence last Sunday. We must write more often, he says. I work jubilantly.

---

* 24th Countess of Sutherland (b. 1921), kinswoman of Lord Chaplin.

Monday, 25th May

Sachie and Gervase Jackson-Stops* leave. Stayed two nights. Sachie extremely forgetful. Repeats his stories and, worse still, asks one to repeat one's own stories, sometimes six times over. But he has pulled himself together miraculously since Georgia's death. Says there is nothing to live for without her. Wakes up in the morning, thinks of something she would be amused to hear, turns over in bed, sees empty space and remembers. I had a bad cold, felt rotten, and did not go out to dinner with the Somersets or lunch with the Barlows.

Anne Rosse wrote me an amusing letter about Lady de Vesci who will be a hundred next year. Lady de V. complaining as usual about the wretched life she had had. 'But Mummy darling,' says Anne in a voice calculated to annoy, 'you had two husbands you loved very much, and two lovely honeymoons.' 'They were horrible, the honeymoons,' said Lady de V. 'I have always hated travelling. In Constantinople I had the curse. Besides, I found all that fiddlin' and heavy breathin' very tiresome.'

The Kaiser's great-grandson brought to have a drink with us. Has married extremely pretty Mancroft daughter. Sweet couple they are. He bright and extremely English, in fact his mother was a Guinness. Knows nothing about the German relations and had not heard of his great-aunt, the recently deceased Duchess of Brunswick, the Kaiser's daughter who published a year or so back the most fascinating book of memoirs. I exhorted him to read them for I said her book gave a very sympathetic picture of the Kaiser. 'Yes,' he said, 'I am afraid there is no book which gives him a fair assessment.'

Friday, 29th May

Went with J.K.-B. to *Salomé* at Coliseum. An extremely good production. The opera excellent and quite unknown to me, as was the whole cast. Next day, having stayed with J., I had Charles Orwin and Richard Robinson[†] to lunch at Brooks's. Found Richard rather too po-faced and very indecisive about what he wishes to do. Is playing with the Victorian Society, I fear. Then meeting at Chatto's with Norah and Nigel Nicolson who most kindly brought a suitcase of

---

* Architectural historian and adviser to N.T. (1947–95).
† Youngest of J.L.-M's Robinson great-nephews, who became a banker.

photographs of Harold and Sissinghurst for Vol. II. Went on to Midi who is out of hospital and back at Cranmer Court. Looking well in spite of heart trouble, but will always be an invalid. Brian[*] came in, wearing a cherry pullover and blue jeans and looking distinguished and handsome with his oval face, sharp quizzical eyes and abrupt manner. Has become an attractive young man.

A. and I motor to Chatsworth for weekend. Take the dogs with us. Also staying dogwise are Pam's dog Beetle and Christopher Sykes's bull-terrier. House so enormous that, so long as they do not pee indoors, Debo does not mind how many there are. We called first at Sheffield to see John Betjeman in Hallamshire Hospital. Has a room to himself which, such is his distinction, they will not allow him to pay for. Room a sort of glass eyrie at top of tall modern block. Like being in a glass box, for the walls are seemingly of white glass. I would find it depressing looking out at view of ugly modern blocks and chimneys and distant grey hills. John sitting in chair, much thinner in face, with slight twist to his mouth which disturbs customary picture of him. Alert but not cheerful and longs to get away, after six weeks. Feeble there, of course, motors in every day and now takes him for drives.

Greeted at Chatsworth by Andrew, extremely well-mannered, welcoming, no longer intimidating. David Mlinaric the decorator, and wife. He has long nose and silhouette like Aubrey Beardsley. She the daughter of Bob Laycock,[†] that charmer of Eton days, and granddaughter of Freda Dudley Ward[‡] that was. Says her grandmother still compos though frail. Confirmed truth of all we had been told about Prince of Wales's caddish treatment of her, that first she knew of being chucked was when the telephone operator at St James's Palace said tearfully, 'Madam, I am very sorry to have to tell you that His Royal Highness will not accept further calls from you.'

Christopher Sykes, nephew of my contemporary Christopher, also staying.[§] Charming, bright, funny, pudding looks. Plays piano well and sang to us his own composition of letter received from Lady

---

[*] Her yr son Brian Gascoigne (b. 1943).

[†] Major-General Sir Robert Laycock (1907–68); Chief of Combined Operations, 1943–7; m. 1935 Angela Dudley Ward.

[‡] (1894–1983); close friend of Edward, Prince of Wales from 1918 to 1934, the circumstances of their rupture being a matter of some dispute. She married, 1st, 1913, William Dudley Ward MP; 2nd, 1937, the Marques de Casa Maury.

[§] Christopher Simon Sykes (b. 1948), writer and photographer; his uncle Christopher Sykes (1907–86).

Spencer* turning down request for information about distant Spencers for his book *Black Sheep*. Uproarious. Heywood and Anne staying. Food by French chef incomparable.

Monday, 1st June

Had hoped to find letter from M. in Bath, but no letter and no telephone call. Haven't heard from him since I telephoned him last Tuesday. Thought I did not mind any more. Find I still do. Damn!

Folly killed a squirrel. Caught it in a flash. I saw a slight tussle in the grass. It was dead in an instant. So curious how dogs do not kill in anger, unlike wild beasts which look angry. Our dogs do not know what hatred is. It is the chase. When I called her she left the corpse, and on our return from the walk she did not nose it out. Do all creatures die with their eyes open? I wish they didn't.

Tuesday, 2nd June

We attended garden party at Montacute to mark 50th anniversary of presentation of the house and village to the National Trust. I remember Oliver Esher† describing to me how he stood on a very small wooden pedestal with the Princess Royal in pouring rain and a howling gale so that neither could hear what the other said. I think my second-hand recollections which I gave the Wessex Office today were passed on to the Duke of Gloucester,‡ because he mentioned these facts which he could not have known otherwise. He is an undistinguished youth, badly dressed in a sloppy City suit and yellow shirt, hair falling over his face which he brushed back with his hand. He made quite a good speech read from typewritten sheet. Was followed by Hugh Grafton§ whose speaking has much improved. Saw a number

---

* Raine McCorquodale (b. 1929); m. (2nd) 1976, 8th Earl Spencer of Althorp, Northamptonshire.

† Oliver Brett, 3rd Viscount Esher (1881–1963); Chairman of Historic Buildings Committee of National Trust; President of Society for Protection of Ancient Buildings.

‡ Born HRH Prince Richard of Gloucester (1944), yr son of HRH Prince Henry, Duke of Gloucester (3rd son of King George V) and Lady Alice Montagu-Douglas-Scott; m. 1972, Birgitte van Deurs; architect and photographer; following death of brother in plane crash, 1972, succeeded to dukedom, 1974.

§ Hugh FitzRoy, 11th Duke of Grafton (b. 1919); architectural conservationist; Chairman of Society for Protection of Ancient Buildings; J.L.-M's colleague on National Trust Properties Committee.

of grisly old faces there from the distant past. I shun them because after
initial words of greeting there is nothing further to say. Was accosted
by Yates the old custodian's son, bent like a crochet-hook, toothless
and purple of visage, but wearing very smart spongebag suit and old-
fashioned square bowler like the Yellow Earl of Lonsdale.* Presented
himself to Duke of Gloucester as son of the late squire who came to
Montacute after Lord Curzon. This must have surprised Baba
Metcalfe† for she was present. Warmly embraced me, and asked us to
meet her when the ceremonies over to accompany her round the
house and be shown her old bedroom as a child here in the 1920s –
for Lord Curzon died in 1925.

Like all talks with royal personages on these occasions, and indeed
my few audiences with popes, my conversation with the Duke of
Gloucester was clipped, awkward and pointless. A. and I were stood
in a line of folk. He was brought up to us by Miss Brotherton,
Chairman of the Wessex Committee, whom we had never met
before. She got our names right. The young Duke shook hands and
stood silent. Then he said, 'I think I have read several of your books?'
I said he might have done. 'Do you still write them?' (I suppose I
looked old and gaga.) 'I don't write books about architecture any
longer, Sir.' 'Why is that?' 'Oh, because the young architectural historians are so clever that I daren't.' 'That seems a pity. Do you really
think they are?' 'Yes, they are so highly trained by the Courtauld
Institute and universities that they become immensely erudite on a
specialised subject.' 'What do you write, then?' I murmured something
about H.N., which he was evidently unaware of. It must be agony for
'them'. I fancy one should be tremendously jolly and crack jokes. That
is what 'they' like.

Taken by Dale‡ to her mother-in-law's house, Lady Sutton having
pestered us for years to see the Sutton pictures. Some of them indeed
interesting. Pair of Gainsborough landscapes now in bank; but the
large Lawrence group of Sir Richard holding a dead pheasant over his

---

* Hugh Cecil Lowther, 5th Earl of Lonsdale (1857–1944); Cumberland landowner and
noted sportsman, president of the National Sporting Club; founder (1909) and presenter
of boxing's Lonsdale Belts.
† Lady Alexandra Curzon (1904–95); dau. of Marquess Curzon of Kedleston; m. 1925
Major E.D. ('Fruity') Metcalfe (d. 1957).
‡ Dale Stevens (b. 1944), dau of J.L.–M's sister Audrey by her 2nd marriage; m. (1964)
James Sutton (b. 1940), yr son of Sir Robert Sutton, 8th Bt.

wife's head a good picture if not an attractive conception. Lady S. a great goose but a good-natured, well-meaning soul. Told me that when first married she was taken to stay at Belvoir. That amidst the great luxury of the household it was amazing there was no toilet paper, as she called it. Instead a basketful of old letters torn in half. She amused herself piecing them together for hours while sitting on the seat.

Thursday, 4th June

Freezing day as usual on this blessed anniversary of George III's birthday. At 10 a.m. went by appointment to see Doric House just below No. 19. A Mr Thompson, tycoon who travels round the world, is the incumbent. Nice man, loves the house, is interested in Barker of Bath* for whom house built by Gandy and has two little Barker oils. You enter spacious hall with curling staircase, elegant and delicate. On right was dining room, now demolished by bomb in War. On left large double cube room with thirty-foot-long fresco by Barker of Turks and Greeks at it in Greek War of Independence, 1822. Not an attractive subject or well executed – I preferred a water-colour copy of 1850 which Thompson has on an easel – but an extraordinarily ambitious work. Barker may have been like Bejamin Haydon I think. He allowed visitors to see his collection of pictures and they had to see the fresco too, an advertisement of his wares.

Rushed to London to lunch with Rosalie Mander. Nice little party in her Buckingham Gate flat – an ex-British Council man from Rome, Mary Lutyens,† and Simon Houfe, grandson of Professor Richardson.‡ The B.C. man talked too much and left early. Better when he went. Liked Rosalie and take back disagreeable things I may have said about her pretensions. She is good in her own house, relaxed. Houfe bright and agreeable. I liked Mary immensely. Very sympathetic. Was born in my year. Has straight silvery hair cut short. Lean face, big bags under eyes, sweet expression. Talked of her artist

---

* Thomas Barker (1769–1847); English painter of rural and other scenes; Doric House is in Sion Hill (*c.* 1818), by the architect Joseph Michael Gandy (1771–1843).

† Author (1908–99); daughter of Sir Edwin Lutyens; m. 1945, J.G. Links, Canaletto expert.

‡ Professor A.E. Richardson, RA, FRIBA (1880–1964); *inter alia*, Prof. of Architecture, London University, 1919–46. There are numerous references to him in J.L.-M's diaries 1946–8.

granddaughter, aged twenty-two or so, who has been living in sin for
two years with another British artist and doesn't know the boyfriend's
surname. The extraordinary incuriosity of the young.

Friday, 5th June

Fetched Perks from Hawkesbury this morning for A. On the way
back he complained to me of interference. 'The Conservatives say we
may not paint the houses in our streets the colours we want to have.'
By this he means conservationists. 'We don't want no interference. We
looks after our houses beautiful.' What is one to do? Democracy is at
a discount in face of such ignorance. Besides, he did not know who
these 'Conservatives' were – the Parish Council, County Council,
Civic Trust, who?

Tuesday, 9th June

Lunched with M. at his flat. A most happy reunion. Was delighted
that he received this morn. the letter I wrote him in the train yesterday and left behind in the carriage. The guard must have found and
posted it. M. full of sweetness and confidences.

Wednesday, 10th June

Bobby Gore,* who was staying last weekend, with George Dix, told
me he has twice seen Anthony Blunt since the scandal. Bobby was
very upset by it and wrote commiserating with Blunt. Blunt replied
that affection remained whereas malice evaporated; made no mention
of the case, and at once continued about Pietro da Cortona whom he
had just discovered and considered a far greater architect than hitherto
supposed. Bobby thinks he is a dual personality, able to switch off one
personality and assume the other at will. I said A.B. must surely have
been terribly upset by the scandal and sensitive about being seen in
public and running risk of insults. Bobby does not think so at all, and
that he is quite indifferent to what the press has written of him.

Went up for Pat Trevor-Roper's dinner party at the Beefsteak Club,
in that absurd baronial hall. At least thirty guests, all at one enormously

---

* Francis St John Gore (b. 1921); adviser on pictures to National Trust, 1956–86; Historic
Buildings Secretary, 1973–81.

long table. Like a Waterloo Banquet,* without the groaning silver
plate. I sat next to Diana Cooper on my right and Pat's left. On my
left a nice man called Michael Howard,† distinguished Oxford don.
Howard said H.N's fault was a desire to be liked. I said it was softness.
He told me that when he was twenty-two he went to a psychologist
and said he feared he was homosexual. 'If that's all, don't waste my
time,' the psychologist said.

Diana talked to me practically throughout, for Pat much occupied
by neighbour on his right, Lady Dufferin, whom he kept pawing and
kissing. Diana wearing a short black veil which just covered top of her
nose. I was very close to her and was amazed by the beauty of her
profile and clarity of her blue eyes. But she talked of her extreme
unhappiness. Began on drugs and ways of ending things. Thought her
friend Randolph Churchill's wife‡ had been so sensible and brave
doing herself in. Said during First War she administered drugs. They
were laudanum then. She only quite likes her biography by Ziegler,§
but wants him to think she is very pleased for she likes *him* so much.
Says some revelations in it about her and Duff which astonish her.
Things she never knew about. Her marriage was a blissful success
because they agreed from the start never to be faithful. They always
loved one another. She was never jealous. Never had been. All children should be brought up to eschew jealousy.

There is something pitiable about Diana who for decades had the
world at her feet, and still has really; but the world means nothing to
her. She is deaf, wears concealed hearing-aid which causes her pain
when noises made like the fire brigade passing (it did while we were
talking) and can taste nothing. Cannot tell the difference between
garlic and eau-de-Cologne. Smell too completely gone. She ate one
course only, namely avocado pear covered with banana and shrimps,
not nice, and drank moderately. I found it tiring talking to her with
so much conversation on all sides. A strain bending down to catch her

---

* The Duke of Wellington's annual banquet (from 1830 until his death) at Apsley House
for veterans of the battle, who crammed around a long table bearing a huge silver centre-
piece, a gift from the Portuguese Government.
† Sir Michael Eliot Howard (b. 1922); Regius Professor of Modern History, Oxford,
1980.
‡ This of course is a reference to Randolph Churchill's 2nd wife, June Osborne (m. 1948;
m. diss. 1961); his 1st wife, Hon. Pamela Digby (m. 1939; m. diss. 1946) d., as Pamela
Harriman, only in 1997.
§ Philip Ziegler (b. 1929); publisher and author.

words. Such a banquet can only be satisfying to the host for his generosity. There is nowhere for guests to mingle and talk. No changing
of seats. At midnight there was a move to go. I had a word with
Gladwyn and asked him why no government would reform the
House of Lords. Surely, I said, it would be sensible to do so before
Benn* has authority to abolish it. Gladwyn did not agree. He said
reform would give the House of Lords power which it now has not
got. As it is, the House does no harm and in fact much good. Any
tampering with it would be a mistake. It must either be left alone or
abolished. He thought Benn would not get power unless unemployment reached the four-million mark. Then anything might happen.
Walked back to Eardley through empty streets.

Thursday, 11th June

Selina Hastings† motored down from London to lunch with me in
Bath and talk about Nancy [Mitford] and Rosamond [Lehmann]
whose lives she is writing. She turned on a tape recorder after luncheon which cramped my style. Although I did not hear it whirling I was
conscious that it was on, and felt constrained. Anyway a dangerous
thing to have permitted. I begged her not to let anyone hear what I
said for the last thing I wished was to offend the Mitfords or
Rosamond. She promised. Indeed I was delighted with her. She is near
perfection. Is gentle, moderate, pretty, intelligent and sympathetic. I
have not been so attracted by a girl her age for years. When she left two
young Broadcasting men, bearded, came to talk about a film they are
prospecting for. Anxious to find a 1700 house with contemporary
garden for filming. Every suggestion provoked an objection. They too
were charming and friendly. Really, how nice the young are to one.

Saturday, 20th June

Watched Nureyev‡ on telly last night, interviewed at a table in a restaurant. Noise of people talking at distant tables in background. He

---

* Rt Hon. Anthony Wedgwood Benn, formerly 2nd Viscount Stansgate, Secretary of
State for Energy, 1975–9, subsequently the leading radical in Parliamentary Labour Party.
† Lady Selina Hastings (b. 1945), d. of 15th Earl of Huntingdon; biographer and journalist.
‡ Rudolf Nureyev (1939–1993), Russian dancer.

was eating like an animal, at a speed I have only seen equalled by Christopher Glenconner. He was also drinking, far too much I would say. Now forty-three. Has lost looks, yet much of the magic remains. Speaks with vehemence, staring at camera with eyes of a fanatic. Radiates self-confidence, not altogether attractive. When asked what he would do when day came when he was too old to dance, he indignantly repudiated the idea it would ever come. 'I can dance now as well as I ever did.' Then throw-backs to scenes from his dancing career, the litheness, the panther-like movements. No one in my time has had these animal qualities so markedly. His determination is ruthless. I understand his colleagues hate him because he treats them abominably. The Russian accent is very attractive. Altogether he is the sexiest person I have ever seen. When asked if he had time for an emotional life, he replied, 'Oh yes, but the people I am in love with have to understand that my art comes first', or words to that effect.

Had a reply from John Phillips* in Monaco to my letter in which I apologised for not asking his permission to quote from Violet Trefusis's letters to Vita. He had been incensed; now mollified by my grovelling letter. Furthermore told me that Violet had specifically left me the George IV gold box, and enclosed xerox copy of relevant codicil to will. Said Lord Ashcombe went off with it and other treasures kept in a showcase in V's bedroom. So I have written to Lord Ashcombe, V's nephew, pointing this out and asking for the box. Interesting to know what his reply will be.

Monday, 29th June

On Saturday the garden open. Fine day, intermittent cloud and sun, but cold wind. Haven't yet worn summer clothes. A. has become a celebrity. People come here in order to talk to her about gardening. Photographers abound, and press ladies like Penelope Mortimer.† I am impressed.

I went to London for the day to take my page proofs to Chatto's, having first had a long interview with Douglas Matthews, Librarian of the London Library, who is making an index of Vol. II as he did of Vol. I. A clever, well-informed man of great modesty. Amazing the

---

* Friend and executor of Violet Trefusis.
† Writer (1918–99); m. (2nd) 1949–72 John Mortimer, QC, playwright and author (b. 1923).

number of small mistakes he found – such as 'awarded the Legion of Honour' whereas it should be 'made a member of'. Main purpose of visit to see M. who goes to Paris again on Thursday. He lunched and I went to his flat for a cup of tea. I said that at times I told myself that I could bear it if he disappeared from my life, but that after three days I had a longing for him, and would be wretchedly unhappy without him. His retort was, 'You will get tired of me first.'

I am saddened that when with Eardley, our old-established delight in each other's company, our perpetual laughter and giggles, seem to have abated. He seems staider, a trifle disapproving, unresponsive. Yet he writes me such affectionate letters. I have so often seen old friends estranged purely through old age. I hope this does not happen with us.

Was told last Sunday by Robert Heber-Percy* that the late Lord Westmorland, Diana's husband, used to put the fire out before going to bed by peeing in it. A pretty trick.

Wednesday, 8th July

The Duke of Beaufort admitted to David that not only had he not written his recently published *Memoirs*, he had not read them. They were written by his *maîtresse en titre*, Lady Cottesloe, and he has not so much as glanced at them, though published under his name. Vicar says it is embarrassing reading.

My Anthology is fated not to be done. I hoped to have this entire week free for it, but no. Fuss with insurance company and garage about my motor accident; fuss about tickets to Mount Athos. These sound trivial interruptions but have taken up more hours than thought possible. Then received letters from both Debo and Diana with helpful corrections of my Nancy piece for *DNB*, which necessitates alterations and retyping. Then comes Douglas Matthews' index to H.N. Vol. II, full of small mistakes which I have to correct.

Friday, 10th July

Motor to Bath on a hot midsummer morning. From all sides the sweet smell of amber hay wafts through the car window. The sun is not fully

---

* Robert Heber-Percy (1912–87), of Faringdon House, Oxon.; equestrian personality, friend and legatee of Gerald Tyrwhitt-Wilson, 14th Baron Berners (1883–1950; the model for Lord Merlin in Nancy Mitford's *The Pursuit of Love*).

up. Through a heavy haze it strikes the distant woodlands powdery blue. Intenser blue conveyed to the landscape by my adored *Geranium pratense*, never in such abundance as this year. But alas, they have cut the road verge between Acton Turville and Tormarton so that only an inner strip is left. I fear this may mean that the geranium has not seeded and that next year the crop will accordingly diminish. How hellishly insensitive highway authorities are, with their hostility to what they call 'noxious weeds'. Very wonderful these midsummer mornings are, but how few.

Saturday, 11th July

Walked from the Preeces' lodge up the old drive to Newark with the dogs. A canopy of green above me, sunlight flickering upon the rutted drive. Overhead a susurration among the leaves from the wind, whereas below all still. Most remarkable abundance this year of stonecrop. It sprawls over the walls, like great yellow sponges. Seems to collect all the sunshine and radiates it when sun is behind cloud, upon the grey days, like heat from the sun stored in those tanks people in the south keep on their rooftops.

Wednesday, 15th July

Peggy this morning told A. that St Swithin's Day was known as Apple Christening Day in these parts. Reason that the rain – and it always rains on this day, come what may – first ripens the apples. As A. motors me to Bath under a grey sky, a gentle drizzle slowly descends.

Poor Ann Fleming died on Sunday. On Saturday I telephoned Susanna Johnson, who was at Heber-Percys' luncheon last weekend telling how she had just come that morning from Ann's bedside, how more growths had broken out in her body, how she still wanted news of what was happening in the world, and how ghastly it was to watch her die, helpless. I telephoned to ask if there was any message I could send Ann, for I had never been a correspondent, yet would like to send my love and oblique thanks for all the kindness I had received from her in the past. Susanna said it was too late for she was now in a coma. It was only lately that I had grown to like Ann. I was a little frightened of her in the past for she was so intensely bright, so 'au fait', so up to date, a little brassy and seemingly hard. Within the last few years since she moved to Sevenhampton I learned to appreciate her kindness, her loyalty to friends, her intense interest in the things of the mind. She must be the last of the great hostesses. I did not like Ian at all, a most unsympathetic and brash individual.

In London yesterday had Dr N. to lunch at Brooks's. Simply a matter of kindness for I knew he wanted to be invited. I had warned him that I had a N.T. meeting at 2.30. On one little finger a huge staring diamond; on the other an emerald; gold bracelets jangling from hairy wrists. We had nothing to say to one another. But he did vouchsafe that H.N. once had an appointment with him, not as a patient but to discuss condition of Michael Clayton-Hutton, one of H's lame dogs, a curious half-genius poet who soon suicided himself (though not before he slept with me).

Friday, 17th July

A. and I motored to Firle for weekend. Lunched en route with Dreda Tryon* near Salisbury. She took us to Heale House, the house which Vita for some strange reason always said we should buy. It belongs to David Somerset's sister and brother-in-law. A disappointing house. Original part of red brick, late seventeenth-century, rather spoilt with ungainly additions of 1920s. A rambling, overgrown garden. She charming, reminding me of E. Winn but less sharp; and is un-smart. She is natural, easy, enlivening. Continued to Firle via Petworth. Dreadful motoring, down twisted, narrow roads, always at end of a queue with slow caravan at its head. Arrived exhausted. The Beits staying. An enjoyable weekend in this lovely, Frenchified house. Clementine [Beit] buttonholes one with long, unpointful stories. Alf I like much, for he is on the ball, interested in everything, and amused if not amusing. A dear man. Rainald Gage older than ever, fat, round, crumpled, inarticulate.† Gasps like a stranded fish and talks to himself, or rather murmurs. Impossible to hear what he says, and Diana hardly easier, for she gabbles.

Saturday, 18th July

Wandered in park this morning with Clementine telling me about her father to whom her grandfather Redesdale was never nice. Her

---

* Etheldreda Josephine (b. 1909), dau. of Sir Merrik Raymond Burrell, 7th Bt, m., 1939, 2nd Baron Tryon (he d. 1976).
† Henry Rainald, 6th Viscount Gage (1895–1982), of Firle Place, Sussex; m. (2nd) 1971, Diana (*née* Cavendish), Hon. Mrs Campbell-Gray.

widowed mother hated the Mitfords and tried to keep her and Rosemary from them when they were children. Before luncheon Madame Matisse brought over. Were told she was the widow of the artist and became excited. But she was in fact the widow of a son, a dull, bourgeois lady. Gages and Beits went to Glyndebourne on Sat. so A. and I dined with Jack and Frankie Donaldson. Frankie told me she was writing a history of British Council and had many questions to ask me about George Lloyd.[*] Produced a review by me in *Spectator* 1949 of Colin Forbes Adam's Life. I had forgotten I had written it. Then said she had been approached by Sidgwick & Jackson through Lord Longford, the recent chairman, to write life of 2nd Lord Esher. Thought him a fascinating subject and suggested my doing it. I thought it over during the night.

Sunday, 19th July

Donaldons come to luncheon. I sit next to Frankie and tell her I am interested in Lord Esher project. She will telephone Frank Longford and communicate with me on Monday.

Go to church at eleven. George Gage[†] reads both lessons. Is quite inaudible. Am handed a Prayer Book bound in red morocco of 1790 with Gage coat-of-arms embossed. In prayers for Royal Family, 'George' and 'Charlotte' are neatly pencilled out and 'William' and 'Adelaide' substituted. Service in Series I of course. Something most feudal about our filing in last, and ushered into two pews isolated for the family. After service we inspect the Gage tombs in Gage chapel. Gages have been here since 1440s.

Before luncheon, A. and I go to Professor Bell's[‡] and buy five of his pottery bowls and plates. Very beautiful they are. Charges us £100, quite cheap. Are given a glass of wine. He charming and belies the impression conveyed over television of pedantic Father Christmas. True, wears long beard, but underneath a sweet and gentle face. Speaks softly, diffidently. She tall, badly dressed, clever, direct. Liked

---

[*] George Lloyd, 1st Lord Lloyd of Dolobran (1879–1941); High Commissioner for Egypt, 1925–9; Chairman of British Council, 1936–40; Secretary of State for the Colonies, 1940–1; J.L.-M. served as his private secretary, 1931–5.

[†] Elder son and heir of 6th Viscount Gage (b. 1932).

[‡] Quentin Bell (1910–96); author, artist and potter; Professor of History of Art, Sussex University; 2nd son of Clive Bell and Vanessa Stephen; m. 1952 Anne Popham.

them both. We also went over Charleston again. It is bought now by
National Trust and work is about to begin. The condition is terribly
down-at-heel. I don't fancy it because the Vanessa–Duncan decora-
tion is of ephemeral sort, which they dabbed over from time to time.
Was never intended to be permanent. A waste of money.

A. and I to Glyndebourne Opera. *Ariadne*. Much Wagnerian
screaming. But lovely music, similar to other Strauss operas. We motor
home, through suburbs from Gatwick to Heathrow, arriving home at
one in the morning. Very tired.

Monday, 20th July

Find in Bath a long, affectionate but depressed letter from M. He is
in a trough and cannot write. Has got himself into a muddle. Am
worried about him.

Tuesday, 21st July

A. and I to London for Buckingham Palace Garden Party. In great discomfort for foolishly put on my best pair of black shoes which pinch
fiendishly. We went with the Berkeleys, driven by dotty George in
their car. A fine day, but coolish. Claps of thunder, but did not rain.
Thousands of guests. We had to walk beyond the entrance to Queen's
Gallery in Buck. Pal. Road to join queue to Palace. Shuffled painfully.
A. dressed in pretty striped black and white dress and white bowler
hat with veil, most becoming. Ushered through the main courtyard
to facing entrance. Fine protective canopy carried by metal struts of
Nash date, and great globe lanterns with crowns thereon. Up staircase
to transverse gallery; pretty Regency staircase, at one end Royal portraits. Through large central room giving on to gardens. Homely yet
majestic. In four corners of this room most splendid Chelsea dinner
service, the Mecklenburg-Strelitz service in blue and white and gold.
On to terrace of garden. This side of the palace is Nash in beautiful
Bath stone. The Edwardian block we see by Blomfield is a brute and
grotesquely disproportionate to the old palace. It is a crying shame
that the Hilton Hotel was allowed, also beastly skyscraper to south.
Both overlook and ruin privacy of gardens. Huge but pretty pavilions
erected on either side to accommodate staff and teas, which we ate on
tables on the lawn. Walked down to the lake but both so suffering
from foot trouble that we could not walk round the lake. Looked at
herbaceous borders however. The best sort of municipal style, a galaxy
of colours.

After waiting for apparently endless stream of visitors descending the steps, at four o'clock the Queen and Duke of Edinburgh appeared, followed by the Kents. 'God Save the Queen' played by a band which was inaudible. The Queen descended steps and mingled with guests. We did not see her again. In fact saw no one we knew, save George Howard, Sir Harold and Lady Wilson, Enoch Powells and Ted Heath. Freda introduced me to latter. I liked his firm handshake and cordial expression of blue eyes.*

Wednesday, 22nd July

Had an interview at Sidgwick & Jackson with Frank Longford[†] who was chairman until lately and is now a director, the new chairman William Armstrong, who did not impress me, and a bright girl called Margaret Willes who spoke of Diana Mosley as 'Diana'. There is always a bright girl with credentials in every publishing house today. They are keen that I should undertake biography of 2nd Lord Esher. Discussed matter for an hour. First thing is for them to find out whether Lionel Esher will approve of me, which I doubt and told them so. Don't think he likes me much since the brush I had with him over Bath. How much do I want to tackle this man's life? He is not romantic. He is an Establishment figure with a skeleton in the cupboard. Longford kept on emphasising this as the most interesting and important aspect. For Lord E. was the *éminence grise* of his time, a sort of Lord Goodman, with immense influence. Lord L. very flattering and friendly. Frankie Donaldson says he is a monster, with a mind set on self- and family advertisement. But if he advertises my book it will be a nice change. He says it is the sort of book which will be serialised.

Monday, 27th July

John Harris[‡] has lent me his file of quotations, but to my surprise they are of little use. Too much historical description, too little concern-

---

* J.L.-M. had already met the former Prime Minister: see entry for 5 July 1974, *Ancient as the Hills.*
† Francis Pakenham, 7th Earl of Longford (1905–2001); Labour Party politician, publisher and humanitarian campaigner; m. 1931 Elizabeth Harman, writer.
‡ Curator, 1960–86, of British Architectural Library's Drawings Collection and Heinz Gallery, and writer on architectural subjects (b. 1931).

ing customs or unusual behaviour. I am not sure what exactly I want
for my Country House Anthology but I do want quotations which
will entertain or surprise.

Met M. at Brooks's. He brought me a present and I gave him one.
Lunched alone with Rosamond who is inundated by biographers of
people she knew. Says there are ten besieging her at this moment,
including her own, Selina Hastings, and she hasn't a moment to
herself. Yet I think she is delighted to be the grand old lady of letters,
to whom the young come and sit at her dear feet. She is having a
swimgloat over the republication of her novels and much public recognition. She complained that her brother John was discontented
with his lot although he has received several honours and she has none.
I wish she could be made a Dame. There is no doubt that everyone
likes recognition however much they may protest that honours mean
nothing to them. We ate smoked salmon and cheese and drank
Malvern water with lemon. M. has written asking to see her about
Sibyl [Colefax], but Ros asked me to tell him that she has nothing to
say about S. who was never in her confidence. Yet M. tells me he has
read intimate letters from Ros to Sibyl pouring out her heart at the
time of her being jilted by Cecil Day-Lewis, which Ros has forgotten. I talked to Ros about her letters to me. She says I should lend
them to Selina who will be discreet. Somehow I don't like the idea.
It may put a constraint on our future correspondence. Like speaking
to Selina with the tape recorder whizzing round.

Wednesday, 29th July

Stayed at home all morning watching and listening to the Wedding
[of HRH The Prince of Wales to Lady Diana Spencer]. A. and I
greatly moved. It was the best form of pageantry. A wonderful experience. The fairy-like beauty of the carriages, the coachmen's liveries,
their cocked hats with tassels hanging from the corners, the grey
horses' manes plaited with silver thread, and the ravishing beauty of
Lady Diana's dress, train of twenty-five feet, gossamer veil, her side-
long glances from those large round blue eyes. She is adorable.

Sunday, 2nd August

Pam brought Diana Mo[sley] to luncheon. Had Rupert Loewenstein
to meet her and a nice young son of Tom Gibson the Vicar, polite,

shy and fair, who is working on the *Wiltshire Times*. Diana holds the
stage always. She is immensely intelligent. Beautiful face rather creased
on closer inspection. Was wearing a black dress; still in mourning
which is strange in England, but probably expected in France.

Diana said her stepson Ravensdale* was furious with the Home
Office for refusing to disgorge papers relating to the imprisonment of
the Mosleys during the War. They declare that the Thirty-Year Rule
does not apply to them. D. wants subject raised in House of Lords.
Ravensdale is writing a memoir of Sir Oswald. D. may write a life of
the Kaiser. She will be careful to be objective, yet thinks a good case
can be made for him in 1914. I told her that Lord Carisbrooke told
H.N. that King Edward VII loathed his nephew because latter sneaked
to Queen Victoria about his affair with Lady Warwick. Diana
remarked that the universal reference to William II as 'the Kaiser' was
meant as a disparaging title. The Emperor Franz-Josef of Austria, just
as much a Kaiser as the other, was never referred to as such by us. She
thinks Britain was jealous of Germany's growing commercial power.
Sidgwick & Jackson are her publishers. She told me how much she
loved Frank Longford and Elizabeth, though she thought E's book on
Queen Mother was awful.

Thursday, 6th August

My seventy-third birthday. A. went to France on Monday to stay with
Rory Cameron† to get some sun and warmth. In her absence I realise
the amount of hard work she has to do – buying food, gardening and
cooking. I have been watering for her these three hot days. Very
exhausting too. I ricked a muscle over the heart on Monday evening
and was in considerable discomfort. The hatefulness of having a birthday alone only made endurable by the sweetness and attention of M.
Sally [Westminster] asked me to dinner; gave me delicious four
courses and claret, and a present of a small malachite dove bought in
Moscow. Deeply touched by her kindness, yet I would have preferred
to remain at home.

She told me that the Prince of Wales is a weak character. At the
Buckingham Palace ball on eve of wedding, he left his bride for several

---

* Nicholas Mosley, 3rd Baron Ravensdale (a title inherited through his mother), eldest
son of Sir Oswald Mosley and his first wife, Lady Cynthia Curzon; novelist (b. 1923).
† Hon. Roderick Cameron (1914–85), Anglo-American travel writer and gardener.

hours to spend the time of night with the Goons in another room. The pathetic little Lady D. was left alone, without an escort, to make conversation to people she did not know. This confirms what I have heard from other sources, that he is not in love with her.

a shit !

Saturday, 8th August

Have always noted that autumn begins on my birthday. Not so this year owing to the cold summer and wet. Trees still green. But today noticed, on walking across playing field with dogs, that the grass was spread with dewy cobwebs.

Thursday, 13 August

A's birthday. Lovely day. We motored to Hidcote and Kiftsgate gardens which she wanted to see. Lunched at sort of Polly's Pantry at Moreton-in-Marsh. Shades of olden days. Hidcote looking well in spite of August season when nothing much out, but crowds so enormous that it was absolutely no pleasure pushing one's way around. Decided I don't ever wish to go there again. Kiftsgate I have never admired. Lovely precipitous site of garden, but hideous house, and planting in bad taste. Called on Mrs Haines* who nearly had hysterics at seeing us, not having heard from one member of the family since January. She makes little sense, being stone deaf and ninety-two. Poor old thing. I had to grit my teeth to conceal my repugnance in kissing her, my dislike of old flesh being as acute as was Mama's.

Friday, 14th August

Dick [Lees-Milne]'s birthday. Drank a silent toast to him while washing up after our frugal evening meal. Frank Longford telephoned today to say that their project of a biography of 2nd Lord Esher is off. Lionel [Esher] has apparently given it to Michael Howard to do, he being a scholar of military history and in all respects well qualified to deal with it. Far better than I. I thanked Frank and thought that would be the end of Sidgwick's flirtation with me. But no. He said, 'Don't

---

* Formerly employed by J.L.-M's parents at Wickhamford Manor, married to Haines the chauffeur, and still living in the village.

think I have done with you. We are determined to get you to write a biog. for us.' Insisted on my lunching with them in London week after next. Meanwhile they are going to think out subjects for my choice. Asked if I would prefer a man or a woman. Said I didn't mind. Did I want a literary character? Rather foolishly I replied that being no literary critic, perhaps not. What I would like is a romantic personality. I can truthfully say that I am more interested in and excited by M's projects than my own.

Saturday, 15th August

Diana Westmorland told me that her younger brother Charles Lister was a very great friend of Alan Lascelles. She couldn't think why, they were so unlike. Charles, she said, was not handsome but charming. Lascelles proposed to Diana once. She rejected him. As a young man he was physically unattractive. I asked about her elder brother killed in Africa. She said he was very handsome. She remembers his coming home on leave as a hero: this must have been eighty years ago. Extraordinary thing was that her parents followed the drum. They accompanied their son during the Boer War, keeping just behind the lines.

We dined with Ian McCallum at Claverton. After dinner Ian said the most monstrous things – that there was no more freedom in this country than behind the Iron Curtain; that he strongly advocated unilateral disarmament on our part; that the police incited the blacks; that we tortured people in Ireland; that Mrs Thatcher was responsible for the anti-Conservation movement; that all politicians were rogues – and expressed the sort of sentiments one associates with Guy Burgess and A. Blunt. I was furious. Argued vehemently. The Briggses* who were present agreed with me. Isabel, sitting next to me on the sofa, said Ian's was a policy of despair, and most reprehensible. That England still maintained the decencies of life and was the happiest country to live in. I told Ian he was talking rubbish when he affirmed that one could no more express one's beliefs in this country than in Russia. I have never liked this man and always suspected he might be a traitor. Now I am certain he would be for twopence, to his personal advantage.

---

* Michael Briggs, businessman, connoisseur and aesthete, of Midford Castle, Bath; his wife, the novelist Isabel Colegate.

Sunday, 16th August

Spent hours searching in botanical books for name of a common yellow flower which grows profusely on walls. Botanical books are very hard to find one's way about in. Finally, convinced myself that it was *Corydalis lutea*, which I shall try and remember, though by this time tomorrow shall have forgotten. Is it a waste of brain space cramming the head with information of slight importance? Or does all knowledge acquired by a certain effort amount to treasure laid up in heaven?

Mary Pless,* staying at Badminton, called before luncheon. She is a friendly, jolly soul, a 'captain's daughter' and former wife of Hanzel Pless. They no longer live together but remain close friends. She told us how she had just visited Poland in order to see Pless Castle and another castle taken from her husband by the Bolsheviks. She found Pless Castle furnished with his pictures and other priceless things. She explained who she was and asked, at Hanzel's request, to be allowed to take photocopies of letters written to his ancestor by Catherine the Great. But the curator indignantly refused. She said the guide who accompanied her and translated was a bloody woman. Mary called on some old servants who said how devoted they were to the family and how happy they had been. While the interpreter was bound to translate these words, she told Mary not to believe a word of them, that these people had of course been downtrodden under the old regime. Mary replied, 'How can *you* know?'

Wednesday, 19th August

Brian Masters motored from London to lunch with me in Bath. Talked of his new book on English hostesses of this century. Talked of Sibyl, the Londonderrys. I said what a nice man I found Robin Castlereagh.† He said, 'But you have not read the letters he wrote his father. They are the unkindest, most unfilial letters I have ever read.' Brian M. is a nice young man. Extraordinary how he has adopted the manners of the aristocracy whom he has made his great study. Even

---

* Mary Minchin (b. 1928), m. 1958 (m. diss. 1971) Henry, Prince of Pless (d. 1984).
† Edward Charles Stewart Robert Vane-Tempest-Stewart, Viscount Castlereagh (1902–55); son and heir of 7th Marquess of Londonderry, to whose titles he succeeded 1949 (though by whom he was disinherited to greatest possible extent); Unionist MP for County Down; 1931–45.

so, one can see his origins are proletarian. I say this without any disparagement. His new book on Georgiana Duchess of Devonshire, which is excellent, well written and witty, has had no reviews and sold a mere hundred or so copies. How is it that good books like this one receive no acknowledgement whereas trash sells? Or rather, had this book been written by Antonia Pakenham,* who can't write for nuts, it would have had huge sales. I have written the Lit. Ed. of *Sunday Telegraph* begging him to review.

He told me that the present Lord Londonderry suffers from blue devils, an affliction inherent in his line since the time of Castlereagh who suicided himself in an access of despair. The present Marquess for no accountable reason retires for days on end to an inner room where he sees no one, eats little and sits with his head in his hands. He is totally abstemious having determined to avoid as far as possible his father's faults, of which alcoholism was the worst.

Have received a charming letter from Lionel Esher. Says I would surely not like his grandfather who was a detestable character. He thinks an American biographer will write it, but is not sure and will let me know. Decent of him to write. Norah writes that she would like a third volume of my diaries.

Friday, 21st August

My dear Uncle Robert's ninety-ninth birthday. God rest his pure soul.

Today Charles Orwin brought his lover, Nicholas Cann, art historian lecturing at Bath University, and Stuart Preston to see me. I took them for lunch to the Vendange. Cann an extremely handsome young man, immaculately dressed, intelligent, well-mannered and wearing a small moustache, the only moustache I have ever liked. Stuart told of his visit with Harold Acton to Gertrude Stein's house in Paris. Said that Alice B. Toklas was a midget. He was sitting on a high stool when he saw below him pass what he took to be a basket of fruit, oranges, lemons and grapes. Was about to pick a handful of the last when it dawned upon him that the basket was the hat worn by Miss Toklas. Stuart said the two chapters of M's book he has read are first-rate. Also praised highly Derek's portraits and landscapes. Thinks him one of the best living artists. When they left I telephoned M. in London. In a

---

* Better known as Lady Antonia Fraser (b. 1932), dau. of 7th Earl of Longford; m., 1st, 1956, Rt Hon. Sir Hugh Fraser (m. diss. 1977); 2nd, 1980, the playwright Harold Pinter.

euphoric state about the book, now going very well. Says he has written 130,000 words so far whereas the allotted length is 75,000.

Wednesday, 26th August

The two lady gardeners from Sissinghurst* lunched at Bad. and spent the day on Sunday. Delightful they were too. Sibille Kreutzberger told us of her life experiences. Her father was a Lutheran pastor in Hanover, her mother a Catholic. In 1938 the father and mother brought Sibille and her sister over to England where after a desperate search they found a kind family to look after them. They had foreseen war coming. When it broke out the father felt his duty was with his parishioners, and returned, accompanied by his wife. On the journey home the wife gave birth to a son, who remained in Germany and lives there now. The father was sent to Auschwitz camp where he somehow survived the War, only to be killed by an army truck the moment he was released. He had not known that his wife had been killed in an air raid during the War. Sibille was loved and cherished by the English foster parents. She went to Waterperry Horticultural School where she met Pamela Schwerdt, from whom she has not parted. The foster parents died last year and left Sibille a tidy fortune.

Last night we dined at Henbury with the Hewers.† Highly civilised couple. Have fashioned a marvellous garden in a dell. The village is now engulfed by Bristol. The grounds of Blaise Castle on one side of their garden fence and village church. Only two hundred yards away, workers' skyscrapers. Tom Hewer told me that his greatest achievement was the discovery of a cure for yellow fever in Central Africa. Another was an antidote to rabies. Said he loathed the Shah of Persia's family. Really bad lot. The brother trafficked in heroin, amassing a vast fortune. All the relations made fortunes out of the people and country. No sympathy need be wasted on them.

Thursday, 27th August

I lunched with Frank Longford, Armstrong and Margaret Willes at Gay Hussar in Greek Street. Delicious and expensive luncheon. I eagerly awaited suggestions for book they are determined I shall write

---

* Pamela Schwerdt and Sibille Kreutzberger, who went to Sissinghurst as head gardeners in 1959.
† Professor of Pathology, Bristol University, 1938–68 (1903–94); m. 1941 Anne Baker.

for them, if it is not to be Esher. Their suggestions however quite pre-
posterous. A Memoir of Vita; a History of the Mitford Family; a
Biography of Cyril Connolly. Since I have written two enormous vols
about Harold and Vita the first is out of the question, especially in
view of Victoria Glendinning's forthcoming biog of V. I pointed out
what they already knew, that Jonathan Guinness is writing history of
Mitfords, and another would neither be welcomed by the family nor
was called for. As for Connolly, I never much liked him and was not
qualified to write about an essentially literary figure. A wasted
meeting. Nevertheless I liked them all. They explained that the publishers of today could only afford to produce books on subjects widely
disseminated on television, such as Royal Wedding, the Mitfords, or
Bloomsbury or Nicolson scandals. Deeply depressing.

I have a tendency to fall asleep half an hour after I begin reading
a book, whether in bed at night or in my armchair in the afternoons
at home.

Friday, 28th August

Rosemary Chaplin, with whom I condoled on the death of Sir Alan
Lascelles, said she was sad, but since he had lent her two books which
she could not for the life of her find, he being extremely fussy and
listing names of borrowers and even asking for return of books after
a fortnight, she felt extreme relief. Nevertheless she was reproaching
herself for these callous thoughts.*

Thursday, 17th September

Derek smitten with hernia trouble which necessitated putting off
jaunt to Mount Athos. I was relieved because I was suffering from
extinction de voix and a bad chest and was alarmed by temperatures of
90 in Athens. But troublesome to get back some of the money spent
on expensive ticket, through insurance.

Took Derek to Long Crichel† for three nights instead, he anyway

---

* Lady Chaplin's late brother, 2nd Viscount Chandos (1920–80), had m. (1949) Caroline,
dau. of Sir Alan Lascelles.
† A long lease of this property, on the Crichel estate in Dorset, was granted in 1944 to
three friends of J.L.-M. – Eardley Knollys, Eddy Sackville-West and Demond Shawe-
Taylor. Some years later, Eardley and Eddy (the latter now Lord Sackville) dropped out,
being replaced by two other friends of J.L.-M. – Raymond Mortimer and Pat Trevor-
Roper. Following Raymond's death in 1980, his place was taken by Derek Hill.

having paid since April his share of that house. Desmond delightfully welcoming. I lunched with Janet Stone in her new house on the river with view of Salisbury Cathedral. Terrace house with garden leading down to river Avon, her bedroom with bow window projecting over water. Sweet daughter Emma staying with newly born baby looking less revolting than usual, rather like a doll. Much nostalgic talk of dear Reynolds. Janet said he was no saint, I having claimed sanctity for him. He knew he was a genius and put work before other considerations as true artists do, which means they are selfish people. Met Derek at station and brought him to tea with Janet, who has got over phase of intense grief and is reconciled to widowhood.

Regime at Crichel more settled than during my last visit, but lugubrious without Eddy and Raymond and their nice things. But Derek has already lent some of his pictures, a Sickert and other masters, as well as paintings of his own.

Got an 'up' on Desmond whose cheerfulness, fun and intellect impress me. Revealed that Lady Gregory was his aunt which I never knew. Remembers Yeats well as a comical figure with his fairies, pixies and Celtic twilight talk. Is sure there was no sex between Yeats and Lady G. But there was with Wilfrid Scawen Blunt who seduced her within months of her marriage to Gregory.* Desmond told me that his relations with Jack [Rathbone] were now impossible. Jack apologises, is unnatural, irritable and a different person. Des says he cannot get back onto the old beam and it is agony for him to be at Furlong Road. This is a sad conclusion to a friendship based on a deep love of fifty-five years.

Was expecting M. to return the day I went to Long Crichel so, accompanied by Honey, paid innumerable visits to the village callbox, ringing his London flat in vain. But on Friday received a letter from France to say he was returning Monday in time to dine with me at Brooks's, which he did. Lovely dinner and heaven to see him. But disturbed that he has not yet finished his book.

Instance of mental decline that Desmond has spent nearly a fort-

---

* Isabella Persse (1852–1932); m. 1880 Sir William Gregory (1817–92); Irish playwright and associate of W.B. Yeats in foundation of the Abbey Theatre, Dublin, in 1904. Wilfrid Scawen Blunt (1840–1922), poet and traveller, was notorious for his *amours*; he m. 1869 Lord Byron's granddaughter Annabella King-Noel; like Sir William Gregory he was an enthusiast for Egyptian nationalism and the cause of Arabi Pasha; in 1888 he was imprisoned for activity in the Irish Land League.

night reading through one admittedly thick and weighty tome about Verdi. He picks it up, puts it down, any excuse to defer reading it, yet protests it is interesting and important, which I am sure it may be. It will be another two weeks before he begins writing his review. Just the condition I remember Raymond falling into in old age.

Saturday, 19th September

George Lloyd's birthday. That dapper, taut, vivacious being, motivated as if by an electric current, would be 102 if still alive.

There is bad news about Diana Mo. Derek told me she had had a stroke. I telephoned Pam who confirmed it, but said it was slight and she was recovering well. Debo gone out to be with her. Then Pam telephoned again. Diana has had a second stroke, and is now paralysed all down one side. This saddens me very much indeed.

John Saumarez Smith to whom I talked in the Shop [Heywood Hill's bookshop] when in London on Monday has written me a long letter with suggestion for my next book – on why the writers of the Thirties became aesthetes, Communists and homosexuals. A good subject but I am not sure I could tackle it. Don't know enough about the English literature of the period. I could only write, superficially, about the personalities of my friends. Meanwhile I hope to finish the wretched Anthology within a few weeks and am editing my post-war diaries.

Last night watched on television a young German pianist playing Rachmaninov concerto at Leeds Competition. A beautiful player, aged twenty-one, sulky face *à la* Desmond Parsons, treacle-coloured hair, wavy and long. Attenuated, slender fingers. Plays with the pads, the line of fingers stretched low over the keys. Curious thing was that he was wearing a jacket with long floppy sleeves, covering wrists and part of the hands. Surely a pianist needs to have hands free from incumbrances like this? When he rose for his well-merited applause I saw how young and callow he was. Like Michelangelo's David, not grown to extremities, almost cloddish. Yet so elegant, so earnest, so fearful, making faces of agony during performance. I hope he wins.

Sunday, 20th September

The following night I watched a blind French boy, aged twenty-two, playing Schumann concerto. A miracle how well he played. Blind since he was three. Also handsome, with lost look of totally blind.

Unlike the others', his slender fingers were crooked at the ends. He felt his way over the keys when first starting. But how he managed to bang both hands down from a height I don't know. Audience much moved. He received great applause; tears in eyes of Duchess of Kent who must be a sweet woman. He came third; my German second; English boy first.

Janet Stone was amusing about having both her Archbishop and Bishop brothers to stay in her cottage. Both are fervent protagonists of Series III, which she hates. She insisted on taking them to Evensong, the only service in Salisbury Cathedral which is Series I. They reluctant to go, and were both dressed so casually and scruffily that she sent them upstairs to put on full canonicals. These they did not have with them, but they managed to fish out purple shirt-fronts. She marched them on either side of her into the Cathedral, the vergers agog with excitement.

Saturday, 26th September

Bamber and Beauty (David Ford) made a rush visit to Bath to arrange an exhibition of Bath prints and engravings at the Victoria Art Gallery next summer during the Festival. By which date they will have our *Images* printed and on sale. Bamber says it will be the best of the series, and already people are enthusiastic. To his surprise the Twickenham volume is selling even better than the Chiswick one. Says that already the Richmond *Images*, the first of the series and his own, is selling at inflated prices when it turns up in second-hand bookshops. He is pleased with my text and is coming down one day to go through it with me. Those damned commas again! When they arrived, Beauty gave me a warm embrace, and to my immense surprise Bamber followed suit. They want me to allow presentation of the leather-bound expensive copies, which will follow the linen-covered copies, in the Library in Lansdown Crescent. I agreed, provided the numbers were not excessive.

The same afternoon my cousin Ruth Wysierska came to tea bringing Professor George Rousseau, a great-grandson of Douanier Rousseau. A nice little midget with face like a baboon, indeed like the jungle animals the Douanier painted. He informed me that he was one of the leading literary critics in America and anxious to review the two vols of H.N. which the Shoestring Press (what a name, he guffawed) is due to bring out in the United States early next year; but Norah writes that the Americans are holding up the printing.

The following day an author called Brian Roberts called to talk about Randolph Churchill whose life he has been commissioned to write by Hamish Hamilton. Middle-aged, lives with friend in Frome. Affable, but a flat character. Randolph would not have liked him. He told me that his book on the Queensberry family which came out recently received good reviews, but the family gave it no publicity and it was overpriced, like mine, at £15.

Chatto's, whom I see next Thursday, have received a favourable report on my old, knocked-about *Countess and Cardinal* from a great Stuart expert, Professor Kenyon of St Andrew's University. To my surprise, they offer to take the book provided I correct, add, amplify and do all the things the learned professor recommends. The prof. is a Cambridge man and I have asked M. to find out about him for me.

Have finished Count Tolstoy's *Stalin's Secret War*. The enormities committed by Stalin make him a greater monster than Genghis Khan, and far worse than Hitler in that he brought about far more murders. The evil of Russian Communism is beyond all belief.

Saturday, 3rd October

Last weekend John Fleming and Hugh Honour stayed. Hugh, so short a time ago youthful and handsome, now puffy about the face and middle-aged. A. asked them how they managed to write a book together. Hugh said that he worked out the synopsis, gave it to John who ploddingly wrote the text, then passed it back to Hugh who polished it. I have often wondered how two could do such a thing.

Eardley and I lunched in John Cornforth's flat on Wed. J.C. wanted information on how we managed to arrange country houses together in N.T. early days. E's memory better than mine. Told how the Trust was so poor and so unwilling to spend money that when offered Thomas Hardy's violin and writing table, he was told to decline them as there was not enough money to transport them from Dorset to Montacute.

Then visited Diana Mosley in London Hospital, Whitechapel. As I entered the ward, she espied me through her open door, and I heard screams of laughter and cries of 'Jim'. D. lay in bed with Pam and Margaret Willes in attendance, looking extremely well, with good colour. Others left and we talked alone for twenty minutes. Her left side, which a fortnight ago was paralysed, is improving. She can already feel it, and even use the left hand. I gave her a clip-board for letter-writing, with which she seemed pleased.

M. lunched on Thursday. For a glorious hour and a half we were together. Next Monday he is off to Paris, his book still unfinished. But he showed me appreciative letter from Weidenfeld. I warned him not to lie back on strength of their approval of work so far done. Sometimes I feel tempted to stick pins into him.

oh, Sod!!

Tuesday, 6th October

Simon and Tricia [Lees-Milne] lunching on Saturday told us that brother Dick [Simon's father] has much aged. They were shocked by his stoop, his pot-belly, inability to walk from car to shops. This saddens me very much. They feel sure he will die before Elaine. She, poor thing, will go to South Africa to live. What a lonely prospect. The children will of course never live in Cyprus which is what the parents banked on, they having gone there primarily to save money for Simon and avoid death duties on their demise.

Then Clarissa* for the night, looking huge and wizened about the eyes. She is leaving London and her husband Michael in a fortnight for France where she has a twenty-five-year-old lover. A's attitude is too extraordinary. She encourages it. I of course do not criticise, and merely say to myself that the affair will end in tears. Such affairs always do unless they are platonic which I gather this one is not. I told A. that the wife of J. was having an affair with a youngish journalist whom we met when lunching with the Js on Sunday. Apparently the J. children took against this man and put messages under his pillow saying, 'Please leave our Mummy alone'. J. had them up and told them they must allow their mother some romance in her life. A. approved of this story and asked why Michael Luke could not show the same enlightened attitude towards Clarissa. I merely remarked, 'Because he is wildly jealous'. I refrained from pointing out that she had behaved in a similar way towards me in the past, and the not-so-distant past either.

Friday, 9th October

Received a letter from Margaret Willes that Diana Mosley has had a sudden operation. The scanning of her head revealed a large cyst. This

---

* J.L.-M's stepdaughter, Hon. Clarissa Chaplin (b. 1934), m. 1958 Michael Luke.

has been removed, and she has come through well. But it was a near thing and the family much worried.

This evening I motored A. to Heathrow whence she embarks for Australia. We dined at the airport and I left to stay with Loelia Lindsay for the weekend. An emotional farewell, both of us almost in tears.

 # Derek Granger directed. *Monday, 12th October*

Dined with Sally [Westminster] to see the first instalment of *Brideshead Revisited* on television. I thought it could not have been better. The principal characters – Sebastian Flyte, Charles Ryder and Anthony Blanche – were true to life as I remember their prototypes. Sebastian reminded me of Desmond [Parsons]. Blanche the living spit of Brian Howard.

Having now sent my typescript of the Anthology to OUP I can say that I have three books written and awaiting publication. Harold Vol. II comes out on the 22nd. It is true that I expect the Anthol. to be returned to me with suggestions and requests to shorten.

Friday, 16th October

OUP has now written about Anthology. Judith Chamberlain seems genuinely pleased; likes Introduction, but says the text must be short-ened. Also received a charming letter from Kenneth Rose* about Harold II.

Walked the dogs in the Bath Golf Course this afternoon. Was searching the ground for a notebook I lost there last Monday. Not much hope, but one never knows. I found another important note-book unexpectedly in the bottom of my car yesterday. While searching, the winter sun full in my eyes, I noted that the edge of every contour of the grass (and the golf course is the old Bath Common, a series of ridges) was etched in white gossamer. Looking closer, I realised that the gossamer was my old friend, the autumn spiders' web. It was the most beautiful sight ever seen. An undula-tion of silken waves. Then at my feet I saw the spiders, little red things like ants. Of course, the reason this golf course has them is

---

* Journalist and author (b. 1924); writer of *Albany* column in *Sunday Telegraph*.

that it is not sprayed. But why do they literally cover a whole field?
– for it is not merely the contours that have them. They are everywhere. What is the purpose? And if it is a windy or a rainy day,
what do they do then?

Pam has just telephoned me to say that darling Diana has had another
slight stroke, even after the dreadful operation. This is very serious and
sad. Alvilde will be distressed when she hears. Had a letter from her
yesterday, posted in Bahrain on way out. I am missing her.

Saturday, 17th October

This morning a girl named Shuttleworth – a step-granddaughter of
Roger [Fulford], I imagine – telephoned to say that he had taken a
bad turn and reluctantly had to put me off. Roger insisted on speaking to me. Was very breathless. I imagine the poor old thing is very
ill. I doubt I shall ever see him again. This means that I motor straight
from here to Phyllis Holt's for luncheon on Wednesday morning,
several hundreds of miles. And from her to Rupert [Hart-Davis] is
another forty miles over the Pennines. So I shall arrive at Rupert's
dead tired, always a pity when one pays a short visit.

M. rang me this evening wondering why I had not been in touch.
I told him I had telephoned but the Maître had answered, so I put the
receiver down. M. thinks this foolish, but I can't face up to explain-
ing to this extremely percipient, clever old lady.

Monday, 19th October

Great-nephew Henry [Robinson] dined with me Friday. Was full of
chat about his father's drinking habits and his own love life. Has sacked
his girl. He gave a hoot of delight that it was all over. Says he has no
wish to be married and tied. But of course he will have when he falls
properly in love.

Have begun typing out the 1946 diary. It lacks the sparkle of the
ones already published.

Wednesday, 21st October

Set off punctually at eight. Folly very miserable; always knows when
one is off for the night. Wouldn't eat her breakfast, and lay with her

head on my foot, gazing reproachfully at me, while I ate mine. I need not have fussed about distance. Arrived at midday. Stopped on an old bridge within sight of the Old Rectory, Lower Tatham, where the Holts live. The most beautiful country, this. River Wenning rushing below me as only moorland rivers rush. On my left, Hornby Castle, of red sandstone. Landscape like Claude. At 12.30 a car drove up, stopped, and a middle-aged, ex-good-looking man said, 'Are you J.L.-M.? I am John Holt. Please come along, and don't wait here.' So I went on. Holts live in a nice rambling old rectory. He very bedint,* nice farmer, she rather bedint which surprised me a little, being the daughter of a very well-off squarson and heir of the Thurland estates. She is my third cousin. Also present her first cousin (and again my third) Olive Wilson of Rigmaden, over from Windermere and not the least bedint. All very friendly. Phyllis has no Lees portraits, and what she has in silver, furniture, etc. comes from the Browns, no relations of mine. However she has a miniature of James Lees, our great-great-grandfather, with hair neatly plaited on the back. A duplicate (and rather better) version of Frieda Lees's one. They were both very interested in my old Lees album and produced albums of their own. What emerged of interest was that Dora Livesey, who married their grandfather Eric Brown Lees, was one of the little girls beloved of Ruskin. Cousin Olive possesses a hundred and fifty unpublished letters to her grandmother from Ruskin, also drawings and sketches by Ruskin and by Dora, who was an art student. This discovery would interest some Ruskin scholar, did I but know one.

Phyllis confirmed what my father always told me, that John, her great-grandfather, brother to mine, Joseph,† was very eccentric. Had to arrive in the drawing room on, say, his right foot. If he arrived on his left, would go upstairs and start all over again. The process was repeated if he did not succeed the second or third time. The three Lees brothers, John (hers) the eldest, James (of Alkrington) and Joseph (of Lower Clarksfield, mine) were known as Nimrod, Ramrod and Fishing Rod, after their attributes. They thought of nothing but sport, and my father told me that, left orphans, they defied their tutors, never went to school, and were completely uneducated and philistine.

---

* From the private language of Harold Nicolson and Vita Sackville-West, implying unsophisticated manners.

† Joseph Lees (1819–1890), m. 1843 Sarah Anne Milne: their son, the diarist's grandfather James Henry Lees-Milne, was the first bearer of that surname.

Phyllis let me take away an account in *Oldham Chronicle* of 1864 of her grandfather's coming of age at Upper Clarksfield, filling a whole page of closely printed words. Evidently they were well-off for the time, employing 2,000 workmen in the coal mines discovered beneath the Clarksfield estate.

At four I left them and motored across the Pennines to Swaledale, arriving at Marske Old Rectory at twilight. Warmly greeted by Rupert and his sweet wife June. She is a darling, simple, good, kind and adoring R., a sort of secretary-housekeeper-companion. His fourth wife. He is a lucky man. Rupert little changed in appearance. Still very hale. With his natty grey moustache more like a retired major than the doyen of Englishmen of letters. Wanted to give me his edition of Sassoon's diaries, but I had brought my own review copy which he wrote an affectionate *dédicace* in. For hours we talked and talked about books and writing. He told me that the 'P' in the diaries, the second lover of Siegfried, was Prince Philip of Hesse, Harold's friend, with whom they were all in Rome in 1921 when the affair started. Since the Prince is still alive – must be ancient – Rupert did not spell out his name. Rupert told me he is about to sell his library complete, subject to a life interest, to an American university. They have offered him £250,000 which he does not think enough. His condition is that the books be kept together, representing a unique collection published within half a century or more.

Took me to see the grave of his third wife Ruth and gravestone by Reynolds [Stone]. It lies behind the house in a graveyard detached from the church. Said her death was the worst tragedy in his life after that of his mother when he was nineteen. She died in a taxi which they had to run to catch on their way to a wedding. She had no suffering, no death rattle, just laid her head back and was gone.

Thursday, 22nd October

Left Rupert most affectionately and drove to Flintham. Passed signpost of Womersley and turned down the road to the village. Telephoned from a call-box, Anne [Rosse] having told me she would be there this week. Lady de Vesci answered and said Anne in Ireland. Had she asked who was speaking, I would have told her, but she didn't and I supposed at her age – ninety-nine – she could not possibly have wished to see me.

Today Vol. II comes out. Bought *Telegraph* and *Guardian* in

Richmond, and no review in either. Haven't looked at *The Times*, and . . .

Saturday, 24th October

. . . haven't heard a word by letter or telephone from a soul about the book. I imagine it is out, and just ignored. Feeling depressed all day. So silly. Bad mood not improved by luncheon with poor Eliza Wansbrough.* Hoped to be alone with her because she is so deaf, but she *will* always have others as she prefers to sacrifice the possibility of conversation with one person to the conviviality of a party at which she hears not a thing. Today she had just her neighbour from over the wall, Richard something, too ready to please, though I'm sure generous and kind.

Sunday, 25th October

M. rang last night that he was going to buy the Sunday papers at midnight to read reviews of H.N. I told him not to bother as there would be none. Today I went to church at 9.15 and just before I left to take Diana W. to lunch with Nan Bernays, Freda Berkeley rang to say there was a rave review in *Sunday Times*, another in *Observer*. *Sunday Times* review by Michael Howard ends, 'If there has been a better biography in the past fifty years, I would like to know which it is.' This evening I heard from Victoria Glendinning, Frankie Donaldson, Bamber, Rachel and Nan Bernays (to whom I sent copy because of frequent mentions of her Rob), all telephoning to congratulate. Very cheering. M. is as thrilled as I am.

Wednesday, 28th October

The picture of Rupert at Marske is ever before me, in his armchair, semi-recumbent, right foot on a gout stool *à la* Lord Holland, June crouching beside him as though eager to do his slightest bidding, I in the visitor's chair opposite him, in his long library, the only library I know which is literally lined with books on all four walls from floor to ceiling. Not an inch of space for a picture. He told me that last year he published four books, this year three. Amongst other things he told

---

* Dau. of Sir George Lewis, 2nd Bt, of the famous family of solicitors.

me that he was considering destroying the diaries of Duff Cooper (his uncle) which were left to him. He said they contain nothing that redounds to his reputation. Mostly snippets of his affairs with women, going into unnecessary detail. Little about politics or literature. Of no value. Thought John Julius, who stood to inherit them with other papers of his father, might be distressed and shocked. What should he do? I said that as a rule I was strongly against the destruction of papers. Not having seen the diaries, my opinion could not be of much use. But my answer would be no, don't destroy.

Tonight, having brought the dogs back from Bath and let them into the garden, I unloaded the car and put it away in the motor-house. Alvilde's car was outside, which I had taken out to enable Perks to fetch the ladder, and I put that away too. Then I had a sudden panic that I had left the dogs behind in Bath on the pavement. Was about to return immediately to Bath, when to my amazement I saw both dogs in the garden at the gate. All was well – but my memory! Senility stalks ahead.

Thursday, 29th October

Drove to Chippenham to meet a man from Wiltshire District Council to look at The Ivy, a Baroque house now in desperate plight. As usual on such occasions there were other people there, and slowly we went over the place in pouring rain. Already they have ruined it. Concrete block of new houses built in garden with Council's consent. House in terrible condition, riddled with dry rot, windows out, stairs unsafe, etc. It has now been bought by a young man who intends to restore it provided the Council prohibit the speculators who own the remainder of the garden from building within twenty yards of the house. The young man amazed me. He looked like a yahoo plebeian, appallingly dressed, filthy, pot-bellied, dirty crimped hair. But he turned out to be educated, a gent, and rather sympathetic.

Saturday, 31st October

Bamber and David Ford came at tea time, bringing Midi, to go through my typescript of *Images of Bath*. While I was getting firewood out of the cupboard below the stairs, David came in from the car and I embraced him. At that moment Bamber walked in from the drawing room. But I don't care what anyone thinks.

Sunday, 1st November

I lunched with the Robinsons* at Moor Wood. Ted seemed recovered, but the meal was sticky and I thought the new wife looked subdued. No drink offered, only water. Walked round the property with Nick and the dogs. He told me that his father's latest outbreak of drink came as a great surprise to Primrose. She felt distressed and betrayed. If it recurs, she may walk off. Small blame to her. Nick now quite adult, so easy to talk to. I can say anything. I feel there is a real bond of affection and understanding between us.

Monday, 2nd November

Expecting to have a clear day's work, went to Bath wearing my old jeans and looking a sight. Had just arrived when *Bath Chronicle* telephoned demanding an interview with me immediately. Nice, intelligent girl arrived with photographer. Talked unguardedly and freely. Forgot that I was being interviewed.

Tuesday, 3rd November

Bath Chronicle interview published. Not too bad. Nice girl had been discreet, but caption – 'James says, Publish and be Damned' – a fabrication of course. Photograph of me almost flattering. That is a relief.

Dined with Alex Moulton at Bradford. Made him watch *Brideshead Revisited* on TV. He kept interrupting with questions. Are those young men meant to be in love? Why does Sebastian dislike his mother? Throughout dinner Alex told me that he was about to administer chastisement in his role as President of the Bradford-on-Avon Preservation Society to the members at their AGM, some of them having criticised his work on re-roofing the Hall. I advised self-restraint.

Wednesday, 4th November

Motored to Oxford this afternoon. Met M. and Charles Orwin at station. They took me to tea with some young men in Holywell. All

---

* Major Edwin Robinson, MC, husband of J.L.-M's niece Prudence (who d. 1976; he had since remarried); their sons Henry, Nicholas and Richard.

very polite and charming to me, but I find such encounters awkward. We went on to the Bodleian, to a party given by Granada Television for an exhibition (costumes and photographs) of the *Brideshead Revisited* serial. I was asked because I suggested Castle Howard to them. Greeted by the producer, Derek Grainger. Talked to the young director, a very clever man, and a few of the cast who were present – not unfortunately including Charles Ryder and Sebastian Flyte. Talked to Count Nikolai Tolstoy about his *Stalin's Secret War*. Liked him. He is prim and Edwardian, wearing high-cut waistcoat and watch-chain. Said his father had escaped from Russia in 1922 at age of nine. I told him that this very morning I had selected his book as one of my three choices for the year. Dropped M. in Hyde Park Square and C. in Exhibition Road. Latter parted rather emotionally because he was returning to an empty flat, having had a break with his lover.

Thursday, 5th November

Dentist at 9.30. Feared an abscess under remaining dog-tooth. Nothing of the sort. Same old trouble of plate rubbing against gum and causing sore. Met M. at his club at midday. Talked affectionately. He promised to finish book by end of year. I betted him £5 he would not. Victoria Glendinning lunched with me at Como Lario. Much enjoyed our talk. She wanted to know whether Harold was aware of the true cause of Vita's muzziness. I told her I was sure he knew about the sherry addiction but that he would not admit it even to his diary. She told me that Vita did not by any means always tell Harold the truth about her affairs. Had more than he ever knew of. Victoria herself has never experienced the twinges of lesbianism or written about a lesbian before. I said I hoped she liked V. She assured me that she did, and hotly defended her against her critics. She is not going to mention the word 'snob'. We embraced warmly on parting. She wants to see A. alone. Quite right.

Friday, 6th November

Found Derry [Moore] on return, come to stay for two nights. Delightful having him. No trouble. On contrary, helps with cooking. Again hoped to have a free day working in Bath. Meryl Secrest telephoned that she was in Bath from America and wished to see me.

Reluctantly invited her to tea. To my horror, doorbell rang at 12.45. This was Margaret Willes, due to lunch next Monday. She had made a mistake. I rushed out to buy food from delicatessen and a bottle of white wine. Object of her visit to persuade me to write memoir about Mitfords. Told her how difficult I would find this. She said that Diana, when she thought she might be dying, gave her blessing to my doing it. Margaret gave me little help how to do it. Mrs Secrest came. A voluble, gushing, friendly lady. Has finished K. Clark biography. Told me that K. asked her to include all the love affairs. Now she is writing about Geoffrey Scott and wanted to know about Pinsent the architect. I was able to give her some information and told her about Vita's affair with Scott.*

Had unusual experience motoring home along the M4 Thursday evening. A beautiful late autumn day. The sun ahead of me larger than ever seen. An enormous orange of tawny gold. As I approached bridges, watched cyclists crossing silhouetted against golden sun, black, strongly delineated. As they pedalled earnestly, intently, I imagined I knew who they were and on what errands bent. One was in a hurry to get to her lover. Another in a hurry to reach the post office before it closed. Another worried about his mother, ill with cancer. In such a flash did these pictures come and go, as I sped at 80 mph and they flicked across the sun. Yet the reality of these people was imprinted across my mind; they were more than shadows, they were alive to me. And all the while the autumn mist was rising from the valleys on either side of the motorway, like sheets about to envelope my silhouettes for ever.

Saturday, 7th November

Derry gets up early. He laid the breakfast table and made the coffee, then left for Berkeley Castle to continue yesterday's photographing. Is superbly happy with his photography, and his wife. John [Kenworthy-Browne] came at midday and stayed until 5.30. We walked around the park, the dogs on leads, for hounds in the distance were drawing Apsley Wood. John had never been to Essex House before. He went around looking carefully at everything. Said that if ever by mischance

---

* Cecil Pinsent (1884–1964), architect and landscape designer; worked at Bernhard Berenson's I Tatti and the Villa Medici, Fiesole, with Geoffrey Scott (1883–1929), biographer and architect.

I should be widowed, he would look after me. We have now known each other twenty-three years. He is fifty, the age (as he reminded me) I was when we first met.

Margaret Willes told me that Diana, while awaiting her operation, talked about her childhood. She vividly recalled Tom playing the piano in the barn at Asthall, she sitting listening to him and watching me with a book beside the fireplace. Diana said she believed annihilation followed death, distressing for Margaret, aged thirty-four, who is a Christian herself.

Monday, 9th November

To Armistice Day service in Badminton Church yesterday. Usual procession of ex-servicemen and girl guides. Mrs Punter, and Don, the chauffeur at the House, in the blue uniform of the British Legion, each carrying a banner which they lower slowly while the Anthem is sung. There is still much feeling about this day. Church nearly full.

Saw no one all day. Motored to Saul in early afternoon, a longish way, and walked by the wide canal. A lovely walk on the towpath. Heard Saul church chime the quarters when I was a mile or more away. Can't be as deaf as I think. Sinking sun casts peculiar oily golden lights on the waters, gently rippling, though no wind and no navigation. Moving experience. Felt away from the world, more away than I do walking in the park or fields at Badminton.

Thursday, 12th November

Met Mrs Foster in the village and condoled on the death of her father. Instead of tears her face lit up and she said that never had her father enjoyed himself more than he did in the last two years of his life, after losing his wife. He had been able to do all the things he had wanted to do, chief of which was to see the lights of Blackpool.

Sunday, 22nd November

A week ago I collected A. from Heathrow at 8 a.m. I was late because her plane from Sydney arrived one hour in advance of scheduled time. Having parked the car I went into a seething mass of brown, black and yellow arrivals. Just heard tail-end of a message to me. Then saw a figure waving. My first sight of A. a great shock. I saw a white-faced,

drawn old lady. This separation of five weeks is the longest we have
had in our thirty years. I was very upset, and still am, by her appearance. True, she was full of spirit, having enjoyed the tour immensely,
and on the way home chatted like one possessed. And this I think
explains what happened to her so soon afterwards. Before evening she
had collapsed with exhaustion and developed a high temperature.
Bronchitis, her dreaded ailment, had developed.

On Thursday, although she was by no means fit, she had reduced
her temperature, and insisted on coming to London in order to see
the Denis Thatcher play* for which I had got tickets, this day, 19th,
being the thirtieth anniversary of our marriage. We meant to go and
come back in the day. I had Selina Hastings to lunch with me.
Delicious luncheon, delicious girl. Not beautiful, but a sparkling face,
lovely skin and huge, liquid, enquiring eyes. Much talk about the
Mitfords. She says that Nancy's letters to Palewski† make very pathetic
reading, letters of pleading, ungovernable love on her part. I'm glad I
don't have to read them. In the evening I went to see Anthony
Chaplin. Grey, gaunt and I would say dying. Tossed about in his bed.
Very depressing visit. Poor Rosemary.

A. picked me up and took me to Brooks's where we had a rather
nasty and expensive dinner. On to Whitehall Theatre. Then arose the
awful business of parking. Having dropped A. at the theatre I desperately drove round and round blocks of ministerial buildings. Finally I
found an empty place at end of a dreary street and rushed back to
theatre. When the play was over – a rather unfunny farce – it was
pouring with rain. I had no umbrella. Went in search of car. Could
not find it. Gone. Returned to now emptied theatre where poor A.
was hugging herself and coughing her heart out on pavement. Told
her car either impounded or stolen. We went to West Central Police
Station where a nice, efficient sergeant policewoman, to whom I gave
number of car from my pocket diary, pressed buttons, rang bells, and
declared that no such car had been impounded and it must therefore
be stolen. By now A. was shivering with cold and misery. We telephoned the Berkeleys, mercifully just returned from dining out, and
they said we might both stay night with them. All our belongings were
in the car. Then I said, perhaps I was mistaken in the street, so at enor-

---

* *Anyone for Denis?*, written by and starring John Wells.
† Colonel Gaston Palewski (1901–84); Chef de Cabinet to General de Gaulle, and French
Ambassador to Rome.

mous cost we got taxi to take us back to Whitehall. There was the car
all the time in a street parallel to the one I had gone to earlier, intact.
By now it was after midnight and we went to the Berkeleys'. A. has
been very good about this lamentable evidence of my senility.

Last night I felt so tired, dispirited and drained that I wondered if
death were near at hand. When people say with astonishment of
someone that he died suddenly without warning, having been talking
and laughing three hours earlier, that signifies nothing. He may well
have felt drained, worn out, exhausted, but was able, as we all are, to
rouse himself to make a final social effort before giving up the ghost.

At Holy Communion this morning in Acton Turville I wondered,
now the temptations of the flesh are rapidly abating, whether I would
undergo a resurgence of holiness and spiritual uplift and become
totally reconciled to God.

Sunday, 29th November

Had a lovely visit to London this past week, staying with Eardley
whom I had not seen for seven weeks, since slight coldness on my part
over his refusal to have me and dogs to stay at The Slade. M. lunched
on return from Paris, looking gummy-eyed because he will stay up at
night and rise at midday. But a joy to see him, and we talked in
Brooks's library till 3.30. I went on to exhibition of Julian Barrow*
paintings in St James's. He there standing in a corner. Every single
painting sold. A highly competent and intelligible painter, like
Graham Rust, and consequently popular. Wish I had bought agreeable picture of Beckford's House, Lansdown Crescent.

Walked to tea with Diana Mosley in Debo's house in Chesterfield
Street. Amazed how well she seems to be. She was wearing a snood
over head, just a touch of hair growing over the forehead, as she had
to be shaved for operation. We talked about Tom [Mosley] whose
papers she is sorting through before selling to Warwick University.
Before I left Nicky Ravensdale came. Nice middle-aged greying man.
Is writing memoir of his father† of whom he is palpably fond though
not liking his politics. There ensued an interesting conversation about

---

* Julian Barrow's painting of J.L.-M. in the garden of Essex House was used for the dust-
jacket of *Ancient as the Hills*.
† Published under the name of Nicholas Mosley in two volumes, *Rules of the Game* (1982)
and *Beyond the Pale* (1983).

Fascism which I had never before had with Diana. I told her I could not stomach those dreadful pre-war Albert Hall meetings, with Tom in black uniform, lights trained on him, him declaiming like Mussolini. Her explanation was that the sort of people to whom he was trying to get his message across liked uniforms, were sentimental, enjoyed the drama and could only be reached by ranting oratory. The accompanying thugs were a necessary bodyguard for without them he would never have been heard. They were there to eject the Communist rowdies sent to break up every meeting. I suppose some truth in this. She said that those of his contemporaries still alive agree he was right in all his prognostications. He was a great thinker. He would walk alone round the Temple,* working out projects in his mind. He thought more than he read. Moreover he bore no resentment against his critics. He was in that sense a big man. Ravensdale occasionally took out a notebook and jotted down. She says the office is still in being. Doing what, I asked? Issuing literature, including a regular magazine, *Action*.

Delicious evening at Eardley's with Richard [Shone]. I went and bought odd assortment of cold food in Sloane Street and E. provided wine and did the work. Always hilarity with Richard and amusing and edifying conversation. The following day, Friday, spent the morning at Hayward Gallery at Lutyens Exhibition. Very well displayed but exhibits of architects' work necessarily difficult, for a mass of photographs becomes boring. But furniture and objects interspersed. I can't take those early Lutyens Great West Road suburban villas with half-timbered gables and inglenooks. His versatility and maverick qualities were a weakness I think. Upstairs an exhibition of paintings of the old Sickert. Marvellous full-length of Edward VIII in Welsh Guards uniform, carrying bearskin, stepping out of Buck. Palace with harassed, still youthful face. The usual number of coruscating mud canvases. A smiling full-length of Gavin Faringdon descending stairs, and a horrifying one of ghastly Lord Castlerosse. Richard told story of Lady Astor meeting Castlerosse at a party, tapping his stomach and saying, 'If that were on a woman what would they be saying?' To which C. replied, 'It was on a woman last night. And what *were* they saying?'

Ros lunched with me at Como Lario. Usual table. She told me something which upset me very much, namely that, two years ago, A. wrote an accusing letter to M. which he immediately took to Ros for

---

* Temple de la Gloire, the Mosleys' house at Orsay.

advice on how to answer. She emphatically said that she dictated his reply, which was to the effect that he was not behaving in a way which could possibly harm her marriage and saw no reason not to continue seeing me. I said to Ros, 'But this is awful. Most young men of twenty-six would have been terrified away. It is a miracle that he still does see and correspond with me.' On my return to Badminton I found A. suffering much from bronchitis, but so upset was I that I fear I could not be as affectionate and solicitous as I should have been.

Monday, 30th November

Selina Hastings, who knows Brian Masters well, told me his life story. He is the illegitimate child of a barmaid in Whitechapel. The father a bus driver. The mother saw from the first that the child wanted to learn. She managed to send him to a good grammar school. He got the required grades and did well. He managed to meet Gilbert Harding* who took to him, practically adopted him and taught him how to speak. Hence his almost perfect accent. To Harding he owes nearly everything, probably also a small legacy. For he owns a house in Kensington where he takes in lodgers in an inefficient way. There is a woman who is in love with him, and a Spanish waiter with whom Brian is in love – the unshaven, dark, silent dwarf we met at Peggy Münster's.† He is terribly jealous of Brian and won't allow his friends to the house. Selina has somehow gained entry. She is fond of Brian who, she is sure, is a masochist. Brian always wanted to mix with society people in high life, something he has achieved. They like him and he likes them.‡

Wednesday, 2nd December

Walking with the dogs in the garden in front of Somerset Place I noticed that the chestnut trees have little buds already. They are

---

* Gilbert Harding (1907–1960), the first British television star, famous for his sparkling wit and often belligerent manner. In private life, he was notorious for his rudeness, drunkenness and homosexuality.
† Margaret Ward (1905–82), m. 1929 Count Paul Münster.
‡ Brian Masters is content, on literary grounds, for this entry to be published as it was written, but points out that some of its details are inaccurate. He is in fact the legitimate son of a family in domestic service in Camberwell; it was his father who was the illegitimate son of a bus driver. He received no legacy from Harding.

soft and sticky. Is the stickiness to prevent insects eating them, or what?

Thursday, 3rd December

John Harris telephoned to ask if I would beg the Devonshires to withdraw their request for the return of half the Palladian drawings loaned to the RIBA, the other half having been given to the RIBA by the 8th Duke. I said I could not possibly interfere. It would be gravely resented. Instead suggested that the RIBA have photographs made of the originals before returning them. John hadn't thought of this.

Went to Seabright's bookshop in Bath and asked the young attendant of about thirty if they had *Who's Who*. 'Who is it by?' he enquired. 'I can't exactly say,' I replied. 'Is it humorous?' he asked. 'Not exactly. It's a reference book, like *Debrett*.' 'What's *Debrett*?' 'Oh, never mind,' I said, and walked away.

✳ *N.B. tell Robert - E.*   *Monday, 7th December*

Although I do not care much for Henry Moore's work I respect him as a deeply serious artist. Interviewed on Radio Three by Lucie-Smith,* when asked what sort of artist he would like to be if given a new life, he said a writer. That words were the greatest medium of art in the world. That communication between humans was the greatest gift and favour conferred on them. He quoted the Bible as the most moving literature to his knowledge. He said the advantage of sculpture over painting was the third dimension, the fact that the artist was able to create something 'real'. He has lived forty years in Hertfordshire, and said he would never have developed as an artist had he lived in London. He must be surrounded by nature. Nature was the basis of all art. The human form was the essential thing around which all art revolved. He would not be anyone else, or have had a different upbringing – he was the seventh of eight children, and his father was a miner. An impressive talk, spoken with much modesty.

Tuesday, 8th December

Went to London by ten o'clock train. When we reached Didcot, the country covered with snow. Train an hour and a half late in typically

---

* Edward Lucie-Smith (b. 1933); poet and art critic.

British way. Never prepared for the inevitable cold of winter. John K.-B. lunched with me. I ploughed my way round London streets in snow boots, for streets and pavements impacted and slippery. Duncan Grant exhibition at d'Offay's gallery. When I see an artist's work *en masse* I appreciate him far better than when coming upon an isolated work. One grasps the technique at once. I would have liked to buy a sketch of wrestlers, but beyond my means.

Went to tea with Hilary Spurling*, in Ladbroke Grove, walking there from Notting Hill station as I used to years ago. For the first time since Jamesey's death saw his No. 9.[†] It is still empty, very melancholy, sinister in fact, with a For Sale board between the windows. Walked up the Grove to No. 48. Thought this mid-Victorian house seemed familiar. It was Dame Una Pope-Hennessy's. She moved there on the General's death in the War, as an impoverished widow. Yet she lived in the whole house. Now the Spurlings have two floors. Mrs Spurling has had three children since I last saw her and she published Vol. I of her Ivy Compton-Burnett book. Her immediate interest now is Margaret Jourdain. Showed me a slim volume of Margaret's poems, privately printed in 1911 by her friend, the subsequent wife of Ernest Thesiger.[‡] Margaret was the daughter of a poor parson. It was expected of her to become a governess. Family disapproval alienated her. Lived for years with old mother, earning perhaps £40 a year writing articles. Always wanted to be a writer even after she had won renown as a furniture expert. Happily she met Ivy just after Great War. Ivy had some money. Thereafter she was free of money worries. Hilary went to see Joan Evans,[§] sent by me. Joan told her why she detested Ivy. Reason that Ivy took Margaret from her and poisoned M.J. against Joan, who apparently, though younger, expected M.J. to live with her. There must have been strong latent lesbian tendencies among these bluestocking ladies, though Hilary S. is sure that I.C.-B. and M.J. were never lovers in the rude sense.

The beauty of the garden trees in the twilight which assumed a sad mauve in the snow. Dined with M., off to Paris tomorrow.

---

* Writer and critic (b. 1940).
† James Pope-Hennessy had been done to death at 9 Ladbroke Grove on 25 January 1974.
‡ Ernest Thesiger (1879–1961), actor, m. 1917 Janette Mary Fernie Ranken.
§ Dame Joan Evans (d. 1977), dau. of Sir John Evans, KCB, FRS; writer on art, and first woman President of the Society of Antiquaries.

Admitted that he might not finish his book by the end of the year. This is dreadful.

Saturday, 12th December

A severe spell of cold weather. Much snow and frost. Tony Mitchell* was to have taken me to Kingston Lacy† yesterday but decided it was unwise. Today a beautiful morning with sun and we risked it. Roads all right, but severely cold. Spent afternoon in house. Of course the original Pratt building quite overlaid by Barry. The Barry work very interesting in its own right, notably the grand staircase. For how much was Sir Joseph Bankes‡ himself responsible? Architectural drawings of his survive in the archives room. In the library Tony produced folios of Bankes's drawings of Egyptian monuments, very good, in colour. An interesting character who might merit a book – Byron's friend and correspondent (much of the correspondence still unpublished), traveller in Middle East, amateur architect, had to leave the country for 'the usual'. I am interested. Important pictures in bad condition. In acreage, this is one of the largest properties left to the Trust.

On our return the full moon incredibly bright and clear, I suppose on account of the sharp frost. Between Tormarton and Acton Turville we stopped the car and looked at the moon through Tony's field glasses. Every lineament observable. I have never seen it so clearly before. Amazed that the topmost circumference of the moon was jagged with mountain ranges. Now surely this is an extraordinary thing to see through ordinary field glasses.

Tuesday, 15th December

A. and I motored to London for the day. Unfortunately, soon before we got onto the motorway, a large car approached us too fast and

---

* Local N.T. Representative, based at Dyrham Park, Glos.

† House in Dorset, recently left to N.T. together with its contents and park; built by Sir Roger Pratt 1663–5 for Sir Ralph Bankes, cased in stone and altered by Sir Charles Barry, 1835–41.

‡ *recte* William John Bankes (d. 1855: see *DNB*); J.L.-M. must have confused him momentarily with the botanist Sir Joseph Banks (1743–1820), who accompanied Captain Cook on his voyages.

skidded into us sideways. Driver's side of my car ripped from front door to rear. Maddening. The driver of the offending car was a nice man however who said he was a motor mechanic and would repair the damage himself without our having to go through insurance agents.

We lunched at the French Embassy in Kensington Palace Gardens. Lovely house, huge red and gold reception rooms. Charming Madame de Margerie.* About twenty-four guests. Our names on cards in front hall. I sat between Lady Antonia Pinter and Joan Haslip, who is writing life of Marie Antoinette.† Lady A. has beautiful fair complexion and lovely piercing blue eyes. I liked her. Her next book about notable seventeenth-century women.‡ She told me she did not use the services of a researcher, but was once helped by Anne Somerset whom she described as a clever girl. The Stephen Spenders§ present and friendly. He said he had taken some splendid photographs of me when we met at Rory's for Christmas three years back.¶ We agreed it was a mistake to read reviews of our books.

Dashed away before coffee to N.T. Properties Committee, item which concerned me not yet reached. This was Kingston Lacy. But there was no need for me to raise my voice and plead. Committee agreed without dissent to recommend acceptance.

Jonathan Guinness** came to Brooks's at 5.30 to talk about Mitfords for his book. Chiefly wanted to know about Tom, the mystery figure he barely knew. Said that when he was a child of eight, Tom was deputed to take him for a walk. He made no concessions, treated J. as an adult, did not slacken speed. The child became exhausted and fell behind. When asked on return whether the walk a success, T. replied not really, Jonathan lagged behind and conversation was uninteresting. J. thinks Tom was the lynch-pin of the family who kept the sisters together and that only after his death did they

---

* The ambassadress.
† Writer (1912–94); her biography of Marie Antoinette was published in 1987.
‡ This was *The Weaker Vessel* (1984).
§ Sir Stephen Spender, poet (1909–95); m. (2nd, 1941) Natasha Litvin. A coolness had sprung up between him and J.L.-M. in 1976 when the reviewer Alistair Forbes mischievously sent J.L.-M. a letter he had received from Spender, abusing J.L.-M.: see *Through Wood and Dale*.
¶ See *Through Wood and Dale*, entry for Christmas Day 1977.
** Eldest son (b. 1930) of Diana Mosley by Bryan Guinness, 2nd Baron Moyne (whom he succeeded, 1992); author, with Catherine Guinness, of *The House of Mitford* (1984).

drift into camps. Not quite true, for their fanatical and opposing political views were not the cause of their differences. We talked about the two grandfathers, Lord Redesdale and Tommy Gibson-Bowles. I liked Jonathan immensely. He is over fifty, round-faced, a little faded, with bushy, thick hair flying Einstein-like from his brows. Great charm, and like all Diana's sons has forward-looking manner, welcoming, affable. We were talking happily in the Library when at seven the hall porter approached me with 'Madam is waiting in the car outside'. This 'Madam' nowadays very old-fashioned. Was sorry to part from him. I think I was right to tell him that Tom had a limited sense of humour, was inclined to be morose, moody, caviare-to-the-general, disliked people, but dearly loved his friends to whom his loyalty was touching.

Friday, 18th December

At breakfast A. said to me that during the night she had a vivid dream that Anthony was dying. She was with him. She was very upset. It is true that Clarissa had telephoned yesterday that he had had a relapse. Then at 9 a.m. Clarissa telephoned again to say Anthony had died in the night. A. replied, 'It was at twenty minutes to three?' Clarissa confirmed that that was the time, the very moment A. awoke from her dream. They talked, then poor A. turned away and wept. I wept too. She apologised. I said, 'But it is not wrong, to shed a tear for those we have loved.' Poor Anthony. Never has there been a more wasted life. He was gifted, clever, well-informed. But intolerably idle, disorganised, opinionated, unwilling to enter public life. Never took his seat in the Lords where he could have spoken for the causes he had at heart – music, wildlife, botany. He is the last of the Chaplins. He achieved little. I may be wrong, for he did compose a cadenza or two for Mozart operas, and he may have discovered some unknown species of creature in the Far East, which discovery may be registered at the Zoo. Not only did he play the piano very well, but he painted birds with talent. He could have achieved so much; that is what is so sad. He was one of those endowed with that fatal charm. The last time I saw him he was exercising it. 'How is our wife,' he asked, 'which art in Heaven?' How well did he know that within a month he would be there himself? For I am sure he will go there after a minimum of purgatory.

NR

Monday, 21st December

Ghastly weather, freezing cold, snow, blizzards, sleet, ice – we have had them all without abatement. I went to London to dine with Kenneth Rose, he having written a charming appreciation of my Vol. II in 'Albany'. What pleased me most was the tribute he paid to Harold's golden character, saying what nonsense the charge of snobbishness was.

The event of the past fortnight has been the military coup in Poland.* The only encouraging result of this disastrous event is the unanimous condemnation of it, not only by the entire European Community but by all the parties in Britain except the extreme Left, which doesn't matter because they are the common enemy of mankind.

Sunday, 27th December

Spent our usual Christmas at Parkside with the Droghedas. Derry, Alexandra and Burnet [Pavitt] present. The Moores not getting on well with the parents; little tearful scenes and misunderstandings. On Christmas Day we went to St George's Chapel. This time we were given seats in the front row of the nave, I on the end seat of the central gangway, next to the inserted stone with inscription recording the Duke of Windsor's lying-in-state on that spot. When the royal family left by the West Door I was within spitting distance. Queen wearing hideous turquoise blue dress, Prince of Wales with scar on left cheek, Duke of Edinburgh shorter than I had supposed, and lined. Princess Pushy of Kent, as they call her, in hideous hat. Prince Michael's beard a mistake. Princess of Wales sweet. Old Duchess of Gloucester a sweet, shrunken old lady. After chapel we had a drink at Adelaide Cottage with Sir John Johnston[†] and his wife. He a good-looking, frank, decent sort of chap. She has a vocal chord missing. Daughter of Alec Hardinge of Penshurst. These royal posts are hereditary, which is quite right for they are born to courtiership. She collects nineteenth-century photo-

---

* In response to Soviet pressure, the army under General Wojciech Jaruzelski overthrew the civil government which had been making concessions to the Solidarity reform movement.

† Lieutenant-Colonel Sir John Johnston (b. 1922); m., 1949, Hon. Elizabeth Hardinge, whose father, 2nd Baron Hardinge of Penshurst (d. 1960), had been Private Secretary to King Edward VIII and King George VI; Assistant Comptroller, Lord Chamberlain's Office, 1964–81; Comptroller, 1981–7.

graph frames. Has forest of them, mostly filled with present-day royalties. Adelaide Cottage built by Nash, *cottage orné* all right with bargeboards and veranda. Pretty outside. Nothing left inside.

Boxing Day we went for drinks to the Martin Charterises at Eton. That beautiful gallery with boys' portraits against greeny-gold walls. In the evening Sir Robin Mackworth-Young,* wife and handsome doctor son came. Sir Robin asked me what I was writing next. This gave me the opportunity of reminding him what he had forgotten, namely the snub he administered to me when I asked for permission to see the Stuart papers. He excused himself by saying that they had to be particular not to let random writers have access to the Queen's papers, but I would be a different matter, etc. So now I have only to write to him formally. Have written all this to M. who will consider me a traitor.

Joan, I fear, is verging on senility. She hears badly and cannot concentrate. Is too intent on being agreeable, appearing to be responsive while not listening to what one is saying. So sad when I remember how bright and on the spot she used to be. She has become like Anne Rosse.

On our return the telephone rang. A. answered and told me that a Mr Haines wanted to speak to me. At once I guessed what had happened. He said, 'I have some bad news to tell you, Sir. Mother passed away on Christmas Eve.' She had been in hospital a fortnight without my knowing, and died sitting in her chair. Poor old darling, she was ninety-two. As Audrey says, that is the last link with Wickhamford broken. And if they do go ahead with the outrageous scheme of wrecking the manor we need never go near the place again. Unfortunately I love the church. Sad though I am at Mrs H's death, having known her all my life – she was a housemaid at the manor when I was born – I was made sadder by reading of the death of Patrick O'Donovan. He was in my company in the Irish Guards, likewise a platoon commander. He was the only friend I had in those dismal, wretched days. Ten years younger than I, he was gay, amusing, amused, very bright and clever, always with a smile and giggle. A pious Catholic, yet ready to laugh at his religion. He really was adorable, and as queer as a coot in those days. I seldom saw him in later days, being shy of him because of the miserable part I played in the Regiment. I remember him telling me that, while he stood at the salute of the King

---

* Librarian at Windsor Castle and Asst. Keeper of the Queen's Archives, 1958–85; then Librarian Emeritus to HM The Queen; b. 1920; m. 1953 Rosemarie Aue.

and Queen at the Victory Parade, the upper part of his body out of his tank, his soldier servant was fellating him below. He married very happily soon after I believe. Freda Berkeley told me today that he had been ill a month with cancer. Poor Paddy, he was entrancing with his ugly, jolly face, his gallantry, piety, humour and good brain. He became a very successful journalist. I remember his worry about what to do when the War was over, and his delight when the *Observer* took him on. He hadn't a penny then.

Thursday, 31st December

This year has been a fairly productive one. *Harold Nicolson* Vol. II has been published. So have my contribution to *Places*, edited by Ronald Blythe, my entry on Nancy Mitford for the *DNB*, which I shall not live to see, my piece on Henry Green for an American magazine, my article on Worcestershire for the *Illustrated London News*, and several reviews for *Book Choice* and *Apollo*. Also I have written three books in a manner of speaking – *Images of Bath* for Bamber Gascoigne's series, *An Anthology of Country Houses* for OUP, and a third volume of my diaries, to be called *Caves of Ice*, 1946 and 1947, for Chatto's. I think it is far less entertaining than the previous diaries; lacks sparkle, contains too many pedestrian descriptions of houses visited for the National Trust, with in-filling of gossip about people met. Then there are the occasional items of a private nature. How much should I disclose? I feel they may embarrass A. Besides, is it of interest to mention that one went to bed with so-and-so thirty-five years ago without an account of the affair or even of the actual experience? And I was not in love during these two years. That is the difference. Love is one thing to write about, lust another, and the latter is uninteresting unless the circumstances are amusing, horrifying or titillating, my affairs having been none of these things.

Appendices

Appendix I

Visit to Mount Athos with Derek Hill
September 1979

This was the second of four occasions on which J.L.-M. accompanied the artist
Derek Hill to the Holy Mountain. The first, in September–October 1977, is
described in Through Wood and Dale.

Thursday, 13th September

On arrival at Salonika, Derek and I order a taxi to drive us to the
Mediterraneo Hotel where we stayed in 1977. On reaching the site
find the hotel totally destroyed in recent earthquake. Nothing left but
a heap of rubble. Stay at City Hotel after desperate search with taxi-
driver who is either a fool or a knave. *or both.*

Friday, 14th September

No one would believe the trouble and fuss entailed in getting permission to visit the Holy Mountain. First a recommendation from the
British Consul is required. He makes sure that one's reasons for
wanting to go are not frivolous. Second, the Ministry for Foreign
Affairs in Salonika raises every objection and assures us that the quota
for the week is already full. Third, the police examine one's credentials and passport. Fourth, the authorities on Mount Athos examine
one's papers and satisfy themselves that one's hair is not too long, that
one is not a hippy and has brought no musical instruments and will
solemnly undertake not to whistle or sing in any monastery. Fifth,
only the Governor of the Mountain can grant permission for one to
stay longer than the allotted four days. Derek Hill, being *persona grata*
and a VIP on the Holy Mountain, usually succeeds. In fact this time
the Governor assured Derek that we might stay as long as we liked.

Derek is very concerned that I should not look too much like a hippy in Salonika and makes me wear a tie and jacket. I think he is afraid I may let him down. But I am scrupulously conforming, obedient and complaisant. In fact I behave like a subservient mouse – (a) to avoid trouble and (b) because I am wholly dependent on his knowledge of the Holy Mountain, his command of languages, and of course his friendship.

The heat in Salonika is very great. A beastly city like Tel Aviv of unsightly cement blocks and the occasional boring, dusty little Byzantine church with an oversize head of the Pantokrator bearded and solemn glowering over one from the stained and rain-streaked dome.

We sit for hours in the Ministry while a beastly female official like the Nazi lady at the Auschwitz camp shouts at us and tells us it is impossible to give us a pass today. D. is very determined and stands up to her valiantly. Insists on her telephoning his friend the Governor while impressing upon her his importance as artist, man of letters, society figure, companion of the late Lord Mountbatten and confidant of Kings and Presidents. I am impressed by his persistence and laudable lack of modesty, and think how much I liked the gentle British Consul Michael Ward – more than I liked his Greek wife who spoke disdainfully about the Greek monarchy last night at dinner. We gave *them* a very good and expensive dinner in a taverna on the seashore, of red mullet and grilled sole with sweetish white wine.

'To think', Derek exclaims petulantly, 'that the Governor of Mount Athos calls me "Sir" whereas this bloody Nazi woman treats me like dirt and keeps me waiting.' Impressed, I condole.

At last we get the Governor on the telephone. While D. complains to him about our treatment I extract a sly smile from the Nazi lady. D., catching me in the act, frowns. He hands the receiver to the Nazi lady who instantly caves in to the Governor and grants us all facilities in the most ingratiating manner. We shake her hand; her steel blue eyes beam upon us like sparks from a blow-lamp; she bows, and ushers us out.

We taxi to the Police Station. There Derek rather grandly sends for the head policeman who years ago befriended him on Mount Athos, gives him half a bottle of whisky bought on the aeroplane,* asks tenderly after his wife and children, and gets our passports stamped

---

* Footnote in text: 'Actually he forgot to do this and walked away with it.'

instantly. We then go to the museum and see the gold treasures recently excavated from Philip of Macedon's tomb, third century BC. Exquisite they are too.

Ghastly bus drive from Salonika to Ouranopolis of 3¾ hours in sweaty heat; no windows open on modern buses and pop music blaring non-stop. At Ouranopolis we are greeted by sweet Martha Harden, Mrs Loch's* Swiss *dame-de-compagnie*, who gives us dinner in the Tower, a medieval fort jutting into the sea and, when the Lochs first came to live here in the 1920s, the only building in the place. Mrs Loch, now bedridden, does not at first recognise D. D. put out.

I am very distressed on undressing to find that the screw point which holds the lead of my gold pencil hanging round my neck is missing. Must have fallen off while pencil on its chain. Pencil useless for ever more; and given me by A. in 1951.† Damn!

Saturday, 15th September

Breakfast in the beamed kitchen hung with archaic cooking utensils and strings of onions, of toast and honey and coffee. Present, Martha and a bearded Swiss gentleman lamenting loss of ring while bathing in the sea – 'my family ring with seal', he moans. So I mention the loss of my pencil-end. To my utter astonishment, Martha comes up to me an hour later while I am talking to old Mrs Loch about her childhood in Australia, holding one hand behind her back and saying, 'Guess what I have got for you.' It is my gold pencil-end she has found glistening in a crack in the floorboards. A miracle. I call her St Martha and embrace her. 'I have no wings, only horns,' this delicious woman exclaims.

The taxi we have ordered to take us to Ierissos, on the way to Esphigmenou on the east coast of the Peninsula, fails to turn up. Finally the postman consents to take us the two-mile journey in his van. I throw my haversack among the mailbags. On extracting it, I find that half the contents have fallen among the mail. D. and I eat yoghurt sitting on the pier waiting for the boat.

Beautiful white boat takes us on a glossy sea round the projecting point of Cape Arapis (which marks the frontier between Greece and the Holy Mountain) to Esphigmenou with what looks like a ruined

---

* Australian widow of the writer of the standard book on Mount Athos.
† The year of their marriage.

castle on a promontory, and behind it a very tall watch-tower, functional and supported by perpendicular butresses. Meet Father Mitrophan on board, D's great friend and joint Abbot of Chilandari, an important monk on the Holy Mountain. Father Mitrophan has a wiry beard and whiskers, a large nose and deprecating manner. We are met on the quay by a truck and taken up a rough track, like a dry riverbed, to Hilandari Monastery.

On arrival we and a Yugoslav doctor are given luncheon with Father M. on a projecting veranda overlooking an enclosed valley and forest scrub. The meal consists of boiled potatoes in oil, tomato and onion salad, uneatable hard bread and resinous white wine. When we finish it is 3.45 and Father M. takes us to Vespers. Very tiring. An hour of standing or (when not observed) perching on a misericord. Dull chanting and strange ululations. Worn out, we are shown by an upstage, opinionated monk with rabbit teeth the treasures recently displayed thanks to an American millionaire benefactor, no longer admitted to Holy Mountain on account of unspecified misdemeanours. Permission to visit Mount Athos is often inexplicably withdrawn and sometimes never granted again to certain persons no matter what generous services they may have rendered in the past. Twelfth- to fourteenth-century icons, manuscripts and jewelled and enamelled panels. Huge needlework panel of Christ given by Ivan the Terrible.

At 5.30 dinner, for which I have no appetite. More potatoes and aubergine swimming in oil and goat's cheese (presumably imported, for no goats or cows allowed on the Holy Mountain).

Before dark – the doors of the monastery are firmly locked at dusk – we wander with the charming Yugoslav doctor. Enter mortuary chapel in which hundreds, even thousands of monks' skulls are packed tightly and veiled by cobwebs on shelves. Oddly enough there is no musty smell in this enclosed space. We see autumn crocuses speckled blue (at Ouranopolis yellow sternbergia was in flower), and are given walnuts (freshly picked) with honey from a tube by a man sitting on a wall.

Sunday, 16th September

D. and I have to share a cell because of an unexpected invasion of Austrian pilgrims last night just before the closing hour. Often pilgrims arrive after dark and, no matter what their extremity, are obliged to sleep on the bench in the porch ourside.

We are called by the guest-master at six by a banging on the door. 'Liturgy has begun,' he says. The worst moment of the day is shaving and washing in pitch dark in an open cloister. No hooks to hang one's towel or shelf on which to put one's soap or sponge. No looking-glass of course. A queue for the four wash-basins. No plugs. I feel a way across my face with the razor. I shamelessly strip (strictly speaking not allowed), but cannot wash my feet because of the puddle in which I am standing. The loo consists of 'little feet', the floor awash with water or worse. Stink appalling. Suddenly the dawn creeps grey and muggy.

We descend to the church in the great courtyard behind the tallest, slenderest cypress ever beheld. The service has been on for half an hour already. We attend the last hour. Much chanting, lowering of candelabra on pulleys, lighting and extinguishing of candles. Priests and guests troop out and climb to third floor. Under a sort of canopy sits Father Mitrophan like Jehovah. Ottoman seats round the four walls. From a large silver tray we are handed by a servitor in drag a glass of water and one lump of Turkish delight coated with coconut dust. Then a thimble of Turkish coffee. This is breakfast. D. and I return to our cell, open a tin of pâté (by no means *de foie gras*) and spread it on Petits Beurres biscuits.

Chilandari Monastery is enormous and beautiful like the one I visited with A. in Bulgaria this spring. A large central stone tower with top corbelled out and supported by brackets. Open and closed walks on three floors. Walls either plastered white or painted to re-semble red brick. A fountain in the court under marble columns supporting a lead dome. Moorish arches to the arcades. Large marble bowl under the dome approached by steps set in lotus pattern. Floor of court is of rough grass and *pavé*. Whole building on outside is tottering; the galleries with their perilous timber supports inspire fear.

Visitors' gallery on third floor recently painted white and grey, very pretty. Walls hung with lithographs of Serbian King Milan and Queen Draga who were defenestrated* and their fingers cut off as they tried to cling to the sills. Also King Paul and Queen Frederika of the Hellenes. (Guest rooms of other monasteries furnished with similar portraits of Balkan royalties.) I write this from the central projecting

---

* In 1903.

window. Gallery might be at Haddon Hall or Knole. Monastery is set in a wooded dell. The silence broken only by a swarm of wasps nesting under an adjoining window and a soft-tongued bell which somewhere strikes the hours. In the sunshine I read *War and Peace* while D. retires to draw a portrait by memory of the hated Nazi lady and of an ancient, bent old priest, nearly a hundred, seen in church with a stick. The guest-master tells us he is a saint. He became a monk just after the First World War, when he walked here from Serbia, and has never left since.

To our surprise, a bell rang at eleven and we were told luncheon for the guests was ready. Monks other than guest-master and Abbot seldom speak and direct one by signs. We are Father Mitrophan's special guests and are obliged to conform. Sat at a large table with the Austrians who arrived last night. Because it is Sunday there is fish for luncheon today (never meat), and grapes. The same sour white wine. I sit next to a lawyer from Salzburg. When the meal is over dead silence reigns until three. Monks resting. They have little sleep at night, rising at 2 a.m. for Compline.

Weather changing – wind rising and sky overcast. During dinner at six it rains cats and dogs. And the ceiling immediately above my bed in the Bishop's Room to which I have been transferred begins leaking. D. says it serves me right for wanting to leave him.

Monday, 17th September

When D. left me last night it was 8 p.m. Dense silence had descended on the monastery. I could not read the small print of my *War and Peace*, so tried to read the first five sonnets of Shakespeare as though the words were unfamiliar, and to remember them by heart. Clearly these sonnets are in the wrong order; should not come so early, for they are reproachful of the young man for not marrying; are not words of love, which starts with Sonnet XVIII in my old edition.

I watch the misty sunlight strike the topmost trees of the rim of the hill outside my window and rapidly strike downwards, becoming less and less opaque and more and more golden every minute. How quickly sunrise and sunset happen here. Last night's tempest has quite gone and already the sky looks as though it will never have a cloud again.

A great deal of waiting and hanging about while Derek feverishly discusses plans with Father Mitrophan in the passage outside my cell

– jabber, jabber, jabber – just like George Chavchavadze's[*] eternal discussions with his old mother Princess Troubetskoy and sister Marina on whether they should have tea or coffee to drink, in the old days in Ashburnham Gardens. I suppose all Slavs are the same.

On the Holy Mountain Byzantine time is observed. All clocks are $4\frac{1}{2}$ hours ahead of Greek time, which is 2 hours ahead of British Summer Time. No one will explain to me what Byzantine time is.

One of the younger fathers leads us and a pack of dreary Germans laden with cameras and light meters up the hill to a ruined skete[†] and chapel with fifteenth-century paintings. These paintings look as alike as a pack of hounds and are mostly so restored that I give them a cursory glance. But the situation is superb and totally isolated. A sheer cliff protects the chapel on one side. Someone has carved a cross at the very top of the cliff, seemingly out of reach. Cypress trees grow round the skete, straight as pencils. The path to the skete is shaded by pines and desultory shrubs. D. strips, as he passes, some pods of Judas tree and says, 'Give them to Alvilde'. Pink oleander flower has a strong smell of vanilla. Everything smells delicious this morning after last night's rain. Pale cyclamen abound.

Lunch at eleven. Bean soup, and the usual tomatoes, potatoes and rock-like bread. We talk to jovial Brother Simeon who looks like Falstaff in his wine-cellar. He gives each of us a mug of red wine from a huge vat. I feel intoxicated and retire to my cell, rather hurt that Father S. should have said to D., 'Your friend is much older than you'. Poor dear Derek, as Queen Victoria would say, may be eight years younger but he is far fatter.

We walk in the afternoon to the shore and enter another skete, this one on the water. We examine more murals – as like as a row of pins – in the chapel of St Basil and wander across a little sandy bay. Not a building other than the skete and the deserted harbour-master's house is to be seen in this wide landscape. Derek bathes naked, contrary to the rules. I turn aside my face in modesty and wash my feet in the sea. We wander back, examining exotic butterflies with brown wings, a border of gold, tails to the wings and blue peacocks' eyes. Camberwell Beauties or Purple Emperors?

---

[*] Georgian prince and pianist who married the Philadelphia heiress Elizabeth de Breteuil (*née* Ridgeway); both were killed in a car crash in the 1950s.

[†] Footnote in text: 'A skete is a small appendage to a monastery, housing 2 or 3 monks. They are usually on remote sites.'

I go to Vespers and on coming out see Brother Simeon in his old overall still washing the funnel-shaped wine vats. He speaks a little English having years ago visited Birmingham. 'Thank God for wine good,' he says – though all Athonite wine seems to be perfectly awful.

Tuesday, 18th September

Got up at 5.45. D. comes into my bedroom announcing he has had a dreadful night of stomach pains. I tell him I have had a bad night too, could not lie comfortably and had semi-dreams of being unable to carry my pack and being obliged to chuck Harold* and go straight home. Yet when standing on my feet I feel all right. Neither of us the least interested in the other's troubles. Breakfast off Earl Grey tea, with biscuits and D's disgusting pâté.

We bid fond farewells to the sweet monks, particularly to Father Luke the smiling guest-master who has been so kind and remembers meeting us at Karyes in 1977. We give him 500 drachmas. We set out at eight laden like mules. D's luggage is made heavier by his digging up a young cypress and picking up large pebbles from the shore.

We climb for two hours. Most of the route is along a narrow gulley, so narrow that it is impossible to carry our hand luggage at our sides. Very hard walking, over boulders. Must watch the feet. Pass through scrub and the usual southern *maquis* until the summit is reached. Whereupon the landscape changes to northern vegetation. Walk through overarching rides, as it might be in Surrey. D. ahead of me reaches a second summit and is outlined against the blue sky. I call him Stout Cortez who with all his men (me) stands silent on a peak in Darien. He is not amused by the analogy, and is out of sorts today. He is laden with bags on strings, a heavy camera, light-meters, coats and jerseys tied to different parts of his anatomy so that he looks like the White Knight in *Alice Through the Looking Glass*, lacking only the Knight's saucepans and kettles.

Eventually we see towering above us the Monastery of Zographou on a pinnacle. But we have to descend a steep path before climbing again up to it. We meet a solitary Austrian actor on his way to Daphni, and a mule carrying firewood by itself. This monastery is Bulgarian whereas Chilandari is Serbian. It is picturesque and down-at-heel. In

---

* J.L.-M. was to visit Sir Harold Acton in Florence before returning to England.

the courtyard one old monk sits telling his beads. He waves us upstairs. A servant takes the letter addressed to the Abbot on our behalf. The Abbot is away but we are told that Father Mitrophan has warned him of our coming. After a prolonged silent wait, we are brought cognac, coffee and three pieces of Turkish delight. D. takes the largest piece, the Austrian the next largest, and I the smallest. The Austrian clicks his heels, says 'Happy Athos!', and strides away into the unknown. Presently D. and I are given luncheon on a terrace overlooking the valley, consisting of runner beans swimming in oil (which give me wind), one rotten tomato each and chunk of the brick-like bread. We eat sparingly and drink Earl Grey from our tea bags.

We are shown a cell with three beds. We have to share. Youth-hostel iron bedsteads. Old iron stove in middle of room with pipe running into a wall, blackening wall and ceiling. Sheets none too clean. Hope no bugs. D. falls fast asleep while I lie on my bed writing this and thinking of M.

There is a deathly silence about this huge Bulgarian monastery which is most lugubrious. Not a soul to be seen in the court but two ancient workmen. We stroll down the path, sit on a bridge and watch the butterflies. D. says how much he enjoys doing nothing for a change, not even reading. He has brought no book. We return and persuade the guest-master (who is not a monk) to boil us water in an old chamber-pot over the kitchen fire of faggots. He is amazed by our use of tea bags.

We attend Vespers at 4.30. There are in all eleven monks, ten old and one beautiful young man with red beard, mischievous eyes and seraphic expression. He escaped from Bulgaria two years ago and has just received the tonsure. What will his future be when the other ten are dead?

Two Austrian professors studying manuscripts arrive. They say there are still 2,000 undocumented ones on the Holy Mountain, all in bad condition. We eat together – noodle soup, tomatoes and yoghurt, a great treat. After which the Abbot appears from nowhere with dishes of mackerel out of a tin, which he hands us himself. He has the expression of a saint. I cannot eat my mackerel and D. puts it in paper bag to throw down the lavatory in order not to offend the kind Abbot's feelings.

Oh how I hate sharing a room. D. is very good but disturbs me as I disturb him. He falls asleep instantly and does not snore but breathes heavily. He insists on keeping the oil lamp alight all night which makes the cell hot, the windows being shut because of mosquitoes. In the neighbouring passage, a dozen workmen drink and shout until midnight. One becomes disgustingly drunk and the Abbot, instead of scolding, comforts him.

Lav. here a simple hole in the floor, but there is no water and the hole is consequently dry – better than Chilandari. With my torch I can see down the hole into a bottomless pit. D. had an odd experience – when fumbling for some lavatory paper in his wallet, a thousand-drachma note flew out and down the hole, but a gust of wind blew it up again and he was able to catch it.

Wednesday, 19th September

D. wakes at 5.30 saying we must get up if we are to catch the boat on the west coast to Daphni. I say it is half an hour too early. It is pitch dark. I shave and wash from a sink of icy water in the passage. D. eats pâté, which I cannot face at this hour. Instead I drink a mug of tea and munch a biscuit. I never feel hungry here. We have great difficulty winkling a priest out of church at Matins to unlock the great door and slide the immense bar into the wall. He is cross about being disturbed at his devotions.

A most beautiful walk to the harbour down a ravine. I have never seen more splendid cypresses. One has to watch each step for fear of twisting an ankle. At a bend in the path there appears our first view of the Holy Mountain itself, pink in the east, silhouetted against the rising sun. We sit on the quay waiting for the white boat, and listen to the gentle lapping of the water. The peace and serenity of the scene unsurpassed. I take out and read the opening lines of Sonnet VII:

> Lo! in the orient when the gracious light
> Lifts up his burning head, each under eye
> Doth homage to his new-appearing sight,
> Serving with looks his sacred majesty . . .

On arrival at Daphni we look forward to fried eggs, which we so much enjoyed last time at taverna on quay. There is indeed a pile of eggs on the dirty counter. Alas, we are not allowed them because it is a fast day. I graze my left leg painfully against the step getting into the bus.

We keep meeting the same companions. Two jolly Germans from Chilandari get on the boat at Dochiarou. They are walking from

Daphni to Iveron. D. points out from the boat the gallery of
Dochiarou on which a Greek colonel invited him to waltz in 1963, to
an ancient gramophone playing numbers from *The Merry Widow*.

At Daphni we catch the only bus on the Mountain to Karyes where
we go through formalities at police station. Hair examined for length,
etc. Call on the Governor who is away, mercifully. D. is vexed.
Luncheon at taverna in town. Filthy noodle soup and potatoes.
Squalor of Greek taverns, which my Graecophil friends find beguil-
ing, revolts me. I think Greeks the dirtiest and ugliest race in Europe,
and like the Irish they are maddening in never giving one a straight
answer. One is either an Italophil or a Graecophil. I am the former.

We wander up the hill to Kondak, the Chilandari 'town house' at
Karyes. Charming Father Iohannes gives us coffee and stale Turkish
delight. Arrangements are made for us to stay here Friday and Saturday
nights. Meanwhile D. goes to sleep upstairs. I sit on the terrace under
an awning of vine and bunches of unpicked grapes, overlooking the
red roofs of Karyes, the powdery blue sea, the folds of heavy wooded
hills and Mount Athos towering in the background, as clear as day and
seemingly as close as my outstretched hand. I hear mule bells in the
distance, the raucous call of a raven. No other sound but bees in the
ivy and the breeze in the vine. It is the most divine day imaginable, a
cloudless sky but by no means too hot. The scene before me is more
sublime and tranquil than any I have experienced. It is what I have
come all this way for. There is a strong, sweet smell of ivy-flower in
the fresh air. I should be inspired at this hour of solitude to noble
enterprises or themes for future books. But no; I fuss about whether
the boat for Karakallou will really sail on Friday so as to get us back
to Salonika in time on Sunday.

While D. continues his siesta upstairs, Father Iohannes scuttles on
to the terrace and cuts two large bunches of grapes with what looks
like a scimitar, which he takes into the house and brings back in a bowl
of water. One bunch is of fat white tasteless grapes, the other of small,
purple, strawberry-tasting ones. He stands beside me grinning in a
polite but hideous manner. Mercifully the telephone rings and he
scuttles off.* I resume *War and Peace*. Father Iohannes however returns

---

* Footnote in text: 'There are a few makeshift telephone lines between individual monasteries, a handle in a box being turned by the caller to make the bell ring at the other
end. These machines are constantly out of order, the slightest variation of the weather,
or an incident such as a falling tree, rendering them unusable.'

with a bowl of hot chestnuts. I thank him profusely and say how greatly I admire the view. He grins uncomprehendingly.

D. and I walk down to Karyes to collect our bags left in the Governor's house and sit on the shady side of the bus for Iveron. We realise what a mistake we have made in bringing so much luggage for a two-day excursion from here. D's bag weighs a ton. When I expostulate with him for packing unnecessary things, he protests indignantly. However I persuade him to leave behind a huge pot of honey. But where to put it meanwhile? The bus will leave in an instant. We find a disused drainpipe and hide it there.

At Iveron we take the boat to Karakallou. The monastery lies well above the harbour. A tractor refuses to give us a lift from quay to monastery. D. is incensed. I say that all natives despise foreign tourists, that I hate the Japanese who swarm into London buses so that I have to stand. Plodding up the hill we sweat profusely. D. pants. He tells me his doctor has warned him never to take violent exercise, that his heart is tired and one day soon he will drop down dead. He would rather that than linger as an invalid. A note of self-pity comes into his voice and a tear into my left eye. 'I am a failure anyway,' he says. I tell him he is less of a failure than I am, that most of us are failures. He says he has not yet painted his masterpiece which he knows is there waiting to be released. I say I have not yet written *my* masterpiece which I hope but am not sure is there. I remind him of the eminent people he has immortalised. I advise him to put himself on a proper diet and stick to it. He says he is not that sort of person and moreover enjoys being greedy.

We are delighted with Karakallou. It is well kept and spotlessly clean. There are only five or six monks left and we wonder whether they are entirely sane. A burly guest-master ushers us into a spacious refectory and within five minutes brings us a delicious aubergine and a tomato each, and the first resinous wine I have liked. It tastes of ginger wine. He tells us the Abbot wishes to show us the monastic treasures. This is unusual for the Abbots are generally reluctant and have to be cajoled to do this. Our Abbot is a dear old man with a very long white beard, twinkling eyes and a deep voice. He unlocks the treasure room with several keys after much fumbling. There is a smell of mothballs and camphor. From neatly stacked glass cases he produces a bound parchment book of the seventh century with minutely illuminated capital letters; a thirteenth-century Testament with miniatures of the Evangelists of utmost delicacy and vivid colouring and gilding, protected by silk covers bound in. These medieval miniatures, absolutely unrestored and in mint condition, move me profoundly, far more than the ubiquitous wall ikons people rave about, most of which bore me stiff.

The Abbot with his podgy fingers taps, pokes and scratches (he has long uncouth nails) these precious images lovingly, in a fashion which would horrify the keepers at the V&A. Yet he is intensely proud of them. The genial old man shows us the Church, which is meticulously cared for. It contains a marvellous brass candelabra, seventeenth- or eighteenth-century, with hand of God in blessing at the base. It and the usual brass coronal hung from the dome are burnished and polished like the sun, a condition I have not noticed in any other church on the Holy Mountain. For these points Karakallou deserves full marks.

Again we are given one small but clean cell to share. No sheets. Only thick horse-blankets. Towels provided, which is uncommon. On mounting the gallery stairs I notice in the gathering dusk what at first I take to be a pretty woman in a dressing-gown reading at the end of a gallery. Then I see it is a youth with sloe-like eyes, evidently a novice for he has no beard. As we are to rise so early next day I prepare to shave at the stone trough in our gallery. While I am searching for somewhere to put my towel, the novice appears from nowhere and calmly starts washing his hands and arms at my trough. Perplexed I observe this intrusion, my face covered with soap. The novice makes no comment or apology. A bell rings for Vespers and he goes off. D. calls out to me that he is attending Vespers. I follow. He and I are the only guests here.

The exhibition which ensues in the church is quite extraordinary. It is very dark in the nave, the only light coming from oil lamps and candles. The novice is conducting the service – that is to say, he reads, recites and intones. Only three monks in attendance, including the Abbot. It is impossible to tell whether the novice, who is apparently under tuition, is drunk, ill, simple, or downright bored and rebellious. For with a black hat jauntily set on one side of his head and a lock of hair straying roguishly down one cheek, he sways from side to side in a dancing movement, and sometimes lifts up his soutane to scratch his bottom. Once while reading from the Gospel he looks up and shouts at the Abbot what sound like words of abuse. The genial Abbot pays not the slightest attention. In turn he delivers the responses but in a most astonishing voice, more high-pitched than Alfred Deller* could

---

* Alfred George Deller, OBE (1912–79); English counter-tenor; Benjamin Britten created the role of Oberon in his *Midsummer Night's Dream* with Deller in mind.

have reached, and he too nods, sways and dances. A third monk joins in by barking like a Pekinese. Their behaviour is like that of three lunatics. What one earth can it mean? There is no sanctity. It is like a Communist mockery of the Mass with ludicrous emphasis on the liturgical phrases and symbolism, accompanied by grotesque genuflections, prostrations and signs of the Cross – in fact playing the fool with the holy gestures and ritual.

We go up to bed bewildered. It is eight o'clock and pitch dark. The novice follows us into our cell asking for matches to light the passage lantern. While D. searches for some, he makes me hold the lantern while he adjusts the wick. In indicating how I should light the lantern, in one rapid movement his fingers interlock with mine. Then the novice starts to fumble in our bags for the matches which D. cannot find. 'For God's sake get him out of here and shut the door!' shouts D. with terror in his voice. As the youth retires he throws me a look of deep hurt and despair.

I feel sorry for this poor boy immured in this very inaccessible community with only five or six dotty old men. How has he got here? Is he simple? Has he been abducted by the monks, as ill-disposed newspapers often accuse them of doing? D. thinks he is like St Anthony, seeing us as grotesque monsters, tempters, as through the eyes of Bosch. I rather see him as a sort of male Susanna with the Elders* in reverse, so to speak. Anyway I take a long time to get to sleep and cannot help wondering how I might have behaved if I had been alone and not under the eagle eye of Derek.

Thursday, 20th September

I have a disturbed night. We rise before five having heard the community go to church again at three. Woken by the customary clatter of the wooden board beaten by a hammer – presumably for our benefit, but we pay no heed.

I manage to swallow three biscuits and some of the jaded pâté. As at Zographou we find on descending that the huge entrance door is firmly locked and bolted. Not a monk to be seen or heard. We drop our bags and go upstairs, down long passages in search of someone to let us out. We hear neighing and smell incense. Another service is in

---

* In the Old Testament, Susanna was falsely accused of unchastity by two old men whose advances she had repelled, and was rescued by Daniel.

progress in an upstairs chapel. D. boldly enters, sees and seizes the acolyte and begs to be let out. Acolyte smiles blandly, but nods head negatively. I detect an air of disappointment in his demeanour. D. then seizes only monk not neighing and drags him out of the chapel. Non-neighing monk is affable. Conducts us into kitchen insisting on making us coffee. We explain by signs that we haven't time and must leave to catch boat at 6.15. Monk roars with hideous laughter like demented hyena. We plead, at last successfully. Monk extracts from cupboard a bunch of Brobdingnagian keys and thrusting into our hands postcards of the Abbey – as it might be 'filthy pictures' – and a couple of sticky pieces of Turkish delight, follows us downstairs and lets us out into the darkness. We thrust into his hand 200 drachmas each, and wave goodbye.

Hurried descent to harbour down very rough, stony path by aid of our torches. Torches are essential on Mount Athos. We arrive before boat. Still pitch dark. Sky pierced with twinkling stars. Gradually a pale primrose rash appears in the east, followed by a dark mauve strip above horizon of sea, followed by rosy band, followed by brilliant orange flare. From the boat we see the sun bob out of the distant ocean like a cork, but hugely, then a golden balloon still tethered to the globe. In this rotund and anchored condition it can be looked at without discomfort by the naked eye. Once launched and become smaller it cannot be looked at. But what a vision of the castellated harbour on its promontory as we sail away! – and the misty pearly edges rising from the livid water into the gilded peak of Mount Athos – a landscape by Claude or even an early nineteenth-century romantic artist, less subtle, more dramatic, like Friedrich, detailed, clear and clean and classical.

D. ticks me off for not saying 'Herité!', the local greeting, to passers-by. He is quite right. 'You never say it,' he complains.

He is extremely observant of faces. Much taken with that of the captain of the boat, a striking blond Viking, whom he photographed and to whom he said he would send a print. And I bet he does. Viking delighted, poses unselfconsciously in every attitude. At Chilandari D. closely studied a very ancient and shy monk at prayers in the church and afterwards at grinding coffee, the only job the old man could still do, and made several excellent sketches of him. Sometimes he does rapid, surreptitious sketches of monks – as he did of one on the quay at Karakallou, by the light of a sickle moon.

We get out at the harbour of Stravronikita and walk to Monastery.

We stayed here two years ago and met an English drug addict who on saying goodbye kissed me on the lips to my surprise. We are given a large room with five beds, high on the cliff sheer above the sea. From my bed I have a view along the serrated coastline of the Monastery of Pantokratoros.

This is a coenobitic monastery.* We lunch in the large refectory at long table on benches, eating from pewter bowls and platters. The monks sit apart at opposite table, some thirty of them with their hats and cloaks on. One monk reads from the Gospel. Otherwise silence enjoined amongst all. When the monks have finished eating they demurely close their eyes and hold their heads down. The Abbot raps the table when he decides the meal is over. The monk stops reading in the middle of a sentence. We all rise. Grace is said. We cross ourselves over and over again. Being a slow eater I rise unsatisfied. The monks file down the room. The Abbot passes down the double line and they make low obeisance to him. We shuffle out as unobtrusively as we can.

Unadventurous day. Afternoon very hot. Have a siesta and short walk along the shady cliff path towards Pantokratoros. Sit on a bench and think. Could I possibly lead a monastic life? Could I endure the sparse and horrid food? The lack of physical comforts? I have a yearning for M., hardly a day goes by when I do not have a vision of him.

D. photographs the monks hoeing. The Abbot on a tractor sternly signs to D. not to photograph him. D., who cherishes this abbatial friendship, is upset and assures Abbot he had no intention of doing so, though I regret to say had been poised to (though why not, God knows).

Tomorrow is a Feast Day – Birth of the Virgin, who is highly esteemed on this womanless peninsula. We guests are given an evening meal, but not the monks. They have to fast, having worked in the fields all afternoon. And very good for their souls too. D. talks to Abbot about roads on Mount Athos. Abbot says he is very tired and will have no sleep until tomorrow night, for the service tonight lasts from 11 p.m. till 7 a.m. We watch a monk banging the wooden plank with a hammer with all his might to announce Vespers, which only last half an hour.

Three Greeks occupy the other beds in our cell. One nice, clean

---

* One in which monks lead a communal life, as opposed to one in which they live as anchorites or hermits.

married man who speaks a little English is next to me, and a pair of ferocious brigands, who we imagine are members of the Baader-Meinhof Gang,* keep to the other end of the room. We have window wide open – because of the brigands – but light a serpent† to keep out mosquitoes. Cannot read after eight. Take a pill and lie like a log. Not a sound until four, when one brigand starts snoring like an express train plunging through a tunnel.

Friday, 21st September

Am woken at 5.15 by the flashing of torches by the four occupants who are discreetly dressing so as to attend the end of the all-night service. Everyone behaves with exemplary propriety. I let them go, then shave and make my ablutions alone, dress and descend in the dark. Forget to see whether the Plough, which before I went to sleep was neatly framed in my window, is in the same position. Imagine not, for the world presumably goes round with it.

Slink into church and stay in a stall at the back. Continuous chanting of very devotional sort. Priests in vestments of gold and silver embroidery, priests in black trailing cloaks and veils from hats reminding me incongruously of my mother back from hunting in a riding habit with tangled veil drooping from her top hat. These monks' hats are called *kallimafi*. Much movement. The only light, from a few oil lamps and large candles carried by priests, makes a poor show against the trickle of grey dawn. Kyrie eleison chanted a hundred times so rapidly that it becomes a yodel. Congregation prostrate themselves on the stone flags before the Miraculous Mosaic of St Nicholas which floated across the sea and has a hole in the forehead where an oyster was embedded. The process of crossing oneself according to the Orthodox rite mystifies me. Seems one cannot do it too often. The ikons, usually bad ones (perhaps once good but made bad by centuries' osculation), within reach of lips are worn down to the wood from kisses. A priest brings a small table close to me with a trayful of what at first I mistake to be money but turns out to be unleavened bread in small triangles. I eat a piece. The priests take a triangle each and so break their fast since midday of yesterday.

---

* Urban guerrillas, 'Red Army Faction', active in the Federal Republic of Germany from *c.* 1969.
† See Appendix III, entry for 24 September.

We wait on the terrace. Monks standing on high stools cut branches of grapes with sharp, curved scimitars, their black figures silhouetted against the golden wall of the mule stables, lit by the morning sun. The sun has now risen above the sea. The island of Samothrace, invisible hitherto, is suddenly revealed – a hump in the hazy plateau of sky and water. A bell rings. The guests are beckoned by a monk to move to the refectory. The monks sing joyfully as they mount the stairs ahead of us. At the door they stand aside, with seraphic faces, and allow us to enter first. Are the community at Karakallou likewise standing with seraphic faces at this moment I wonder? It is eight o'clock. Here each place at table is provided with a plate of swordfish, a plate of tomato, a glass of wine, a hunk of bread – not the sort of food I relish at this hour. I leave half my fish and all my tomatoes. Derek, having already consumed tinned beef and biscuits in the dorm, eats everything. A monk reads from the Gospel throughout.

We take our luggage down to the quay because the Viking assured us yesterday that his boat was calling at nine this morning for Iveron. It does not come. We return to the Monastery at ten. It is already extremely hot. The monks consent to send our luggage to Karyes by mule. We walk ahead. D. gets very puffed and palpitating, although not carrying great weights this morning. At Karyes the monk unloading the mule refuses to accept money – poor man, he has been up all night and now, fortified only by some swordfish and tomato, has to walk home. (When we left the Monastery the guest-master did reluctantly accept our 500 drachmas.)

Filthy luncheon in Karyes tavern of tepid potatoes and fizzy lemon squash. We pick up the honey pot still in the drain where we had left it. Climb the hill to Kondak. This building stinks of cats. Cats only are allowed to breed on this peninsula it seems; indeed nothing could stop them. D. draws me asleep on the terrace, one arm supporting my neck. Result a good likeness but expression disagreeable and cross. 'No one could say you are a ray of sunshine exactly,' he says to me.

At Kondak I wash properly all over for first time in a week. Then sit on terrace reading Sonnets. Admire Shakespeare's modesty about his verses. 'Although they be outstripp'd by every pen/ Reserve them for my love, not for their rhyme.' Can he have believed this? Was he sincere, he, the greatest poet in the world? D. thinks not.

Really the Greeks are filthy. I wander round Karyes, the only town, if it is large enough to be so termed, on the peninsula. Muck, dilapidation, offal, squalor, tatters. A land with no women cannot be wholly civilised, certainly not clean.

In the evening the Governor's Secretary summons us for a talk. We sit in the Governor's plastic-upholstered room drinking Armagnac. The Secretary is a very devout man. Discusses whether Christ was born God and Man. I say, of course. D. says No, he became God because of his sanctity. The Secretary says Nonsense. Of course I am right. He tells us much about the condition of individual monasteries. Ninety per cent of the monks are very holy men. This I well believe. We do not sneak on the monks of Karakallou because we like them and do not want them to be investigated and scolded. Secretary says that unfortunately the community squabble among themselves. Some refuse to recognise the Patriarch of Constantinople and are termed Schismatics by the Zealots. The Zealots, very strict and puritanical, come from Esphigmenou Monastery where they fly a black flag and have taken over one-half of Dochiarou Monastery, the other half (the two nicknamed Sodom and Gomorrah) refusing to be taken over. Governor apparently furious with Zealots for this unprecedented interference. Zealots however a powerful body, self-appointed censors of morals on Holy Mountain and feared by the Community, on which they decline to be represented. Secretary tells us that although few young Greeks now go to church they are all religious – what I would call superstitious. The windscreens of the buses on the peninsula are plastered with ikons, red lamps and holy postcards, with smattering of football players; and the bus conductor from Daphni to Karyes, aged twenty-five I guess, crossed himself during an argument with the driver.

D. and I are running out of money. Foolishly we did not cash enough travellers' cheques in Salonika. Dined in our room off sardines and Kendal [mint] cake. In bed and lights out at 8.15.

Saturday, 22nd September

Wake at 6.45. Leave at 8.30 in Daphni bus. Get out at Xeropotamou Monastery, sadly deserted and dilapidated. Large part destroyed by fire two years ago. A filthy old rascal of a caretaker conducts us down endless galleries, all stinking of lavatory, and gives us coffee. We ask to see church, rebuilt in eighteenth century. Monk takes us behind iconostasis and shows us the most precious treasure, within a safe – three fragments as large as my little finger of the True Cross, mounted in gold and silver and embossed with precious stones. Marvellous object. Also fourteenth-century paten of hard green stone called steatite mounted in silver; and very ancient manuscript book bound in silver. They come out of a large box of embossed silver fashioned to look like an outsize Bible.

Several fragments of ancient Greek and Hellenistic sculptured plaques inset in walls of courtyard. Also Turkish tiles, sixteenth-century, of red carnations, very rare D. assures me, he being expert on Islamics.

We walk above the sea through groves of olive, chestnut and oak. At a fountain we meet a hermit in tatters with sweet collie dog. Reach St Penteleimon, the Russian Monastery, large and rather ugly and mostly nineteenth-century. Before 1914 it contained 2,000 Russian monks, now about ten. Monk takes us straight up to bell-tower. An enormous embossed bell dated 1894, pinnacle year of this monastery's flourish. Derek doesn't like bell-towers because he was seduced in one, aged fourteen, by a cousin. I do like bell-towers, not that I was seduced exactly but I had a romantic tryst in a Portuguese one *aetatis circa* XXIV. The chapel's onion domes newly painted yellow, would once have been gold. Old priest accosts us in pedantic English. Tells us he is an artist and known to famous artists the world over. 'Who do you think my great friend be in England? He is your great friend too, no?' Both of us imagine he is going to say Graham Sutherland. 'Who?' we enquire. 'Robin Hood,' he answers. Given tea and Turkish delight off a table with oil-cloth cover designed and signed by, of all people, Picasso.

Both monasteries visited today half-deserted and lugubrious. Guest room at St Penteleimon hung with portraits of Czar Nicholas II and Czarina. Nice that they survived several anti-monarchist Greek governments.

Alas, the mechanised saw has reached Athos. Its hideous, raucous whine offends my ears as I write this from terrace at Kondak. Also since my last visit I have remarked innovation of motor tractors, and paths turned to tracks to accommodate them.

D. on tenterhooks lest the Governor of Mount Athos, due to return today from Salonika, might not telephone. Should he ring him up and ask if he wishes to see D.? I advised not to unless D. had something to communicate to a doubtless busy man. No, he hadn't, but he would like to pay respects, etc. I suspect that D. did in fact telephone because later he says jubilantly, 'The Governor has asked to see us at eight.' 'Oh Lord,' I say, 'that is our bedtime. Need I go?' 'What!!' exclaimed D., appalled, 'not want to see the Governor?' So I obediently accompany him. Clear to me that this harassed, pink-faced, pink-shirted young-ish man, efficient and polite, has little to impart beyond the news that he has miraculously recovered from a serious motor accident through the intervention of Our Lady of Mount Athos, his wife and four chil-dren in Salonika thereby being spared an irreparable loss. D. impressed by this wonderful intervention, which is not the sort of thing which impresses me. Our Lady of Mount Athos might well have decided otherwise. A toss-up. However, the Governor tells how he has scored off the Zealots by sacking them from Dochiarou and filling the mon-astery with thirty monks of his own choice. Is also going to put more monks into Karakallou, which will doubtless spoil the fun of the present community of six. He tells me that no layman is allowed to own property here; one can only rent and most of the tenants are poor, hopeless creatures whom the good Fathers wish to help and give employment to.

After half an hour of these *politesses* the Governor's secretary bustles into the room announcing the unexpected arrival of the Bishop of Athos. We discreetly rise and make our departure. D. very concerned. Who is this Bishop of Athos? He has never heard of such a person. Was this a ruse of the Governor to get rid of us? I suspect so. Just as the Governor of Gibraltar might tell an importunate visitor that one of the Colony's monkeys was waiting to see him.

Sunday, 23rd September

While D. rushes down to church in Karyes I stay behind packing in the daylight. Now at 6.45 awaiting his return and our departure by bus for Daphni. I sit on terrace for the last time. I shall never return. The sun hidden by a band of mist is reflected in a golden splodge on the calm sea. A mist cloud swathes the middle distance, and the peak of the Holy Mountain rises dark and sombre from behind. The cloud accentuates its height. Already the bees are very busy among the ivy flowers.

There is always angst waiting for buses and boats here. Are they coming, or have they already come and gone? Usually the former anxiety is resolved for if bus or boat does come it is usually late. The drive from Karyes to Daphni is like being in a small vessel on a choppy sea. Priests and pilgrims are hurled together from one side to the other. This morning I am bruised black and blue.

At Ouranopolis heavenly St Martha and the willing, taciturn and rock-like Fanny, the maid, greet us in the Tower. We are given coffee, newly baked bread and Mount Athos honey as a sort of brunch – far and away the best meal since we were here eight days ago. Into the kitchen where we sit come at all hours of the day Holy Fathers, shepherds, beggars, young boys, old boys, riff-raff of every description – and all are given something to eat or drink, from the enormous iron saucepans and vessels brewing over the log fire, while old Mrs Loch, the hostess, aged eighty-eight, lies dying upstairs and desperately trying to frame some important question which is on her mind and won't form itself into words.

Twice during the long bus drive back to Salonika the doors of the luggage-hold burst open, splitting suitcases and a crate of fish onto the dusty road. Each time yells of protest and indignation from the passengers. Crossly the driver is obliged to stop. The passengers swarm out of the bus and trot along the road to retrieve the scattered luggage. Mercifully ours was spared each time, and complacently we heaved sighs of relief. Peasants on the bus are sick into plastic bags.

D. and I dine together at a decent restaurant on the pavement overlooking the sea at Salonika. He gives me an illustrated book on the Holy Mountain with an affectionate *dédicace*. He is an ideal travelling companion – efficient, sweet-tempered, amusing, informative and generous. Has organised everything and been infinitely patient with my inefficiency, ignorance and muddle-headedness. I have come to love Derek.

Monday, 24th September

I am called at 5.30 for my flight to Rome. Greatly touched that D. comes to my room at six to ask if I am all right and say goodbye. We embrace fervently. From Salonika I fly to Athens; there change aeroplanes and fly to Rome, where it is pouring with rain. Lunch at station and take the *rapido* for Florence. Reach Villa La Pietra and stay with Harold Acton. Blessed peace, and luxury.

Appendix II

Tour of Normandy with A.L.-M. and David and Rosemary Verey
September 1980

Sunday, 31st August

The Vereys call for us at 5.15 in large, grand white car which like so many cars of this size has little room for legs inside and is cramped. We pack our luggage into the boot and sorrowfully shut and lock the front door on the dogs, whose wistful, perplexed eyes of abandon cause me pain. We drive to Southampton docks, drive car onto an enormous ferryboat which holds 220 cars and lorries, and seek berths. A. and I share one, adequate but confined. I don't look forward to this jaunt at all,* and think longingly of M. who is flying to England probably this very evening.

Monday, 1st September

It is very stuffy in the cabin. We turn on a vent in the ceiling which blows delicious cold sea air and makes a noise as of the Fleet Air Arm dive-bombing the Normandy beaches in 1944. Called by rude banging on door by steward at 6 a.m. which is five our time. Alvilde who has not slept one wink fetches me – still sleepy under sedation – a glass of orange juice. She is always solicitous over these *petits soins*. She met couple at bar who on being told by A. what she was doing remarked, 'But you make a great mistake in spoiling your husband.'

The Vereys, after we have packed selves into their car, announce that they are taking us to breakfast with unknown French lady in Le Havre. Mme de Rufenacht is most distinguished rich widow of

---

* Footnote in text: 'Did enjoy it in the end.'

ship-owner living in large late nineteenth-century house in the smart residential outskirts of Havre, 189 rue de Félix Faure. Why celebrate a President whose only claim to fame that he died in the arms of his mistress? Mme R. has some rare things bought at the Grosvenor House Antiques Fair, including candlesticks of Derbyshire bluejohn mounted in ormolu and a most desirable bookcase shaped like a tall pillar with an urn on top. An old friend of hers is staying, a Mr Currie, Scotch, who has lived most of his life in France. Rather senile and totally blind. Told me he was about to leave for America to marry third wife, with whom he was in love fifty-five years ago. Foolishly I asked him if he had seen her since then. 'No,' he said sadly. As we left, Mme R. said with some bitterness, 'I hope he may be happy. His first two wives were bitches.' These *bien* old French ladies come out with some startling observations. To our surprise, Mme R. smoked the most foul-smelling English cigarettes.

Manoir de Coupersarte. Must be very little known. A moated manor, now farmhouse, fifteenth-century, of half-timber, close upright studs, with very small herringbone bricks in the panels like Roman bricks. U-shape with *cours d'honneur*. Gables with projecting hoods and doors for hoisting provisions. Steep tiled roof; at rear two corner *tourelles* with shingled conical caps and finials of glazed terracotta, perhaps even faience. Pigeons perching on roofs. Geese parading in courtyard. Ducks in moat, heads in wings, dozing and floating with current. *Tourelles* supported by four long rickety struts joining at corners of stone base over the water. *Dépendences* also of half-timber, but panels filled with wattle and daub, the daub consisting of red impacted mud. These certainly of sixteenth century if not earlier. We ate picnic on stone bridge by moat, drinking sweet cider.

Château de Grandchamp. Long Louis XIII wing tacked on to tall half-timbered structure with mansard roof and a chimney sprouting insanely from the lantern. Absolute serenity and tranquillity. At first we thought tall extremity nineteenth-century by Viollet-le-Duc but decided not. Merely heavily restored. Not open. Gazed through grille – long untidy garden and ugly hedges planted to prevent public looking through. French taste in hedges often leaves much to be desired and they have a passion for concrete posts and wire.

St-Pierre sur Dives. Benedictine church, cool, white Caen stone. All these French churches lack monuments which give interest to English parish churches. Merely rows of mingy little plaques with 'Merci', initials of grateful recipient of benefits from BVM and date. David looks for beak-head moulding over arches which he claims came over with Conquest to Gloucestershire churches.

Château at Assy. Remains of splendid late eighteenth-century house with portico of disengaged columns. Pediment has empty space for noble arms of family, not carved because of intervention of Revolution. Poor owner guillotined. Was once a vast peristyle, like colonnade of St Peter's. A detached chapel in Flamboyant style. Along ridge tiles little figures of horsemen in faience. Only once seen before by me, on Bredon Rectory, Worcs. Son of present owner, bedint young man lying supine underneath old wreck of car, mending its anatomy, told us his father had bought house from d'Aubigny counts. Lives in one minute wing, kindly allowed us to enter low-ceilinged hall. Stairs curved down to stone chequered floor, ending in twirling brass newels. Upstairs ruinous but through key-hole of one bedroom spied splendid wallpaper in tatters. May be *toile d'Harfleur* and looked like Jacobean crewel work. A sad spectacle. Splendid park trees. Elm disease already ravaging Normandy. Was told it had not reached here before I left. But untrue.

Château de Bénouville. Drove far out of way through ugly outskirts of Caen to see. Told by Colin McMordie it was a 'must' by Ledoux. It is palatial, cold, dull with vast portico. Now a Foundling Hospital and so institutional and spoilt. Wire protection on *grand escalier* and at windows to prevent children falling to their deaths. Nothing of interest remains except curved flights of stairs and noble dome over stairwell. Was formerly Harcourt property. Always impressed by elegance of French eighteenth-century stair treads, curved at each end in concaves and convexes to suit feet.

Château d'Audrieu. Stay here for three nights. Charming seventeenth-century château run by owner and wife on grandest of *grande luxe* lines and will cost us the earth.

Tuesday, 2nd September

Château Balleroy by Mansard, said to be his first building. Louis XIII. Reminds me of a sophisticated Ashdown Hall, i.e., very tall centre of two rooms thick and wings of one room thick. Steps in ellipses and

counter-ellipses. A dry moat, probably always dry, like that at
Blickling where I found seventeenth-century account book mentioning orange trees kept therein. Balleroy built of layers of slate
treated as though of brick, and Caen stone dressings. Effect a twilight
under cloudy moon. Tall window of small square panes. Staircase
occupies one-half of centre block, as at Ashdown. *Le Grand Salon*
ceiling of carved wood as though plaster. Walls of *toile d'Harfleur*.
Pictures attributed to Mignard too bad to be original. Faces in portraits all the same. Originals sold perhaps and then copied. Garden
layout attributed to Le Nôtre. Quite impossible, must be later. Very
remarkable house.

Abbaye Cerisy-la-Forêt. Romanesque and empty. Sleeping rather than
dead, mournful rather than sad, as though God has left it temporarily. Simple upright pews of unvarnished silvery oak. Elegance of few
eighteenth-century additions, viz. altar steps in curves and rails of
wood, rounded arcades, very delicate, and imitating ironwork. We
picnic outside Abbey, spreading rug on a base of a pier of demolished nave.

Bayeux. Nice old town, smaller than horrid Caen. Cathedral recon-
ditioned in nineteenth century. Disappointing. On other hand Bayeux
Tapestry (needlework really) more wonderful than I ever supposed.
Never seen before. Where was it all the centuries after Conquest?
Fascinating detail. The Normans all dark-haired like M., Harold red-
headed. Whippets depicted. The horses' heads shown over the prow
of the invading boats, with smiling faces in anticipation of victory.
William's troops about to embark wade through the waves to reach
boats, their skirts hitched above waists and only slips covering
pudenda.

Looking for Brécy stopped at *Château Gabriel Brécy*, ancient priory.
Drew sketch of tall tower with *tourelles*. Now school of agriculture.
Young men and girl students singing as they hoed.

Château de Brécy. Delicious château belonging to Jacques de Lacretelle,
who never visits. Garden 1653. Box parterres on either side of garden
front done by present owner from André Molet's book 'Garden of
Pleasure'. Receding terraces leading to wrought-iron grilles, divine;
and two pavilions beside perspective latticed arches on walls. Mass of
urns, finials and double-headed beasts, Cerberus. Most lavish architectural garden so far seen. Only spoilt by flowers against wall of

house. Ought to be uprooted. Empty church only entered from garden. Pavement removed. Earth floor. Disused.

On return to Audrieu, terrible hour spent by Madame telephoning to book rooms for us over weekend. Every hotel is full. Finally booked rooms inland at inn on junction of main road. Poor look-out.

Wednesday, 3rd September

Abbaye de Mondaye. Likewise recommended by Colin McMordie. Very surprised to find Premonstratensian foundation of 1706–27. Built by Père R.P. Eustace Bertout (quite unknown to me) in Baroque style. Façade of church in Gesù motif. High central tower. The Order expelled in 1901, returned in 1921. White-habited monks seen flitting like moths discreetly behind doorways. Now run as boys' school. On entering church spirits rise with strong smell of incense. Baroque organ over West end door – plain wood case – also choir stalls carved *boiseries* in chestnut-wood. In Chapel of Blessed Sacrement, shrapnel marks on wall from last war. Behind altar huge composition of Assumption in plaster, very Baroque.

Tilly. We stop to look at British War Cemetery. Very neatly kept, mown lawn, not a daisy allowed. Strong smell of weed-killer. Too suburban. Pathetic little gravestones in rows, absolutely uniform in shape and lettering. Names of killed and date and age. Many only nineteen. Relatives allowed to have pious quotations added. All very trite and poignant. 'He died that we might live', etc. But did he, poor boy? He died because he had to and was too frightened to run away. Many stones headed 'A Soldier', victim unidentified.

We lunch at *Thury-Harcourt* with Duc and Duchesse d'Harcourt. His first wife Antoinette one of A's best French friends whom I remember well. Daughter of Baron Ferdinand Gérard and granddaughter of the painter. Antoinette was very pretty, very sweet and covered in gold bracelets and bangles. The Germans put her in a concentration camp outside Paris during the War and tortured her. She never recovered, and took to drugs. Became very difficult and died about twenty years ago. Antoinette did not get on with François, a dull, conventional little man.

He lives with second wife who is very beautiful. Deep blue eyes, dark hair scooped back *à la* Diana Mosley; very lively. The château having been blown up with every stick of furniture inside it by the retreating Germans in 1944 out of sheer malice, duke now lives in *Pavillon de Fantasie* in park. Pretty little folly temple recently extended. Exquisite taste. Small salon decorated with painted flowers, birds and animals, early nineteenth-century. Oval dining room in which difficult to hear a word spoken.

Drinks under spreading lime tree in garden, choice of whisky or *jus de tomate*. Chose latter. Duke's sister Marquise de Pomoreu staying. Greeted A. with much affection. A. in her Vicomtesse days* moved in exclusive Paris *gratin* society. Luncheon delicious, waited on by young butler wearing white jacket and white gloves. '*Le déjeuner est servi, Madame la Duchesse.*' Addressed her in third person always. '*Madame la Duchesse veut que j'apporte le café en dehors?*' etc. General conversation at luncheon – round table. No *tête-à-tête* talk permitted. Everyone speaks at once. Only one topic of conversation. Very civilised. I remember this the recognised practice *chez* Marie-Blanche de Polignac and the Chavchavadzes. Only Emerald [Cunard]† followed this habit at her table in London. François d'H. every inch the duke – small, slightly *mesquin*, ugly, purple-nosed, but exquisitely neatly dressed in brown suit and highly polished brown shoes. Very hot day, hottest so far this summer, boiling sunshine, divine. Chic menu cards on table with coronet and cypher.

After luncheon A. and duke exchanged presents. He gave her his little book on gardens – *Les Jardins Heureux* – and she gave her garden book. Walked to ruined château. Duke told me his mother present when it was destroyed. She was so distressed that she died of heart failure.

Drove to *Canon*, heavenly house built just before Revolution by Élie de Beaumont. Now belongs to Madame de Mézerac, *née* Élie de Beaumont. Did not see her. Too old and ill upstairs. But shown round garden and house by charming grandson who is student at Caen University. He comes home every weekend and works in garden. Adores Canon. Uncle and Aunt with their families also live in *dépendences*. Garden traversed by straight rides with temples and statues and busts at end of vistas. Formal *étang* at back of house, with swans. One temple built in perspective; canted end columns to portico. Beyond

---

* A.L.-M. had lived mostly in Paris during her marriage (1933–50) to Hon. Anthony Chaplin – but was only a viscountess between his accession to the title in 1949 and her marriage to J.L.-M. in 1951.

† Lady Cunard, widow of Sir Bache Cunard, whom she m. 1895; well-known Society hostess (d. 1948).

stable block, on which bomb fell during War, walled garden of six separate compartments. All down-at-heel, but romantic.

On return visited very ancient disused church of *Thaon*. Had to
walk half a mile through wood. Called at farmhouse for key. Found
group of teenage hooligans in church having broken through hole in
wall. They were throwing stones at each other. Furious, I shouted at
them and drove them out. David was too feeble to support me but
nevertheless impressed. A. unfortunately stayed in car for she would
have spoken her mind to greater effect.

Thursday, 4th September

Back in Bayeux, an enchanting little town with no hideous outskirts.
Centre apparently undamaged in War. Visited crypt of Cathedral. On
four faces of vaults resting on Romanesque columns an Angelic Choir
consisting of angels blowing trumpets, beating drums, playing organs,
handbells, bagpipes in monochrome. What date? Thirteenth-century?
The crypt is eleventh-century.

On leaving Bayeux (ending our three-night visit at expensive
Château d'Audrieu costing £150 each) we passed through village of
Maisons. Diverted in order for A. to see château where she used to stay
with Antoinette d'Harcourt. Moated and ugly with pointed towers and
spikes and mansard roofs with ill-placed *cheminées*. Nice moat however
and *bassin*. Now lived in by young François, known as Monsieur
d'Harcourt, Duke's eldest son but without courtesy title. He a *député*
busy opposing Government for laxity in dealing with fishermen's
strike. A. addressed *gardien* and wife who spoke lovingly of Antoinette,
and left note for young François who due to return this evening.

Drove to *American War Cemetery at Omaha Beach-head*. Very depressing experience. Was reminded of Forest Lawns in Evelyn Waugh
novel. A thousand grave-stones of Carrara marble (one-upmanship on
British stone). All beautifully kept like super-metropolitan garden and
laid out by Russell Page, that dreary skull-faced landscape gardener.
Gazing down from these shaven lawns and ilex groves and self-pavil-
ions onto golden beach and scrub below, one got idea of what invasion forces had to encounter. Moved onwards to cliff edge where
picnicked. Black-and-white dog appeared from nowhere and shared
our meal. Felt depressed by scene of terrible carnage of 1944, and
some guilt that I had not taken part in it with my regiment.

Caen: St-Etienne or Abbaye des Hommes. Norman church built by William
the Conqueror. His stone in front of altar contains one bone. Rest
exhumed and scattered at Revolution. Quite extraordinary double
arcade of Romanesque aisles superimposed. Vaulting without bosses.
How did Normans learn to do what Greeks and Romans did not know?
Lovely oak pulpit panels carved eighteenth century, and eighteenth-
century clock filling whole of north transept. Elegance of eighteenth
century always improves austerity of Romanesque and Gothic.

Abbaye des Dames. Crypt built by Queen Matilda. Closely packed
Romanesque columns with involuted capitals, the like of which only
found in England on obscure churches of Hereford school of builders – at Dymock, Glos., and Kilpeck, Herefords. – so David tells me.
   Stay night at Meulles, Château de Montford. Most depressing,
hideous building, thin as a pencil and as tall. Built circa 1880 in striped
red brick and stone, François Premier style. Very steep mansard roof
dotted with windows. Down-at-heel. No bedside light, and plugs to
wash-basin broken. Read Hardy story in *Group of Noble Dames* about
Lady Uplandtown's midnight tryst with statue of her disfigured
husband, which she embraced and made love to, like me at Grenoble
and the narrator in the Heine story.

Friday, 5th September

Ate far too much last night dining at a local restaurant highly recommended in Michelin guide – *pâté de foie gras, langouste,* duck and soufflé
with Calvados. Can't eat last thing at night as I used to; and remember how annoyed I used to be when Harold refused more than one
course wherever he might be dining.

Château de Beaumesnil. A gross edition of Balleroy, and on grander scale.
Impression of great size induced by paper-thinness of building. A
heavy Mannerist style, Louis XIII. Effect at distance undeniably splendid and imposing. On close inspection all the detail fussy, even ugly.
The red-brick ground is overlaid with richly carved stone – window
pediments, shell moulds, masks and fat console scrolls, and projecting
roof gables. I don't really like mansard roofs with chimneys popping
out of them like jack-in-the-boxes. A large glass-sided lantern astride
the roof-ridge set transversely. House sits in wide moat which on one
side becomes an island with a yew mound, like an enormous pouffe.

Straight rides in the Le Nôtre manner stretch to the rear and another *bassin*. House a museum of book bindings recently opened. I believe myself not to be a bibliophile until I see eighteenth-century bindings with porcelain inlays, and *petit-point* covers, and seventeenth-century covers of Morocco with tooled coats-of-arms and Popes' tiaras and cardinals' hats in gold. Rainy morning and rather cold.

Château du Champ de Bataille. On arrival not open. So we motored into wood and ordered cider and ate picnic under umbrellas outside bar. At 2.30 château opened. A. explained to *gardien* that Duc d'Harcourt told us not to pay. Man knew for he had been forewarned. Taken round with small party by *gardien*'s small daughter, aged eleven, who gave us preferential treatment. François d'H. complained to us that he had offered château to the state which had declined it. At the entrance he has put up a carved wall-stone with the proud words: *En 1970 le duc d'Harcourt a offert à l'État le Château du Champ de Bataille entièrement restauré avec son mobilier et —— hectares de terrain. Ce don a été refusé.*

Huge house approached by open forecourt. *Basse-court* entered through gateway of Baroque design, broken pediment, niches cut from corners in unusual manner in massive piers. Two long wings face each other. Louis XIV date. Right mixture of brick and stone; strawberry and cream texture, very beautiful, enhanced by base of flint. Genealogical tree of Harcourt dukes shows them to be descended from practically every European royal family including Elizabeth Queen of Bohemia, which means François has a lineal claim to the throne of England. Several Fragonards of which duke told us frames of incomparable magnificence had been destroyed at Thury Harcourt, and one splendid Fragonard portrait. Touching relic the little brick on which Marie Antoinette had kept her feet warm in prison; and copy of her last will written in prison.

Stay night at black-and-white house at Meulles lent us by kind Mme Rufenacht – her country retreat in forest on the Seine. Given scrumptious tea by farmer's wife (who 'does' for her) on arrival. Almost immediately go to dine at Hôtel de Marine at Caudebec. Watch large barges and ships laden with coal chug up Seine to Rouen or Paris. Lovely marine life. Fascinating place beloved of artists. Would like to live here. First night I have had a room to myself. Hitherto unable to write this diary in bed because A. does not like me working with light on. So these notes hurriedly jotted down at odd moments – in the car or in churches.

Wake up. Pull back curtains. A misty, dew-drenched autumn morning. Little sun to start with. More comes later and promises to endure. Delicious breakfast given us by farmer's wife at large round oak dining-table. In addition to brioches and cherry jam, white peaches and strawberries. I face through open window an apple tree bowed to the ground with crabs. Rosemary is so tired she stayed behind to read in orchard beside the brook. David motors us to Caudebec-en-Caux and Villequier further down the river. We walk along embankment. Some of the houses have irises growing from the ridges of the thatched roofs. Come upon a Maison Vacquier where Victor Hugo stayed. His favourite daughter Léopoldine married Auguste Vacquier, an ill-conditioned man judging from numerous portraits and drawings. Splendidly arranged shrine full of relics and likenesses of Hugo. Plaster cast of his hand. I measure mine against it. The same size and shape, viz., rather stumpy and gnarled. Léopoldine was drowned in river here. Don't care for V. Hugo.

At Caudebec visit church beloved of Bonington and other artists. In Flamboyant style and possibly most beautiful church I have ever seen. The prow-shaped *chevet* (peculiar to these parts?) supported by one pier so as to open total view of East end. Organ at West end of sixteenth-century Fontainebleau style. In one chapel of *chevet* are figures showing Christ in tomb, late Gothic, of exquisite poignancy. Strong pervasive smell of hops in this town.

New bridge over Seine far more beautiful than Severn Bridge at Bristol. Cobweb effect of thin struts. At Yvetot so appalled by hotel at which we had rooms booked being on junction of four main roads that we decided we could not sleep there. Continued to Bacqueville and took rooms at an old posting inn. Primitive.

Château de Miromesnil. Red-brick Louis XIII. Shown round by two little granddaughters of owner. Owner arrived, panting with exhaustion because he had missed our arrival, intending to greet us at the gate. Introduced self as Marquis de Voqué. Dear old boy with charming wife, both first-class gardeners. I get fearfully bored with gardening talk, exchange of names of rare plants and experiences with plant diseases and vagaries. Rosemary is relentlessly boring on subject when she gets going. I thought we would never leave. When we did, we went straight to next-door Château de ? owned by Bamberg couple, incredibly rich younger people in jet set. This visit even longer and worse.

Garden crammed with autumnal flowers. She, a sister of Rosemary's friend Vicomtesse de Rochefoucauld, very spoilt and tiresome. Denigrating everything her husband, a sympathetic keen gardener, had done. Talked about her private aeroplane, houses in Spain, Lausanne and Paris, and shooting in Norway and Nicaragua. Bitchy and flirtatious. I could have struck her. Decided I would not visit any more gardens tomorrow, but stay by myself in Dieppe.

On way back to our primitive hotel at Bacqueville – Hôtel de l'Aigle d'Or – went to *Auppegard* and looked at outside of house owned before War by Ethel Sands and Nan Hudson.* Charming small *manoir* by church, decorated by Vanessa Bell and Duncan Grant.† Did not know owner or ask to see inside. Vita and Virginia stayed here in 1924 and Vita wrote Harold long descriptive letter about visit and how Virginia read aloud shocking extracts from her autobiography and the old ladies bridled with enjoyment. Had been informed that house had been destroyed by Germans, who made garden into launching-pad of V-1 bombs. This however not the case at all. Saw facing church a memorial to ten civilians in village killed by explosion of one of these bombs. We saw what we took to be site of launching-pad at end of avenue at rear of house. Strange that I must have been terrified by hundreds of these bloody things which came to London and burst on all sides of us – which came from Auppegard where dear Ethel had lived so happily in the Twenties. She was the nicest and ugliest woman I have ever known, indistinguishable from a neighing horse when she laughed, which was often. In her biography she is quoted as having made a new friend in me. But owing to wartime difficulties our friendship never developed beyond exchange of rather formal little luncheons and dinners. She was a very good painter and Duncan had a high opinion of her.

A. is the most wonderfully efficient traveller and with her perfect French charms everyone she meets and invariably gets her way. But oh so restless and exhausting to travel with. And never lets me out of her sight for one instant – not for fear that I may get into mischief but merely because of her innate possessiveness.

---

* American artist and partner. In *Ancestral Voices* J.L.-M. describes a visit to them in Wiltshire in 1943.
† Bloomsbury artists.

Sunday, 7th September

Glorious, cloudless day. Breakfast in the bar. A red-faced, bleary-eyed farmer comes in and drinks three cups of coffee into each of which he pours a glass of Cognac. Now no Englishman would do this – which goes to show there must be some truth in reports that the French consume more alcohol than the English. Whereas it is the English upper and middle classes who drink, here it is the working classes.

Drive to *Dieppe* which I foolishly imagined looked as it did to Sickert and Jacques-Émile Blanche. The War ruined that image. Gone the striped tents and beach umbrellas and horse-drawn bathing machines. Instead, cement esplanade and blocks of concrete flats of unparalleled vulgarity. We drive westward, past British Museum and site of raid of 1942 to a cove where the Vereys bathe in ice-cold water. A. and I pick marjoram and stones from the shore, orange brick-like objects shaped like sponges, agates, pink flints and snow-white pebbles glistening with silvery speckles.

While the others walk round Princess Stourdza's large Sunningdale-like garden at *Vasterival*, I sit blissfully under an apple tree on a shady lawn and digest the plateful of winkles I ate with a pin at luncheon. Finish Hardy's *Group of Noble Dames*. Like Dickens he gets the upper classes wrong. He is not cosmic in his novels, but an arresting story-teller. After two hours the others join me. They are worn out by the Princess's ceaseless talk and recitation of Latin names of shrubs in this hideous suburban arboretum of rhododendrons and azaleas. I have clearly enjoyed myself the most and they are rather cross with me. Meanwhile the maid, whom I had shocked by entering the house in their absence and making use of the lavatory, had spread a delicious tea on garden table under another apple tree. Before others returned I surreptitiously ate enormous spoonful of honey, carefully wiping spoon on grass so as not to be found out. Then we sat down and all ate brioches and more honey. Princess directed her salvos now at me. Has beautiful false teeth. Rather took to me I fancy because I could not talk gardening and talked about Romania. Was told at next house that she and husband escaped separately after War and agreed to meet at Dieppe if both survived. This they did. She never mentioned husband and we wondered if she was a widow, or divorced. We later learnt he is very much alive and runs a farm.

★

After tea went to see neighbouring arboretum, equally vast, *Le Bois des Moutiers*, belonging to a Madame Mallet, widow living with son, daughter-in-law and grandchildren. Built *c.* 1890 by Lutyens for Mme M's father-in-law, garden designed by Gertrude Jekyll. First house Lutyens ever built. In Early English style. Oak doors with leather thongs on latches. Long windows with small square panes. When nice son conducted us to banqueting hall switched on gramophone record of organ music and when we left turned it off. Mme Mallet very distinguished, handsome, grey-haired and direct. Said she was happier living in this large house with no servants and her family than she would be alone and with six indoor servants, as before War.

Stayed night at humble hostelry at Martin-Église with rushing stream and lush meadow. Excellent dinner. Cross proprietress because Vereys complained of mosquitoes in their room.

Monday, 8th September

Cold and raining. Lunched with Marquise de Pomereu (Liddy to Alvilde) at *Château de Daubeuf.* This by far the best house we have seen, perhaps because not open to public. Wonderful avenues radiate from the four fronts. Ancient lime trees. Arched entrance gateway to forecourt. Brick and stone – Louis Quatorze – plain and no mansard roof. Rooms decorated in such impeccable taste that one wants to cry. When French have good taste it is superb, and nothing in the world excels it. Walls painted faded greys and pinks. Huge gilded mirrors with mauve glass dim with age, relief busts of Talleyrands and Pomereus, portraits by Rigaud and hundreds of miniatures hung together on large velvet frames. Empire bureaus and beds. *Fauteuils Louis XVI* in faded silk with velvet covers; andirons of brass and ormolu. Boulle glass-fronted armoires filled with Sèvres dinner services. Aubusson and seventeenth-century Persian carpets. Everything perfection because it has grown, belongs, is inherited. Nothing new or brash. Yet this old woman lives alone in house, only one gardener in detached pavilion. She showed us an old hammer-triggered shotgun kept loaded beside her bed, which I am sure she would not hesitate to fire on an intruder. Gave us a marvellous luncheon cooked and served to us by gardener's teenage daughter – tenderest fillet steak ever tasted. Has one unsatisfactory son she called Bobby and is leaving house to nineteen-year-old grandson who she says will undoubtedly sell. Such houses as these must be doomed – alas!

She sent us to house of her nearest neighbour and greatest friend,
Mme de Bailleul at *Château Bailleul*. Been in family since built in
1543. Unspoilt Henri II outside but ghastly gloomy nineteenth-
century Renaissance inside. Horrible and forbidding. In *parc*, cement
launching-pad of V-1 doodlebugs remains. (Mme de Pomereu referred to the 'Véuns': I thought a family, and could not understand
why the Véuns had been so destructive. A. told me the Pomereus
were in bad odour after War for being collaborators. She told me
Diana Mosley her most intimate friend in Paris. When Rosemary
went to loo, found *Mein Kampf* among pile of books by the seat.) Best
things about Bailleul are the lead figures on roof of Prudence, Justice,
etc., and leaves of weeds likewise fashioned in lead sprouting from the
parapet. Inside some fine sixteenth-century needlework. Pitch dark
fake armoires and chairs.

We stopped at Etretat. Little spoilt resort. Some old houses on sea-
front destroyed in War. But extraordinary rock formations painted by
Monet unchanged. Climbed to top of steep cliffs and walked westward. Ate shrimps fresh caught and drank white wine sitting on sea-
front in evening sun. Delicious boys parading up and down esplanade.

Drove to Le Havre and boarded ferry-boat.

Appendix III

Visit to Mount Athos with Derek Hill
September 1980

Thursday, 18th September

I arrived [at Heathrow] before Derek who appeared at the desk for Salonika at 7.30, smiling from ear to ear. He was rested, radiant, recovered. Thank the Lord.

On stepping out onto the tarmac at Salonika temperature was delicious – a cool breeze. This means it will not be too hot on the Holy Mountain. On the other hand, beastly Salonika very stuffy. Rooms in Capitol Hotel. Not bad. Slept in afternoon and dined on pavement of Straits Restaurant watching parade of *jeunesse dorée*, not up to much. Ugly youth here. Delicious dinner of melon, aubergine and white wine.

Derek has already in his efficient way telephoned the Consul and Governor of Mount Athos. Latter says we need not go through the normal and disagreeable experience of applying for visas to Nazi Concentration Camp lady at Foreign Office. Governor puts every facility at our disposal. But Chief of Police, Georgio, who agreed to turn up last night at eight, failed to do so and left no message. This put D. into slight pet. He is like a child. His moods pass as quickly and in five minutes he is all sunshine. He has upset me a little by telling me how shocked he is to hear from John Higgins (literary editor of *The Times* with whom D. lunched yesterday) that they are publishing extract about love affair of Raymond and Harold, of which D. knew nothing. Thinks it in poor taste and that I shall be blamed.

Friday, 19th September

The Consul Michael Ward sits in his office blandly smiling. Is a very sweet man, profoundly, integrally British. Would not set the Thames on fire but would, if asked, go to the stake without raising a hair rather than submit to the slightest insult to HM The Queen whose photograph under a crown in bronze hangs behind his desk. He is the salt of the earth and honest as daylight. A trifle ineffectual perhaps but his niceness makes me feel a 'rotter'. If he knew certain things about me he would faint with dumb distress, though would not go purple and inveigh against me like my father.

We went to the Philip of Macedon gold treasure again. 'Inconceivable', D. kept repeating, 'how they made such intricate things as the diadems of beaten gold within oak leaves with acorns, so perfect.' After all, in fourth-century BC they were more civilised than we are now, and as good craftsmen as we were in the eighteenth century.

Three-and-a-half-hour drive in the bus in stifling heat over the mountains to Ouranopolis. From a distance the old Tower visible on promontory. Greeted and embraced by dear Martha and old Mrs Loch sitting on her wooden throne. Last year she was in bed dying and speechless. Now dressed, walking in and out of the Tower, climbing the steep stairs and talking in her broad Australian accent, not always sensibly perhaps. She has lived here since the 1920s when there was no village, not another house in sight. Fanny comes in with welcome tea tray and round, powdery, sweet cakes. We sleep in Fanny's house, a room each.

D. very pleased and relieved to find awaiting him letter from the Governor authorising him as special friend of Mount Athos, and me his companion, to have free access without necessity of permits from Foreign Ministry. He is sending his jeep to meet us at Daphni tomorrow.

I love this Tower – a refuge, a home, these kind women, the cats, the cosy kitchen where we eat fish soup, salad, cheese, grapes for supper.

Saturday, 20th September

My alarm clock goes off at 6 a.m. but I heard D. stumping about unnecessarily at 5.30. It is pitch dark. Fanny has provided thermos of rather nasty Nescafé coffee and thick cheese sandwiches for our breakfast. Stuff clothes into new haversack and sally forth into dawn. Boat leaves at 7.30. Full of tourists, mostly Germans, scruffy and ugly, all carrying enormous orange kitbags bulging with protuberant pockets like growths.

Round the first point a misty view of the Mountain like a drawing by Hokusai. Orange sky over the foreground cliffs quickly dissolves into powdery blue. On arrival at Daphni we are met by Governor's secretary in Governor's jeep. He says we must wait ten minutes. So never knowing when next meal is coming we order fried eggs and coffee in café. Road to Daphni appallingly bumpy like bottom of a river. Secretary drives like a daemon. We are thrown from side to side. He catches up bus but cannot pass. We drive on its tail and are enveloped by clouds of dust.

Long talk with Governor. He says conditions on the Mountain are improving but strange happenings in certain monasteries. Dochiarou telephoned to say the enemy were at the gate. Indeed, a posse of Zealots, twenty strong, advanced, took over community and drove out old gang who, they said, had ceased to adhere to the ancient rules, whatever they were. Another monastery community needed an enemy to unite them. Having divided amongst themselves and resorted to fisticuffs, police called in. After enforced reconciliation they united in making Governor their enemy and are now happy.

We walk in great afternoon heat downhill to Stavronikita. View from corner of path over sea. Like Knole, all towers, turrets and court-yards. The same melancholy guest-master as last year received us. We arrive at the same time as a party of youngish Greeks, very sweet and polite. Offered Turkish delight and glass of cold water. Taken into Chapel, shown cell, same as last year, all five of us together with sheer drop to sea five hundred feet below. One by one the Greeks wash, return and change their shirts. Scrupulously clean they are. They on one side of the room, D. and I on the other.

Tonight there is to be an all-night festival. The waves beat against the rocks below. Delicious soothing hissing sound. Given supper of beans in lukewarm gravy, hard bread and water, and tomatoes, in pewter dishes. Refectory very clean. Monks not eating today because of Vigil of Adoration of Holy Cross. It is dark by 7.30 p.m. Having strolled on terrace eating grapes picked from vine canopy, go upstairs again. Undress, put on pyjamas, perfunctory wash. One oil lamp is lit. Impossible to read. As I get into bed and take sleeping pill, D. asks what time it is. I say 8.45. One of the Greeks corrects me. He says it is 7.45. There is nothing to be done but hope for sleep. The Greeks play cards over the oil lamp. They form a group exactly like the Caravaggio S. Luigi picture (in Rome I think), the lamp illuminating their handsome features, the rest of their bodies hidden in the dark.

Curious shadows cast on whitewashed wall of one Greek dealing cards. Then they brew coffee in a tin mug which they slot into the ring of a wall-light, holding over the big oil lamp. Operation takes three-quarters of an hour. Much hilarity.

Sunday, 21st September

Sleep fairly well. Am awake at five, which I see by torchlight. Decide to get up and go to Church. Had heard beating of wooden board and tinging of bells hours before. Try to shave in wash-house by torchlight. Strip to waist and begin when beautiful German youth with blue eyes walks in. He kindly lights oil lamp for me but it goes out. Return to cell and dress by torchlight. This wakes Derek and he too gets up. Descend by torchlight into Church. Only lit by red lamps, a few candles. Whole monastery of about thirty monks assembled wearing black hats and veils. Chanting but no music. Never is music. Don't know what is going on. Feel tired standing on misericord of choir stall. Gradually grey light of dawn percolates through windows of dome. The candles are extinguished. As service ends monks leave church, each taking morsel of unleavened bread from basket. I do likewise.

At 7.30 a sort of ceremonial breakfast. Monks break their fast of twenty-four hours. Bells ring, the monks holding candles form two rows outside refectory door, and chant. Abbot, resplendent in gold cope, his crimson mantle borne by an acolyte, processes into refectory. We pilgrims numbering about twenty-five follow. Breakfast consists of fish (cold and full of bones), shredded vegetable, goat cheese and bread: one glass of red wine. Priest reads from Gospels in a pulpit. Abbot bangs on table when he considers meal finished. Priest ceases reading abruptly. More chanting. Acolyte walks round room with silver censer. Priest gives everyone something from pewter plate which I cannot see. Being other side of table he does not reach me though I hold out my hand. We file out of refectory, bowing in turn to Abbot who stands at door.

Watch red sun rise slowly out of the sea. This visit to Stavronikita coincides exactly with last year's festival.

Derek in conversation with Abbot last night persuaded him to allow us to stay here another night although one-night visit is the rule. D. still worn out by return journey from Yemen and goes back to bed, somewhat to my embarrassment, for all the other pilgrims have already left. The beautiful German boy's ugly friend tells me he is going straight home. He does not feel in accord with the spirit of the Holy Mountain.

Unforgettable sight of monks lying prone on floor like bats with outspread wings when dawn came and the lights were extinguished.

D. feels so tired that he goes back to bed and sleeps all morning. I too feel tired and limp all day. In late afternoon we started to walk to St Pantokratoros but did not have strength to go whole way. Sat and lay on prickly undergrowth beside the path. D. complained that he received no recognition as a painter and was a failure, etc. Wanted to join *Exit** and suicide himself in a few years' time. This inordinate depression I learnt later was caused by the refusal of the Marlborough Galleries, his agents, to buy two of his landscapes lately on the market, and of the National Portrait Gallery to accept his portrait of Wilfred Thesiger.† He is too sensitive.

Monday, 22nd September

Three different occupants of our cell, of lower category than last, one we call Nero, one a Byronic corsair of terrifying aspect, one a weedy unshaven dentist. All night they shift and turn: and at three o'clock two get up and go to Church. I hear church bells and beating of the board repeatedly. At 5.30 rise. Find no running water in guests' wash-place. All I do is kill a hornet. Desperately search for another wash-place and find what I think may be the Abbot's private one. As all the monks are in church I think it safe to strip to the buff and wash all over. No looking-glass however and I find shaving awkward.

Descend to Church for one hour. So dark on entry that I sit on a monk on his pew. Monk squeals. When it comes to breakfast find the little plastic jam pots I bought so laboriously at the motorway restaurants have burst, and everything in plastic bag covered with stickiness.

Have lost my gold pen with red and blue inks, great favourite which I had for years. Am sure stolen by the corsair. Still have M's bullet biro‡ which I carry round my neck on its leather thong.

Usual confusion about whether the boat for Lavra will come, because of wind and change from summer to winter schedule. Monks

---

* The Voluntary Euthanasia Society.
† Traveller and writer (b. 1910).
‡ Bought and presented to J.L.-M. at Royal Tournament.

never know anything of this sort. So far am not enjoying this pilgrimage much.

See boat approaching from window of cell three storeys up. Hastily throw food and scattered clothing into bags and dash down to harbour. Guest-master refuses to take money but leads us to Church and I put thousand-drachma note on altar table. We just catch boat. It is rough on the shore and boat bumps and jerks against concrete pier. Throw our luggage on board and are pulled onto deck by the arms, rather painful. D. buys two tickets for Great Lavra, the goal of this expedition. When we get to Karakallou harbour the Captain announces that he won't continue to Lavra and is going home. We feel sure it is because he has not enough passengers on board to make it worth while. The bloody man keeps our money. We disembark at first stop on way back – Iveron.

This enormous monastery almost deserted. Those monks we meet not the least welcoming. They say there is no bus to Karyes. D. asks to telephone the Governor. Is told no one can telephone between eleven and four. D. is in despair. I do not mind much, even missing the Grand Lavra. We climb steep stairs to empty guest room and consider what to do. A very dirty lay brother brings a tray of two pieces of Turkish delight and water. No raki offered this year I notice. Lay brother stands speechless, smiling with two rows of gold teeth. Then at midday we are given a meal of sliced potatoes in oil, not bad, and a plate of sad jaded olives which we ignore.

The pity is that D. is quite incapable of walking now, *and* he brings far too much luggage. His haversack weighs a ton. He says his heart won't stand climbs. And I think he is probably right. But it is pointless coming to Mount Athos unless one is able to walk. I could easily manage to get to Karakallou and indeed long to go there again, but D. won't consider it. He is pinning his faith on the Governor sending his jeep this evening.

Tuesday, 23rd September

All Greeks are mad and maddening. I have always thought so. D. says to the gate-keeper that he must telephone the Governor. This horrible old monk who is chain-smoking like a chimney (the monks are strictly forbidden to smoke but Iveron is a lax monastery) says there is no telephone. Then he says there is one but it does not work between four and eight! It is now four and he still refuses. So we force our way upstairs, find the Abbot's room and force our way in. We make him telephone Governor's house. Governor is away but his secretary says he cannot send jeep and there is no bus. In despair we retire to consider what to do when we see crowd of tourists approach with bags. They have come by bus. So there is one. We bundle into it and go to Karyes. Meanwhile I have caught a flea from sitting on a cat-ridden bench and am bitten from head to foot.

At Karyes helpful Governor's secretary informs us that boat from Daphni may sail to Lavra or part of way tomorrow and suggests we stay tonight at Koutloumousiou Monastery, he having spoken, so he affirmed, to the Abbot. On arrival by foot we are left waiting in a dark room for one hour and then told Abbot is in Jerusalem. Finally shown to a pitch-dark cell with no window and sixteen beds. Mercifully we are the only inhabitants. Hungrily we await supper. This consists of one plate of spaghetti soup and the uneatable bread. We get to bed famished at eight. Sleep well until six, only disturbed by occasional bells and beating of wooden board with mallet.

After dressing we hear distant mumbling of prayers but not coming from Church which is closed. Look at courtyard with inlaid plates on wells and even jugs with handles (glazed Turkish pottery either Iznik late sixteenth- or seventeenth-century or Ratachaya eighteenth-century). When monks appear we are told there is no breakfast and because gas cylinder has run out no hot water to make our own coffee. Angrily we pack and on our way out are beckoned into gate-porter's dark room where on table is a cup of Turkish coffee each, glass of raki and Turkish delight. We consume these things with relish.

Am now sitting in sun on wooden bench beside fountain dated 1816 and very pretty, waiting to be allowed to visit the Church. Old mad monk with long white beard sits beside me watching with interest and humming. Machinery has, alas, come to Mount Athos. Workmen are making cement in one of those rotary mixers. There are chain-saws to be heard in the woods.

As well as being mad, the Greeks are utter hell I think. After all the priest's promises they refuse to let us see the Church. The postman in Karyes post office refuses to sell us stamps. Why? There are the stamps in front of him. Is he on strike? He shouts angrily, bangs the door furiously in the face of an old monk. Then calmly proceeds to produce stamps for us. This is typical – just as when taverna proprietor shouts 'no food' and then instantly produces meat and macaroni.

We walk up to Karyes, passing the notice-board proclaiming in English:

Forest is Place of Calming
And God's Smile
Protect it from Fires

We catch 10.45 bus to Daphni where we post cards – mine to A.
and M. We get into a small motor-boat and sail south to Gregoriou.
It is a calm sunny day, very hot on this sheltered side of peninsula.

By dint of D. producing his letter from Governor we are given a
cell of three beds all to ourselves at top of a high tower, clean and
comfortable. WC next door with actual basin and plug. Only WC
stinks of rotten fish.

Gregoriou a flourishing community of forty monks under strict
Abbot with whom D. claims immediate acquaintance while I wait.
Monastery in good order and very clean. Lots of young monks with
I must admit fairly silly faces. At Vespers we are turned out of pew
for being heretics and only allowed to stand in narthex. So our
religious fervour abates somewhat. At six, dinner in crowded refectory with many monks and pilgrims. Best meal so far eaten. Pewter
plates of aubergine, yoghurt and melon. Before going to bed at
eight, stroll through monks' cemetery. Pathetic little crosses give
ages of deceased, nearly all my age or younger. Garden of camellias
and lemon trees.

Wednesday, 24th September

Terribly hot night. Sleep without pyjama top under sheet only. We lit
our mosquito-repellent snakes. Suddenly at 2 a.m. tremendous wind
gets up and windows and doors bang. Since we are not welcome at
church we stay in bed till seven, I having shaved in dark by torchlight
at six. We descend to kitchen with our instant coffee bags and are
given hot water in copper saucepan. Very reviving. Eat nothing. After
watching crowded boat at 8.15 in harbour below (all ranks assemble
to watch this one excitement of the day, like Dorothy Wordsworth
when the post-chaise passed by Dove Cottage), I watch D. in guest
room discussing Ecumenism with young monk who speaks indifferent
English. Monk unyielding in views. Declares that neither Catholicism
or Anglicanism are Christian because our respective beliefs in the
Sacrament are wrong and it is very doubtful whether we shall be saved.
However the ways of merciful God are strange and He may (or may
not) see fit to overlook the enormity of our transgressions. Find this

bigotry in the young unsympathetic, although I was impressed by the little monk's earnestness.

Luncheon at 10.45. Again excellent. Lukewarm beans, rich plum cake and grapes. D. just stopped me drinking a glass of vinegar which I poured from bottle mistaking it for wine.

Walk in afternoon, 1.30 to 3.30, on path to Simopetra. Even without haversacks get fearfully hot. Climb to deserted ledge and saw Simopetra clinging to cliff the other side of a gorge. D. shows me fearful bruises and bloody patches on his leg caused by being hauled on to boat at Stavronikita. No wonder he can't walk, poor thing. He cut and gave me a prickly pear to eat. It tasted of nothing and has left prickles in my mouth and on fingers.

We watched butterflies – red and white Admirals, now extinct in England – and identify wild flowers. Agree no view more idyllic than that of Gregoriou monastery at our feet and peak of Holy Mountain behind it. D. talks of his autobiog. he intends writing and his tuition under Schiaparelli and Molyneux in Paris. Told me that Mrs Byron left him all Robert's books and travel papers. See another notice-board in English as follows:

Forest Ar God's Miracle
Take Care
To be Saved from Fire

Very praiseworthy. Does it refer to Hell's eternal flames as well?

We follow a cavalcade of donkeys laden with faggots on panniers into the first court, through the second court of the monastery. Led by monks who treat them kindly and speak to them. Clip, clop they go on the cobbles.

Evening Vespers last a long time because of visit in private motor-boat of Bishop of Samothrace. There is much donning of crimson and gold vestments in the narthex which we watch with interest. Bishop with snow-white beard and benign countenance is handed silver Holy Poker by our Abbot with nice long dark face and rabbity teeth like Ben Nicolson's. Then dinner at seven, again good, with the same plum cake and grapes.

Waiting for dusk we sit on terrace overlooking harbour. Much activity. Monks unfurling yellow fishing nets and rowing with boats out to sea. D. does rapid three-minute sketch which he will do a painting of when he gets home.

I watch large sun drop. At first like silver florin through the mist. Upon an aquamarine sea below it casts a path of silver straight to me, only stopping short a hundred yards from shore. I realise that this miraculous natural phenomenon is also for the mule-keeper who is three hundred yards away and paying no attention to it. The pathway also leads to him who does not heed it. Gradually the sun gets larger and redder as it sets. The shimmering path turns to gold like the colossal pendant of a corsage of yellow diamonds. Flecks of gold coruscate in the gently lapping waters. The sun, now pure gold, an immense guinea-piece, drops with a loud sizzling sound into the horizon. It is instantly dark.

Thursday, 25th September

I wear M's cartridge round my neck in bed. When I turn over the cartridge digs a hole in my chest and I am reminded of M. and lie thinking of him with affection. D. suddenly wakes up in agonies of cramp. 'I am crumbling to my death,' he shouts. 'I am at the end of my life. I have no future. I must join Exit the moment I get home.' At six I shave and wash by torchlight then return to bed until seven. We have had eleven hours of bed, if not sleep, and no reading.

Mass is still in progress, longer than usual. Full canonicals etc. because of Bishop. When this is over a kind priest gives us hot water for our coffee which is more welcome than any other refreshment. We munch a few biscuits. Monk who speaks English takes us to mortuary chapel, frescoed from floor to ceiling with enchanting scenes of men and animals rejoicing on the Day of Judgement. Monk said thirteenth-century but clearly to our eyes repainted in nineteenth. We ask why so few monks' graves in cemetery. He said because dead are buried in same graves as predecessors, not in coffins but shrouds, after bones of predecessors have been removed and placed in mortuary chapel.

At 9 a.m. enormous and very good meal in honour of Bishop – whitebait, pimento and rice, and wine. My neighbour, an old Greek, clinked glasses with me. After meal two interminable speeches by Abbot and Bishop. Jokes evidently, for sly laughter from monks. I got bored and stuck wooden toothpick provided into D's behind without him realising. When he did, was not pleased.

As I was writing the above, D. rushed in to say, 'Quick, the Abbot's boat will take us to Dionysiou, now. Hurry!' Luckily had already packed. On quay watched departure of Bishop. All monks assembled. Much kissing of hands of venerable Patriarch, holding staff of office and graciously inclining his head to his flock. With dignity he followed his suitcases into dinghy and standing at prow gave a blessing and was borne away.

D. and I clambered into our humbler craft and also sailed away to neighbouring monastery in next creek. Dionysiou. Little Father Filosof, who yesterday had pronounced us irredeemable heretics, accompanied us to quay and poured many blessings on our heads and expressed heartfelt desire to see us again. When we turned the corner of the bay he was still standing, a solitary figure in black, waving. There is something childlike and endearing about these simple monks.

On the boat, D. said, 'How *could* you stick toothpicks into my behind while the Bishop was delivering his lecture?' I said, 'Because you were surreptitiously drawing on your paper napkin a monk with his mouth open who looked like Lady Ottoline Morrell. So there!'

Greeted at Dionysiou with raki, Turkish delight and coffee. Are ushered into a cell with four beds and window embrasure protruding over sea and supported by flimsy sticks. We choose the beds furthest from window.

Walk along cliff to a point where a cross planted on rock over steep promontory. View overlooking creek of St Paul's Monastery where we stayed in 1977. Several folds of mountains rising from sea into a haze above which towers the crest of Holy Mountain. Watch butterflies and crickets with striped legs. D. takes photographs of me on edge of cliffs and I take one of him. We come upon a pool of congealed blood on a rock. D. swears it is human blood.

Athos adopts Byzantine time which is 4¼ hours ahead of Greek time. Thus we go to Vespers at five o'clock our time which is registered by the clocks here as 9.15. Vespers seem interminable, the same old drone and we again relegated to the outside narthex. We agreed we could not last the course if we were young monks. Most of them here old and decrepit. We perch in our stalls and watch them enter one by one and kiss the ikons. The faces or feet of the saints they kiss are worn a nasty brown by generations of old lips. Vespers over, we are denied admission to the refectory with the monks and told we will be fed later. This depresses us, the first monastery where we have been segregated. When we are allowed to eat, we are revolted by the con-

gealed rice, over-ripe grapes, sour wine and stringy runner beans. I
eat little. The church and courts of this monastery are too jammed
together – no space, and no trees like the cypresses and figs elsewhere.
A feeling of claustrophobia prevails.

Then the unexpected occurs, as always here. On return from a
sunset stroll am met by a charming Greek professor from Athens who
is Government Superintendent of works of art on Athos. He asks if I
would like to see the Library. Gladly I accept. Rush to it before sun
sets. Wonderful manuscript treasures. Am particularly struck by
eleventh-century Bible bound in gold-embossed cover of sixteenth
century; and marvellous illumination of St Basil and in margin figures
of the amanuensis and artist at easel, dating from eleventh century.
What is so gratifying to me is that these illuminations are untouched,
while nearly every fresco and ikon on wood has been restored. They
are therefore in pristine condition. One of a saint on a stool reading
and a man bending over him is exactly as when painted in eleventh
century. The gold is still pure unsullied gold leaf, the blue of pow-
dered lapis. Most moving because unchanged, just as the Orthodox
liturgy which we have lately heard *ad nauseam* is exactly the same as
when first defined in the Emperor Justinian's reign. Our new friend
told us that until fifteen years ago, when the Greek Government set
up superintendents to document and list and protect the immense
quantity of Athos treasures, the ignorant monks allowed much to
perish and much to be stolen. Only a few months ago two manuscript
books from Dionysiou Monastery mysteriously turned up in America
having presumably been purloined by a visitor. American dealer
offered to sell back to Monastery for two million dollars, which Mon.
obviously has not got.

New friend, when it was too dark to see more in Library, took us
down labyrinth of passages and through overhanging galleries to visit
youngish monk who paints ikons. His work pitiably derivative though
very competent. D. able to talk to him about process of painting
which delighted monk. D's enthusiasm, knowledge of pictures of all
periods and in most galleries of the world and his prodigious memory
astound me. On leaving monk we sat with new friend on gallery overlooking harbour and talked about Athos until what we imagined to
be a very late hour. Not a sound from huge monastery except our
subdued voices. It was 9 p.m. And it got cold. We went to bed. No
one else in our cell, thank goodness.

Friday, 26th September

Sleep badly. Bed too short and toes cold. Bed also on such a slant that it was like sleeping on a cliff. Went to loo at 1 a.m. with torch down long corridor, through a door, up some stairs, and got lost. By time I returned I was wide awake. Then a vicious wind got up and a Wuthering Heights tempest beat down the gorge behind monastery. Windows, of which one pane missing, and doors hideously rattled. And seemingly all night that sinister beating of wood summoning monks from their beds to prayer at one, three and five o'clock, most disturbing.

At six rose and shaved at stone trough in passage opposite guest master's kitchen by light of torch, there being no oil lamp. Managed to ablute while monks still in church – they being terrified of and shocked by any exposure of bare skin – and few tourists there. Returned to bed till 7.30 – very late for us. New friend who knows way about managed to get us hot water for our instant coffee and also found, spread and gave me a hunk of bread and generous helping of Athos honey, the first met with by me, although there are many beehives.

Although very picturesque outside, the inner courts of Dionysiou have been repainted in sickly colours since last visit in 1977 – church a hot red and well-heads a sickly green and Byzantine columns of cloisters a sticky chocolate. A pity, for nearly all the monasteries charmingly painted. Even shabby Iveron full of pale faded blues, greens and primrose, beside the curiously inset porcelain plates and tiles.

Catch 8.20 boat for Daphni. Very full and low in water. Stand all the way. This boat with single mast resembles those in Bayeux Tapestry. At Daphni, two hours' wait for large boat for Ouranopolis. D. and new friend eat boiled potatoes. D. gets quite cross because I eat so little. He eats voraciously. I am a naturally slow eater, and when I am hungry, which is seldom, have to choke down food and drink to keep pace with him and get my share. Warm welcome at the Tower at Ouranopolis and delicious luncheon given by Fanny in cosy kitchen – rice and pimentos, coffee. Sleep in afternoon, and buy thick knitted cardigan like a dressing-gown.

This visit to Mount Athos the least successful of the three because we were unable to visit Grand Lavra, the largest, oldest and most interesting architecturally of the monasteries. Rough weather the cause. Thus failed to see south end of peninsula and the Hermits, a few of whom still live isolated on ledges of rock and are occasionally given chunks of dry bread by passing priests in a basket let down from above on a rope. One monk, aged ninety-two, has lived like this for forty years. We were told there may also still be a few hermits in the forest, completely naked, living under canopies of tree branches and in caves, eating berries and leaves. They behave like shy beasts and disappear like wild deer at the approach of strangers. Terribly disappointing not to meet these people. Also, to appreciate Mount Athos one must walk from monastery to monastery and this D. quite unable to do now even without haversack and luggage. And I don't think I can any longer do it either with impedimenta for long distances. Shan't go again.*

Yet certain highlights in the expedition stand out vividly and memorably – the incomparably beautiful setting of Stavronikita on a sheer cliff hundreds of feet above the rocks to the sea-shore; the sweep of the bay northwards towards Pantokratoros and southwards towards Ivron and westwards across forests of chestnuts and olives towards the Holy Mountain; the shower of gold coins from the setting sun across an aquamarine sea at Gregoriou; the abundance of butterflies (so nostalgic of my childhood) on our walks, those tortoiseshells, white and red admirals and painted ladies, now extinct in England; the medieval gold Bible and the illuminated missal in the Library of Dionysiou; the old blind priest with the face of an El Greco saint shuffling with outstretched arms into the church at Gregoriou; the sweet, childlike face of Father Filosof, full of forgiveness of our sins and sincere distress at our departure; the sailing of the Bishop from the quay to Samothrace; the fifteen-year-old schoolboy snuggling up to me on a bench at Stavronikita and giving me a photograph as a memento, like a shepherd boy playing a plaintive song on a reed pipe; and the wake and wash made by the boat carrying us from Dionysiou in the early dawn away to Daphni under those towering folded arms of Mount Athos down to the sea and a strange black cloud issuing from the summit and tipped with flame by the sun, like smoke from some sacrificial altar.

These evanescent moments, and they were only moments, snatched from time were worth the expense and effort of getting to the Holy Mountain.

---

* J.L.-M. did in fact accompany D.H. to the mountain once more, in 1982.

Appendix IV

Wednesday, 29th April

Cashed in my dear little Renault car at Bath garage. Saw new one, very dark blue and rather chic, and paid cheque for £1,593 without a qualm. Mr Richardson the garage proprietor drove me to station in old car. I hopped out with luggage, thanked him and never gave the car a pat or looked round. At Paddington was met by M. and we lunched at Italian restaurant opposite station. I went by taxi to collect Eardley and we took train from Victoria, each with new suitcase on wheels. At Gatwick no delay by strikers. Off on time by 4.30 and reached Naples in 2½ hours. E. made mistake in thinking agents had told him that our hotel, Parkers, next to airport. They may have said Air Terminal, for taxi took hours and cost fortune. Parkers v. grand and expensive. Each have our own room.

Thursday, 30th April

Car hired from Avis arrived at hotel an hour late, excuse that traffic held up by strike in city centre. I drove, stopping only at wayside stations for petrol and coffee. When I became tired, E. took over. I was frightened, with reason, for on passing car parked on roadside E. drove into it with loud sound of tearing metal. Mercifully other car was empty and we did not stop, caddishly. When we examined our car we found it to be intact by some miracle. I took wheel again. Drove to Tropea on bunion-like protuberance on foot of Calabria facing Sicily. Desperately disappointed with coast. The beautiful land quite ruined by development, advertising and vulgarity since my last visit with Fleming and Honour more than twenty

years ago. Clean rooms in brand new, unfinished hotel. Disgusting
dinner and bad red wine.

Friday, 1st May

Had not realised it was May Day holiday and all shops shut. Drove to
lakes, hoping to find ideal paradise in which to stay for ten days.
Climbed to Catanazaro, hideous modern industrial town. Hotel quite
impossible. Continued to Villagio Marcuso, high up in forest. Hotel
interesting, half Swiss chalet, half black-and-white Cheshire manor
house, but not yet open. Believed S. Giovanni in Fiori to be suitable.
Saw across valley this most loathsome town, without a church or
tower, every building modern. Dead and dusty, like Nagasaki after
atomic bombardment. Hotel again shut. Overcome with despair.
Thought of chucking tour and returning to Naples. On way to
Cosenza saw road advert of Grand Hotel at Lorica on Lake Arvo.
Drove to it. Hotel open, large, welcoming. High up. Cold at dusk.

Went for stroll before dinner. Lorica without church, bar or shop,
merely a cluster of modern houses, half-built, standing derelict in
patches of such squalor as hardly witnessed in Lebanon. Old broken
perambulators, frigidaires, parts of motor-cars thrown everywhere.
The reason these places are so ghastly is that until twenty-five years
ago they did not exist. Moreover, the frightful unplanned development has been halted, so that buildings remain half-finished as if
national bankruptcy has intervened and arrested them. When we
motored round lake we were struck by its beauty, the wooded banks
down to the shore, the hills behind, the lack of building development.
The moment we came upon a '*pensione*' it was surrounded by piles of
débris and advertisement hoardings. We felt we could not stay in such
surroundings. Yet when away from the frightful development, the
landscape is wild and beautiful. But the damage done since I last
motored here in 1955, or whenever it was, is unbelievable. Really, the
Italians are cynical demons, totally philistine.

Saturday, 2nd May

Woke up to dark morning. On opening shutters saw lake enveloped
in grey mist which turned to cloud, rain and bitter cold. No heat in
hotel. Did not go out till evening for short walk with E., wearing
every jersey I could lay hands on and plastic waterproof. This is not
what we have come for. However I spread out proofs on bedroom

table and in course of day correct 2¼ chapters. Water not hot enough for shower, so go to bed with pile of blankets and wearing socks.

Up in the mountains there are small pansies the size of 'Jackanapes', of two sorts. One deep gentian blue, the other pale yellow. Are they violas? But they are not purple.

Sunday, 3rd May

Still overcast though clearer than yesterday. We resolve to leave immediately after breakfast. Drive along Lake Arvo and descend beautiful mountain of beech, chestnut and oak to Cosenza. Soon reach the sea and fine weather. Make for Cinque Stelle. Before reaching it we see on our right a rather grand hotel standing in own grounds a little above the road. It is like a gentleman's seat of 1880 in stucco. Impressed by lovely garden. We enquire about rooms and are told we can have one each for 24,000 lire a day. So we install ourselves at Grand Hotel San-Michele at Centraro. Lovely rooms overlooking sea, each with balcony and writing-table. While E. sleeps, I finish correcting proofs of Chapter 3 of H.N. II.

In cool of evening – for mid afternoon very hot – we walk behind hotel up a track, which like all Italian tracks ends in impenetrable growth and barbed wire. Nevertheless we pick two different orchids, daphne, a pink flower like convolvulus but growing on the ground, anchusa, ladies' bedstraw, wild gladioli, gorse, broom. The garden of the hotel is full of roses, daphne and orange blossom. The hotel is so ritzy and grand that we know it to be far above our station. What's more, we are the only guests staying. Yet there are servants, waiters, porters and porteresses, housemaids, proprietors galore. We dine in solitary state and sit in the huge hall with lights blazing from the walls. Bath-water boiling hot. We wonder whether, if we were not here, the lights would be on and servants assembled. What we mistook for cars of other guests were the Renaults and Citroëns of the staff.

Absurd conversation in Italian after dinner with handsome proprietor like Ronald Colman* type film hero of 1930s – black moustache, large brown eyes and screaming with virility. We asked whether we could walk from hotel straight into mountains. Yes, he says, *ma é molto pericoloso*. Snakes and precipices. I met a snake about four feet long and

---

* Film and stage actor (1891–1958); played Rudolf Rassendyll in *The Prisoner of Zenda* (1937).

thin like a whip-cord. Black it was. Not dangerous, he said, whereas the short grey ones apparently fatal. He measured the length on the tablecloth and asked the waiter to show us something of similar greyness: waiter produced an ashtray.

Before dinner put a call through to A. Got through during dinner and had to speak to her on dining room extension with E. and waiters all listening. Rather cramped my style though I had no secrets to tell. She is all right and has Clarissa with her. Says weather in England horribly cold again. I guess it is bad all over Europe, for only on this coast is there sun.

E. and I miss art and architecture. He says this is the first time he has travelled anywhere without visiting museums or churches. Here there are neither.

I wish I had a better memory. E. said he remembered vividly how he and I sat after luncheon at Roquebrune alone with Sir Winston Churchill and I kept him amused, a thing I cannot credit. And what did you do, I asked E? He did and said nothing. Sir Winston must have been in his dotage then. He was staying with the Reeveses, whom Lady C. hated, in Chanel's old villa below ours.*

Monday, 4th May

It is extraordinary that E. and I should be staying here in the acme of comfort and luxury, doing what we could be doing at no cost at home. Woke up to overcast day and there has been no sun to speak of. But from bedroom window beautiful view of coast to the south, not unlike view of Monaco towards Mentone. Worked all morning at proofs. After luncheon we walked beneath railway to grey sandy shore with new buildings more than half of which unfinished. Before they put a roof on they set up television aerial. The squalid development here just as bad as any seen elsewhere. The whole coast of Calabria has been utterly, irredeemably ruined. We returned at four and retired to rooms. E. seems quite happy though what he does I am not quite sure beyond reading Dadie [Rylands]'s *Ages of Man* and drawing the wild flowers he picks, with crayons.

Standing on my balcony this afternoon I saw two jet fighters sweep down from the mountains and zoom over hotel. I followed them with

---

* This is perhaps the luncheon party J.L.-M. describes in the entry for 7 September 1957 in *A Mingled Measure*.

my eyes as they turned over and over, dashed out to sea, and returned to disappear over mountains. Suddenly I felt giddy, staggered backwards into room and for two minutes lay on my bed.

There are two astonishing trees on either side of the terrace beneath my window. Conifers shaped like obelisks, their branches rising upwards and their fronds rising upwards likewise.

Tuesday, 5th May

A terrible morning. Black sky, black sea, thunder, lightning, torrential rain. E. comes into my room after breakfast to say we must go to Naples, surrender car and sightsee by taxi. I say we cannot drive two hundred miles in weather of this sort. We are at least comfortable in our luxury hotel. Tomorrow the weather may clear. But it is damnable to endure storms and beastliness in the south of Italy in May.

This morning I correct proofs of Chapter 6. I have written much that is dull and repetitive. It is now nearly lunch time and we have not descended. Already the sun fitfully gleams upon the sea, but the french windows still rattle.

We drive, since we cannot walk, to local town on a hill called Cetrato. From below it looks ancient and picturesque, but there is not a single building worth examination. Failing to find a bank for cashing cheques, we continue to Paolo. This is scarcely more interesting. After wandering round this scruffy place we return to hotel. While E. walks up the hill until driven back by rain, I correct Chapter 7. This chapter does not strike me as dull.

E. and I are never at a loss for conversation. We talk continuously through meals without pauses. He is deafer than I am so I get impatient at times. He gets irritated by me. But our impatience and irritation last no longer than the ripples on a stagnant pool. He denies vehemently that creative artists ever assess their own merit, and considers they should be utterly ruthless in pursuing their work without regard for wife or mate. I say this cannot be, for such reasoning implies that every little twerp of an artist can behave in a totally egotistic manner. Besides, I am certain that Mozart, Shakespeare and Michelangelo were aware of their greatness just as the twerp is aware of his lack of merit. 'There you go again,' says E., 'just like Raymond and all critics. No artist ever pauses to consider whether he is good or bad. He is just driven on by the fire within him.' I suspect that these sentiments are defensive, for E. must realise he is not a good artist.

E. says there is nothing one can't do if one really wants to. One can always find the time and the money. He remembers Olive Rubens. Says she was extrovert and coarse-grained. He also knew Vita's father Lord Sackville and played tennis with him at Knole. Talked about his negotiations with Miss Talbot when giving Lacock to the National Trust.* He found Fox Talbot's manuscript recounting story of his invention of moving photography; the discovery by means of his *camera oscura* on Lake of Geneva that the impression of the image he saw through it could be captured on a negative. Miss Talbot gave this incredibly valuable document to the Royal Photographic Society just as she gave the Lacock copy of the Magna Carta to the British Museum, and for the remainder of her life lived on £300 a year.

Wednesday, 6th May

The morning stalks in like the proverbial Lamb of April. Gone is the growling Wolf of March. E. to my delight agrees we must stay on here another day. We shall start in five minutes on our walk up the mountains. This is what we have come for. It must be done. Already from my balcony I smell the fresh scents of roses and daphne and orange blossom, all newly rinsed in the rain of yesterday. I have slept and feel so well.

Lovely walk in the mountain behind hotel. Not too hot. Warm smells of herbs and musty cistus. We are out for $2\frac{1}{2}$ hours. Climb through wooded track, half in shade, half in sun, between banks of holm oaks, their barks cut for cork. Meet a surly peasant who asks if we are German engineers. Explain we are harmless English tourists. The wife gives us a smile which elevates the heart. Another peasant scowls down upon us from a height because we are walking over his terrain. E. told me afterwards that he had a gun under his arm. We decide to stick to the paths, but it is sometimes difficult to tell when we are on the paths, when off them. Watch butterflies – chalk blues, meadow browns, swallowtails and another beautiful butterly with tail wing like the pincers of a stag-beetle but marked like a zebra, pale cream and black or dark brown. Have never seen anything like it. Many varieties of orchid. Got back hungry for luncheon. Superb view of coastline from the hill, all the horrid development rendered invisible by blue haze. A most lovely walk.

---

* Lacock Abbey was donated to N.T. in 1944 by this descendant of the pioneer of photography W.H. Fox Talbot (1800–77), whose family seat it was.

All afternoon corrected proofs of Chapter 8 which is bad. Am ashamed it has gone to Nigel and Rupert in this condition. Certainly the book deteriorates towards the end.

E. has a rather tiresome dogmatic side which age enhances. Snubs one. After dinner tonight told me that I disapproved of everything and looked at the worst sides of everything. I rose, said I was going to bed and went upstairs without a further word. Trouble is that age makes old friends crotchety. E. has almost Bloomsbury superiority and inclined to dismiss with contumely right-wing views, being naturally ready to espouse the sympathies of all groups who are against authority, just for the sake of contrariness and a show of liberalism. Damn liberty, equality and fraternity, the delusions of history and absolute balls!

Thursday, 7th May

Draw back curtains to reveal a lapis sea and the vigour of a Mediterranean morn. For the first time see a little white boat on the water, for there is no fishing any more in this sea in spite of the waiter last night assuring us that the sole we had ordered had been caught locally an hour before. It was delicious and in fact came, we were later told by the proprietor, from Japan. See E's cheerful face on his balcony pointing excitedly to a far-distant hazy horizon which he assured me was Sardinia. It was nothing of the sort but I refrained from contradicting him. I'm sure one should never correct or contradict one's friends however great the temptation. If on the other hand they ask for one's opinion of their behaviour or actions, then one should give it without fear or prejudice. E. has a censorious, disapproving side which occasionally irks me. But I know I am provocative and often tiresome. Indeed, I am often aware of the devil entering me.

We left at 9.30 along the coast and beastly it was until we struck east into the mountains. More than half the hideous buildings are unfinished. We have been told these are buildings which owners began without obtaining permission and completion of which has been prohibited. But I find this hard to believe because (a) I don't think the Italians have any strict planning laws and (b) so enormous a quantity of houses would not be begun and arrested at same stage of construction.*

---

* A more likely reason is that the builders took advantage of laws whereby local authorities could not require unlicensed buildings to be removed after they had passed a certain stage of construction.

Even the mountains are disfigured by pylons, advertisement hoardings, quarries cut deep into the hillsides, dams, and vast pipes down precipices. Beauty means nothing to the Italians. Only money matters. The *autostrada* restaurants don't exist south of Naples, only snack bars and very bad too. Today we bought expensive sandwiches that tasted of nothing and the bread was stale. When I told the waiter, he said stale bread was better for the stomach than new.

Visited La Padula monastery. Third time I have seen it. At last they are beginning much-needed repairs. The long corridor with monks' cells now inaccessible. Peered into the Library. Books removed and the canvas ceiling-paintings hanging in strips. Guide said all damage caused by damp and neglect.

Reach Ravello at four. Horrible twisty road. This riviera is still unspoilt. We stay at Hotel Palumbo in great luxury. Again the only visitors staying. Told that tourists kept away by fear of repetition of last year's earthquakes. Palumbo was the Bishop's Palace. Hall and ground floor supported by Romanesque columns. Some may be Constantinian. Duomo contains splendid pulpit of Cosmati work, grander than any I have seen. A plain white marble sarcophagus carved with figures of Evangelists, very beautiful, tenth-century. Pursued round Church relentlessly by custodian whom neither blandishments nor curses would dismiss.

Had forgotten the excellent quality of intarsia stalls of chapel in La Padula. Pre-Renaissance, early fifteenth-century I guess, of scenes of the Passion, the eyes of the chief participants being inlaid mother of pearl which gives the faces a curiously alert aspect. The Baroque work here coarse: the façade charming but an architectural absurdity.

Friday, 8th May

Wake up at dawn to see from my window great blood-orange glow of rising sun behind the mountains' jagged range, the vale between swathed in mist. Returned to bed and sleep. E. and I have a room each and bathroom between.

Overcome with beauty of this place. Nearly all the buildings are old. Just the right number. Certainly the most lovely riviera in Europe. The orange and lemon terraces covered with thick black netting to protect the early crop from hailstones, of which one shower can destroy the lot. So they remain until June comes.

I finish proof-correcting today. This is the ideal place to come to out of season if one has work to do and the money to spend on expensive hotel.

We walk to Villa Cimbrone on edge of Ravello, a badly fudged-up house belonging to brother of the owner of this house. Gardens open to public on payment of 1,000 lire. Municipal bedding and some terrible statuary. But one long path with statue at end silhouetted against sky compels one to approach it. When one reaches it, one is confronted with terrace with low wall and sheer drop to sea of a thousand feet. Most terrifying drop ever seen. Overcome by vertigo looking over. Both of us experienced that stinging at back of legs which height-fear brings. It is something one cannot control and is wholly physical, like my legs giving way beneath me during bombing raids in the war.

Saturday, 9th May

Had long talk with proprietor and son last night. Charming people and the father very distinguished and grand. Son gave account of earthquake as experienced in Ravello last November. The epicentre, if that is correct term, was at Avellino some forty miles away. Son was upstairs here. Had no warning signals or premonitions. Heard noise as of very heavy lorry approaching palazzo. Realised this impossible as no road passes hotel, only path. Roaring became louder. House shook like dog having come out of water, then rocked from side to side. He ran downstairs, calling to servants. Was anxious crossing gallery suspended over deep stairwell on slender iron brackets. Nevertheless kept running. Reached marble stairs, taking two at a time. His one idea to get outside building which he felt sure must collapse. Indeed, this ancient building supported by group of slender and ancient Byzantine columns. Quake lasted 1½ minutes which felt more like 1½ hours. Feeling of fear and helplessness overcame him. Many people sick afterwards. For a month, minor tremors would be felt at night, adding to the terror.

Proprietor showed us with pride old visitors' books with signatures of distinguished writers, actors, film stars, royalties. Was surprised to find that of my cousin Isabel Napier in party of Dirk Bogarde and Ingrid Bergman. What could she have been doing with these celebrities?

We left at 9.15 for Naples. Perfect morning. Drove over the mountain pass. Followed directions given to us to Hotel Santa Lucia on front. May have stayed here before, or at neighbouring Excelsior. Having disposed of hired car at Avis — who made us pay for extra charges like personal insurance and local taxes not included in London estimate – took taxi to Museo Nazionale to see frescos, sculpture, etc. from Pompeii. Half museum rooms shut. No sign for instance of dancing faun of which I have eighteenth-century copy. Museum indifferently managed. Some exhibits perishing in glass cases – fragments of black nets, stuffs, wooden implements turning to dust. Some of the Roman paintings bad but others beautiful, particularly still lifes, birds and some pastoral scenes. Fine group of women called Funeral Choir with shawls over heads, as dear Rhoda Birley* used to look, stepping forward in a regimental dance like a painting by Duncan Grant. Silver ewers remarkable, ivory spoons, combs. The earth colours used in painting, lapis blue, yellow ochre, blood red, shown in bowls.

Horrid luncheon in restaurant close to Museum. Proprietor tried to cheat us. Taxi driver had cheated us. We walked down hill to hotel. Stepped into Santa Chiara courtyard. Two youths accosted us. We did not understand what they wanted. Showed us a coat they carried. Then one of them asked E. if he would like a very nice cheap woman. 'No,' he yelled at them, and bolted. I followed at dignified trot. E. said one of the youths nudged against him suspiciously. He was sure he meant to pick his pocket while the other distracted his attention by means of the coat.

Naples has become the most detestable town. The traffic along the front is ceaseless. The squalor of the Villa Communale garden abysmal. Two loud-speakers blare pop music. The trees are broken by footballs. All the statues disfigured by red paint on faces and pudenda. Inhabitants incredibly ugly, haven't seen a pretty face on one. Streets littered with black plastic bags spilling garbage. Din and filth and vandalism. Italy must be in a pretty bad way. Total decay is the impression of the South except for the Sorrento Peninsula. There too the street walls are plastered with Communist propaganda posters. I imagine unemployment is rife. The hotels have notices in all rooms warning visitors against thieves.

Sunday, 10th May

Beautiful day, the sort of hot day one occasionally gets in England in July. But the only good thing to be said about today, which in all other respects was a complete failure. Having paid hotel bill and left luggage

---

* Rhoda Pike, widow of the portrait painter Sir Oswald Birley.

well locked up, we took a taxi to San Martino Museum. Last time I was here I spent a whole morning intoxicated with beauty of exhibits, pictures, furniture and Capo di Monte china, then had delicious meal in restaurant. We intended to repeat this experiment but alas, the earthquake last year caused such damage that only two rooms of rather ugly Venetian glass were open. The Carthusian Church however is intact, walls and floors alive with polychrome marble. By 10.30 we had seen all there was to see, and spent an hour waiting for a bus which never came. No taxis. Started walking down in great heat. Met a man who counselled us against walking through the poor streets because, he explained, 'of the people'. I suppose E. and self look rather absurd and muggable. Finally found Funicular and descended quietly in old-fashioned ancient carriage.

Lunched at Bersagliere. Then read and dozed in only sitting room of Hotel Sta Lucia, devoid of daylight. At five I walked out to look for churches. Found two shut and returned. Long wait in horrible airport. Our plane late because of strike trouble in England. Naples most detestable town, which I hope never to see again. In fact don't want ever to go to or travel through Italy, except Venice and possibly Rome.*

---

* Nevertheless, J.L.-M. and E.K. successfully visited Vicenza and Asolo a year later.

INDEX